*Yardstick Competition among Governments*

# *Yardstick Competition among Governments*

## Accountability and Policymaking When Citizens Look across Borders

Pierre Salmon

OXFORD
UNIVERSITY PRESS

## OXFORD
UNIVERSITY PRESS

Oxford University Press is a department of the University of Oxford. It furthers
the University's objective of excellence in research, scholarship, and education
by publishing worldwide. Oxford is a registered trade mark of Oxford University
Press in the UK and certain other countries.

Published in the United States of America by Oxford University Press
198 Madison Avenue, New York, NY 10016, United States of America.

© Oxford University Press 2019

Library of Congress Cataloging-in-Publication Data
Names: Salmon, Pierre (Professor of economics), author.
Title: Yardstick competition among governments : accountability
and policymaking when citizens look across borders / Pierre Salmon.
Description: New York : Oxford University Press, [2019] |
Includes bibliographical references. Identifiers: LCCN 2018045614 |
ISBN 9780190499167 (hardcover : alk. paper) | ISBN 9780190499181 (epub) |
ISBN 9780190499198 (oxford scholarship online)
Subjects: LCSH: Political science—Economic aspects. |
Public administration—Evaluation. | Government competition. | Finance, Public.
Classification: LCC JA77 .S25 2019 | DDC 320.6—dc23
LC record available at https://lccn.loc.gov/2018045614

9 8 7 6 5 4 3 2 1

Printed by Sheridan Books, Inc., United States of America

For Michèle

# CONTENTS

# ACKNOWLEDGMENTS

Given the time span over which the ideas presented here matured and the range of the domains involved, it is impossible to acknowledge all the discussions and comments that influenced the views I express in this book. The persons (some of them not anymore with us) to whom I most desire to express my gratitude include, in alphabetic order, Ehtisham Ahmad, Elisabetta Crocci Angelini, Peter Bernholz, Massimo Bordignon, Vani Borooah, Albert Breton, Giorgio Brosio, Alberto Cassone, Laura Castelluci, Gérard Charreaux, Roger Congleton, Bernard Creutzen, Francesco Farina, Lars Feld, Mario Ferrero, Francesco Forte, Angela Fraschini, Gianluigi Galeotti, Manfred Holler, Jean-Michel Josselin, Roland Kirstein, Serge-Christophe Kolm, Vikas Kumar, Jean-Dominique Lafay, Finn Laursen, Jacques Le Cacheux, Uskali Mäki, Carla Marchese, Alain Marciano, Alain Mingat, Michel Mougeot, Mancur Olson, Fabio Padovano, Martin Paldam, Scott Parris, Sonia Paty, David Pervin, Werner Pommerehne, Adam Przeworski, Jørn Rattsø, Federico Revelli, Mark Roe, Friedrich Schneider, Anthony Scott, Susan Senior Nello, Stephen Smith, Ragnar Torvik, Marcia Valiante, Roland Vaubel, Stefan Voigt, Bernard Walliser, Bengt-Arne Wickström, Stanley Winer, Ronald Wintrobe, Alain Wolfelsperger, and Stefano Zamagni. One name must be singled out. Without Albert Breton's influence, I would never have written this book. Let me add that I miss him very much.

*Yardstick Competition among Governments*

# CHAPTER 1

# Introduction

The extent to which the inhabitants of a city, region, or country are aware or might become aware of the situation in other cities, regions, and countries is a key dimension of political and policy set-ups at all levels of government. In the context of decentralization and fiscal federalism, the possibility that such awareness exists is now acknowledged and some of its implications studied under the name of yardstick competition among governments—or political yardstick competition. This expression suggests a concern among incumbent officials with whether the governments they lead are well placed in the comparisons that voters, or more generally the people, make or can make across jurisdictions. That concern can have an impact on governmental policies.

Extending or adapting the analysis to the relationship among central governments and beyond public finance is one of the main objectives of the book. The task is both important and difficult. Let me focus first on importance. Yardstick competition is a bottom-up mechanism. It puts ordinary citizens, voters, or more generally "the ruled" in the foreground. It mitigates some of the obstacles they face to make governments accountable. This is the main reason why the mechanism is of systemic importance. Its total neglect is a shortcoming of many books and articles on public choice, political economy, democracy, dictatorship, public affairs, history, globalization, public finance, economic growth, and persistent poverty. Typically, individual countries are discussed as if they were islands. When international linkages are considered, as a rule they have nothing to do with yardstick competition. Comparative studies compare countries but do not mention the possibility that citizens also do so.

With regard to why the task is difficult, let me just indicate at this stage that it implies reconsidering many usual assumptions about politics. It is for this reason that parts of the following chapters are not directly about yardstick competition but about the context in which it becomes relevant.

The idea underlying yardstick competition among governments is simple. Let us apprehend it in a setting which is also relatively simple, that of local finance—its original habitat. Imagine a city in which the local tax increases by 20 percent. Is that increase justified? Citizens would like to form an opinion on the matter. But they have no direct access to the relevant information. The mayor explains why the increase is justified. Opponents claim that it is not. The media, and other sources of information, might be biased.

The problem encountered here is studied in economics as a manifestation of information asymmetry.[1] If a decision-maker, an agent, works for another, the principal, in general the latter will have no access to all the information the former detains. Consequently, it will often be difficult for the principal to detect insufficient effort on the part of the agent or deviations from what he or she (the principal) would decide if fully informed. Office-holders, like the mayor in our example, are the agents of the voters, who are the principals. Ordinary citizens or voters cannot directly observe the true cost of the services that governments provide or, in many policy areas, whether governmental decisions are congruent with their preferences. Obviously, these limitations may have serious effects on the accountability of incumbent politicians and the content of public policies.

Although "information asymmetry" and "principal-agent" belong to the vocabulary of economics, awareness of the basic situation and its implications for the way political systems work is far from new. Both have been discussed in different words by many generations of scholars and laymen—albeit usually under the convenient and tacit assumption of a world reduced to a single jurisdiction or polity. That assumption seems innocuous but it is not.

When the existence of several jurisdictions (cities, regions, or countries) is acknowledged,[2] the relationship between office-holders and citizens changes in two ways , which are related to the exit-voice dichotomy coined by Hirschman (1970). Citizens can react to office-holders' decisions by moving across jurisdictions, which was impossible by definition under the single-jurisdiction assumption. The "voting-with-the-feet" mechanism that ensues was first analyzed systematically by Tiebout (1956). This book is about the second consequence of acknowledging the existence of a multi-jurisdiction setting. Without moving across borders, citizens can improve their assessment of incumbents or policies by making comparisons with what happens in other jurisdictions.

We will discuss later the relation between the two mechanisms. For the moment, let me emphasize a fundamental difference: information asymmetry and accountability are largely irrelevant in the case of the Tiebout mechanism, whereas they are essential in that of yardstick competition. In the first case, cross-border information plays a role but only of a "mobility-facilitating" or "arbitrage-facilitating" kind. Its imperfections are part of the transaction costs that limit mobility. Policy-making is constrained by the "mobility-based competition" (involving not only households but also firms and factors) to which governments are submitted, independently of whether their nature is democratic or not. In the case of yardstick competition, cross-border information has the main role. Whether or not it is sought or exploited, its mere availability has important implications not only for policy-making but also for the way the political system works. By mitigating information asymmetry, it may improve accountability to a degree that simultaneously depends on and affects characteristics of the political regime.

For the moment, let me remain concrete and return to the example I began with and to the context of local finance, still the one in which yardstick competition among governments is mostly studied. The evolution of local taxes is in the domain of facts. Objective and verifiable information about them is publicly available. If individuals in one city get information about what is happening in others, this may influence their assessment of the tax increase decided in their own city. If the said individuals have no reason to think that the cities compared are not approximately similar and subject to more or less common or similar circumstances, the fact that taxes increase more in their own city than in the others may have, by itself, a negative effect on their evaluation of incumbents' performance.[3]

An effect of that kind has a very small chance of changing the vote of any given individual. But if a number of voters reason along these lines, it is likely that some will change their vote. Thus, ceteris paribus, there will be an aggregate effect on the total number of votes obtained by the incumbent. That relation, which is not yet yardstick competition, is now generally referred to as "yardstick voting."

To get to yardstick competition proper, one must consider the effect of yardstick voting on policy-making. It operates along two lines. Elected office-holders are unlikely to remain unaware of yardstick voting or the possibility thereof. This makes them attentive to comparative performance. A concern with where their jurisdiction stands along that dimension will influence their decisions. To remain in the domain of taxation, we may expect them to be more inclined to reduce taxation if taxation also diminishes elsewhere. That first effect operates through the incentives created by yardstick voting. The second effect operates through selection. Office-holders unwilling or unable to do what is necessary to achieve a good comparative performance may be replaced by challengers who might perform better. As we will see, there are interesting models combining incentives and selection.

All this seems commonsensical. It is thus puzzling that two papers I published in 1987 were apparently the first to present the mechanism at length.[4] In one (Salmon 1987a),[5] the mechanism derived almost logically or naturally from a special treatment of the way pressure groups are mobilized and of the implications of that form of mobilization for political accountability (I will return to that idiosyncratic analysis). In the other paper (Salmon 1987b), I related the mechanism to the analysis of contests and tournaments which had been recently proposed by Lazear and Rosen (1981) and others in the setting of labor and industrial economics.[6] The way I addressed the matter was informal. The two papers were contributions to discussions focused on federalism and decentralization, but they also reflected broader concerns. Their reception was limited but I was encouraged by the response of a few scholars, in particular that of Albert Breton, who integrated the mechanism I had stressed in his book (Breton 1996) and of Giorgio Brosio, who had one of the two papers translated in Italian and included it in a collection he edited (Brosio 1996). I will refer later to the work I did on the matter after 1987.

The scientific research program (in a collective sense of the expression) on political yardstick competition started or took off with Besley and Case (1995). Following the example, framework, and agenda (I hesitate to fuse these terms into the concept of paradigm) clearly formulated in that seminal paper, yardstick competition became an object of theoretical elaboration and empirical investigation mainly in the domain of fiscal federalism. A feature of Besley and Case (1995) is a relatively large distance between two components: a formal model and an informal set of propositions studied empirically. The distance has remained a characteristic of much of the work done on political yardstick competition. Both components have contributed to make the mechanism an object of study respectable in the eyes of the profession. On the theoretical side, peer recognition has been enhanced by embedding yardstick competition in a larger program, the use of game theory to study political agency (see Besley 2006 and the references therein). That research strategy has been fruitful inasmuch as possible effects have been derived that a more informal discussion might have missed. Nonetheless, I have mixed feelings about it. I think in particular that it relies too much on the reduction of the electorate to a single representative voter as well as on other theoretical assumptions, like "common knowledge," also unfavorable to acknowledging the possible impact of yardstick competition.

The empirical work on political yardstick competition deserves unquali-fied praise. The studies have been particularly innovative. Thanks to them it is now confirmed empirically that yardstick competition among local or re-gional governments can have a significant influence on their fiscal decisions (taxation and expenditures) and/or on the way these decisions affect the electoral prospects or popularity of incumbents (yardstick voting). It is a fact that if such significance had not been established, yardstick competi-tion would not have attracted or kept the attention of a sizeable number of researchers. Of course, whatever the sociology of the profession, empirical significance is important in itself.

Two patterns are followed in empirical studies involving yardstick competition—both present in Besley and Case (1995) but only one in most of the other studies. In the first, the presence of yardstick compe-tition is detected if the popularity or electoral score of incumbents is af-fected not only by fiscal decisions made in their own jurisdictions but also by the decisions made in neighboring ones. This corresponds to the already mentioned mechanism of yardstick voting, but there is a presumption that yardstick voting will induce incumbents to engage in yardstick competition proper.[7]

In the second pattern, the starting point is a purely empirical regu-larity: fiscal interaction among neighboring jurisdictions. Fiscal choices in one jurisdiction are related to fiscal decisions in others. How is the inter-dependence to be explained? It may be due to a common shock or trend, to expenditure spillovers, to mobility-based (e.g., tax) competition or to yard-stick competition, to mention the main causes discussed in the literature. One way to single out yardstick competition is to test whether some purely political characteristics of the decision context have an effect on the inter-action. Variables used for that purpose include the strength of the majority enjoyed by the incumbent, whether the incumbent can be a candidate again or faces a term limit, and the proximity of the next election. Contrary to yardstick competition, the other mechanisms that can cause the observed interaction have no clear-cut relation with these variables. Thus, if any one of the latter is found to have an effect on the existence or strength of the interaction, this is interpreted as supporting the hypothesis that yardstick competition plays a role in it.[8]

From our perspective, the merits of the two patterns are different. The first (yardstick voting presumed to induce yardstick competition) is partic-ularly convenient for engaging in new reflections. Its versatility or open-ness enables it to enter as an element in different lines of reasoning. It allows that voters' cross-border comparisons, electoral effects of these comparisons, and politicians' response to these effects are sequences that can be investigated or discussed separately. This is an inducement to consider the dynamics and shape of the overall process. The pattern also allows non-coincidence between the variables concerned by voter comparisons (economic growth, say) and the variables involved in incumbents' response to these comparisons (the rate of a business tax, say).

However, in this book we are more interested in policies and policy outcomes than in ordinary politics. This constitutes an important difference between our analysis and the literature focused on the results and determinants of elections, including the important work done on popularity functions, "economic voting," etc.[9] Even if we will refer to the effects of policies on voting, our main interest, closer to the logic of the second pattern (policy interactions possibly caused by yardstick competition), will be in how yardstick competition affects policies or policy outcomes. Only, our perspective being broader than that underlying the second pattern, it will also include the systemic question of how political yardstick competition changes the general capacity of voters or citizens to influence policies—obviously an important matter for democracy.[10]

The two patterns have also a common characteristic, which is their closeness to the observation level. Although increasingly subtle and sophisticated, the work required for investigating the presence of yardstick voting or yardstick competition proper in given settings and data sets is mainly statistical or econometric. Reaction coefficients are usually estimated from the relatively small variations that can normally be observed. It is not really known how the estimated coefficients would fare under much larger variations. In other words, we are on the observation surface or only at a small distance below.[11]

It should be clear from the way I introduced the topic that the approach adopted in this book is broader than that adopted so far in the literature, whether theoretical or empirical. One obvious reason, directly related to the limits of the domain of fiscal federalism, is that variables other than fiscal ones can also be objects of yardstick competition—some laws and regulations, for example, or macroeconomic variables such as economic growth, inflation, and unemployment. Another reason, also mentioned, is that yardstick competition need not only take place among local and regional governments within a country but also at the international level between the central governments of different countries. The most decisive reason, however, is our insistence on systemic implications. To give that matter its proper place, the approach will have to be not only broader but also deeper, that is, less closely dependent on observation.

I was criticized (by a discussant) for having (in a particular context) written that "observed differences in performance are generally limited and voters need not bother to take notice of them." "Why then should we bother with yardstick competition?" I was asked. The answer, of course, is that comparisons may remain important even though they are virtual or potential rather than actual. Their effect then (or the effect of their conditional expectation) may be to constrain policy-making—that is, to set bounds to what decision-makers feel free to do. Voters may be unaware of small differences between their jurisdiction and others. But they would take notice of the larger ones that would come about if incumbents did not respect the constraints. And incumbents, aware of this, do generally respect the said constraints—which makes the observed differences, or their absence, endogenous.[12]

At an even deeper level of reality, let us consider the case when constraints are not binding. Policy-makers may have never contemplated the kind of decisions that the constraints would hamper. They may remain within the bounds for reasons, or under the influence of forces, that have nothing to do with awareness of these bounds. For example, the fact that differences in taxation observed across jurisdictions are small may be completely unrelated to yardstick competition. I will argue that even then, even if triggered only when other influences on policy-making fail to operate, yardstick competition as a latent mechanism remains part of the institutional setup. It is a kind of second-layer security device (like an overflow outlet for example), whose existence is important even though it may never come into actual use.

The overview that follows provides additional information about the main arguments developed in this book. As noted at the outset, the idea of political yardstick competition is simple. But that simplicity is not also a feature of the settings in which the mechanism works. In the characterization of the mechanism presented in chapter 2, several complexities inherent to real-world settings are addressed as openly as possible. My motivation is definitely not distrust of modeling in general or doubts about the role of abstraction and idealization in providing new insights. It stems from the conviction that the real world being complex or even messy is exactly what makes yardstick competition relevant. Information asymmetry faced by voters is not a sufficient assumption. In the stylized framework in which Besley (2006) analyzes political agency, information asymmetry is central; yet, the role of yardstick competition is secondary at best. The world he depicts is not messy enough for cross-jurisdiction comparisons to make a significant difference.[13]

To characterize yardstick competition among governments, much attention is given in chapter 2 to the setting in which it operates. The main distinctive point is that the principals are assumed to be the individual members of large heterogeneous electorates or, more generally, populations of citizens. This makes the principal-agent relationship quite different from the agency relations constructed in game-theoretic models of politics. Heterogeneity has several aspects. The one, related to preferences and often dealt with by reference to the median voter, is not the most interesting for our purpose. What counts most is the existence of differences in the way voters interpret their role, function, or task, allowing the coexistence within the same electorate of different types of voting behavior, not all of them forward-looking. When they face large heterogeneous electorates of that kind, I will argue, incumbents can treat the response to their decisions as an aggregate non-strategic relation between comparative performance and expected electoral support.

Heterogeneity is helpful, perhaps indispensable, to making yardstick competition relevant. However, it has many consequences—like the meaning given to performance, or conflicting individual assessments about it—that are analytically troublesome. An effort is made to deal with the difficulties raised. We will have to concede the likelihood of some ambiguity or even confusion when performance discrepancies among jurisdictions are small. How damaging is that concession? I noted above that small observed differences among jurisdictions are unlikely to have a large effect. I must now add that their effect may also be ambiguous. The main remedy is the same. It lies in the hypothesis of a tendency for both insignificance and ambiguity or confusion to dissipate when differences in comparative performance are larger. This implies a non-linear response of voters to these differences.[14]

In chapter 3, I examine more precisely the relationship between accountability, information asymmetry, and yardstick competition. The chapter is organized around the logical steps involved in that relationship. Political yardstick competition is important if we focus on the question of office-holders' accountability. The accountability perspective is presented particularly well in Manin's (1997) analysis of representative government. It was already recommended in particular by Popper (1945), for whom the main problem of politics is "how can we so organize political institutions that bad or incompetent rulers can be prevented from doing too much damage?" or for whom "democracy is a system in which we can get rid of governments without bloodshed"—that is, in which "the social institutions provide means by which the rulers may be dismissed by the ruled" (pp. 121–22).[15]

Contrary, perhaps, to Popper, I will not interpret these views as conferring a monopoly to accountability. We only need that accountability be one of the characteristics of democracies. To locate more precisely its role, we may refer again to Popper, this time to his "conjectures and refutations" dichotomy (Popper 1963). On election days, many voters do decide on the basis of platforms or visions (e.g., of the "yes-we-can" or "make-America-great-again" kind), personal attributes of candidates, endorsements by parties, unions and other groups etc. However, given strong uncertainty, notably about the relationship between policies and policy outcomes, these decisions may be interpreted as objectively conjectural. Accountability implies that they are reversible at another election on the basis of experience.[16]

Once we have adopted the accountability perspective (without being blind to its limitations), we encounter the information asymmetry obstacle. Neither Popper, nor, for that matter, Manin, analyze how difficult it is for the "ruled" to find out whether the "rulers" are good or bad, whether they have done their best or could have done better. A part of chapter 3 is devoted to showing how difficult it is or would be, at least in some important policy domains, to overcome or mitigate information asymmetry in the absence of cross-jurisdiction comparisons. The idiosyncratic theory of interest groups alluded to earlier plays an important part in that largely counterfactual reasoning. What could be expected from political parties and the media is also considered. When one has taken the full measure of the problem of information asymmetry inevitably arising in any polity supposed to be informationally closed, a role is set for cross-jurisdiction comparisons and with them yardstick political competition to come to the rescue of accountability.

That logic already inspired the way tournaments or yardstick competition were introduced by Lazear and Rosen (1981) and others in the fields of labor and industrial economics. A brief account of this is provided in chapter 3, as is an explanation of why the transposition to the political domain, first, *is* not and, second, *should not* be straightforward. The main reason why this transposition is not straightforward is that in the political case, competition—or the battleground on which competition takes place—is segmented. This is not the case in the original setting considered by Lazear and Rosen and others. There, competition takes place among the agents of a principal for a reward or a sanction given by that same principal. But in political settings one competitive process takes place in each jurisdiction between the incumbent and other candidates for the support of voters and another competitive process takes place, this time across jurisdictions, among the different incumbents for a good place in the relative evaluations made by these voters. The two processes are interrelated. The structure of political yardstick competition is definitely more complicated than that of yardstick competition *tout court*.

The transposition should not be straightforward in the sense that the bilateral contractual element considered essential when the principal-agent relationship is analyzed in the context of firms becomes counter-productive or misleading when assumed to be also present in the case of large-number elections. In such settings, voters, in their role of principals, are not party to a contract, they commit to nothing.

Chapter 4 complements the characterization of political yardstick competition by considering types of relations among governments that can co-exist, interact, or be confused with yardstick competition.[17] Some of the mechanisms involved are summarized briefly, mainly to distinguish them from yardstick competition. But two mechanisms—mobility-based competition and policy learning—deserve more attention. The bulk of chapter 4 is devoted to them. Although each is the object of a large literature, little has been written on their interaction with yardstick competition, which is our main interest in them.

In the case of policy learning, in addition to that interest in interaction, it is necessary to work out a sufficiently clear separation with yardstick competition at the conceptual level. On that matter, two differences seem crucial. First, although both mechanisms involve cross-jurisdiction comparisons, those comparisons are made exclusively by voters or citizens in the case of yardstick competition, principally by officials in the case of policy learning. Second, we will assume citizens to be mainly concerned with policy outcomes, including when making comparisons across jurisdictions, whereas we will assume that officials also compare policies. However, I will suggest that voters turn to policy comparisons when comparisons of outcomes make them durably dissatisfied with the performance of their governments.

As noted, the main strength of the research program on political yardstick competition lies in the serious empirical work accomplished in the domain of fiscal federalism. That work has been successful because it has adopted a precise and relatively narrow framework, centered on local taxation and expenditure. Broadening the perspective is much more adventurous and speculative. I try to show that it is worth undertaking. Chapter 5 is concerned with narrowing, chapter 6 with the challenge of broadening, and chapter 7 with two heuristic models that explore ways to do so.

In chapter 5, a discussion of some major empirical contributions is preceded by a discussion of the state of affairs in the domain of fiscal federalism that motivated interest in the yardstick competition mechanism. Two aspects were important: dissatisfaction with the existing theory of decentralization, of the kind exposed for instance in Oates (1972), and evidence of spatial interactions, as documented in particular in Case (1993). The discussion of contributions is not a proper survey, if only because it glosses over their technical features, which is what makes them interesting in the eyes of many scholars.

The fiscal or public finance setting is very specific, and this has been exploited with success both by empirical work and game-theoretical modeling. Even within the confines of that setting, however, there is a growing interest among researchers for other or more complicated relations than the ones identified originally. A number of points discussed among researchers are analyzed briefly, but in the last part of the chapter, I turn to observations or queries from the outside. They are mostly inspired by a reflection on the relationship between the empirical findings discussed in chapter 5 and the characterization of yardstick competition presented in chapters 2 and 3. In fact, the empirical findings say much less about the forms that the mechanism can take than suggested in many contributions. The statistical work confirms that some form of yardstick competition is at work (an achievement deserving our gratitude) but not much else. In particular, the findings should not be supposed to validate the game-theoretical analysis or the pure mimicking behavior assumption typically associated with the empirical investigation.

The broader perspective is mainly about competition among national rather than subnational governments. In fact, we will have often adopted it tacitly before reaching chapter 6, which is devoted to it. Thus, in that chapter the discussion of yardstick competition among national governments is less about substance than about the puzzle raised by its almost complete neglect in the literature.[18] We consider several possible reasons for that lack of involvement on the part of researchers. To mention just one, the situation of the United States with regard to the possible impact of yardstick competition and the well-deserved influence of US scholarship, when taken together, may have something to do in the puzzling lack of attention given to yardstick competition also in the context of small open economies such as the European ones. Because of its focus on international yardstick competition, the chapter also includes an exploration of how yardstick competition may work in the context of complex and different kinds of political systems—in particular in the case of compound governments, which include a legislative branch in addition to the executive, and in the case of authoritarian regimes, in which variations in bottom-up political support tend to be expressed through public opinion rather than through voting. Of course, the main obstacle to giving more attention to these different extensions is the difficulty of translating plausible informal reasoning, even when supported by casual observation, into a research agenda satisfying current scientific norms.

To a degree, that remark is also relevant to chapter 7, in which the presentation of two heuristic models is exclusively or mainly geometrical. The first model shows how yardstick competition may have an influence on the allocation of government's efforts or attention, in particular how it may reorient that allocation from transactions with interest categories to broader concerns such as economic growth. That influence depends on the specific characteristics of each jurisdiction. Many of these characteristics, such as size, are obviously exogenous. Others, in particular institutional arrangements, may not be. An extension of the model is used to discuss the possibility that institutions adapt to the degree of potency, or potential strength, of yardstick competition. Another extension is used to discuss what we may call productive discretion, as applied for instance to the viability of unpopular policies or international leadership.

The second heuristic model helps to clarify an argument already formulated. One of the main effects of yardstick competition is to maintain office-holders' choice within some bounds. There are many reasons why the mechanism is generally latent—that is, at rest—but knowing that it may release itself at some point is highly significant from a systemic perspective. What factors determine these bounds? The model suggests a rough division of determinants into two categories related to information and political institutions. Constraints on governments generated by yardstick competition can be lenient because of various impediments to comparisons and/or because of institutional arrangements protecting incumbents from their effects. As an application, that distinction is useful for understanding some instances of persistent low economic growth.[19]

Chapter 8 is about vertical interactions. In the preceding chapters, it is assumed that, at any tier of governmental systems (local, regional, international), yardstick competition takes place horizontally without any kind of interaction among levels. Interactions of that kind complicate the working of horizontal yardstick competition. They may in particular introduce elements of top-down yardstick competition. In the case of China, I will argue that two forms of yardstick competition interact: one, mostly top-down, at the domestic level, as analyzed in particular, under a different name, by Maskin, Qian, and Xu (2000) and Xu (2011); the other, bottom-up, essentially at the international level. A central part of the chapter is about vertical yardstick competition, the way it is interpreted in Breton (e.g., 1996, 2006) and the form it may take in unitary governmental systems. The chapter also includes a discussion of the particular context of European integration.

The final comments presented in chapter 9 are divided into three related matters: perverse effects, prescriptions, and arguments. Although the possibility that yardstick competition may not work (in the sense of having no effect) is a central feature of our interpretation of the mechanism, it has no obvious normative connotation. Having perverse effects is another matter. That possibility is one of the propositions derived rigorously in game-theoretic models, in relation with the interaction between incentives and selection. It is mainly discussed in chapter 2 but some additional points are made in chapter 9. Anyhow, there are other, equally important, ways in which yardstick competition can have perverse effects.

That possibility has of course negative implications for the recommendations or suggestions that one might want to derive from the analysis. Indeed, rather than leading to prescriptions or suggestions, I will suggest that the uncovering of yardstick competition as a possibly important mechanism should play a role mainly as an argument in political economy debates.

Although, or perhaps because, I have always been interested in the philosophy of science and in economic methodology, I know that most readers, whether scholars or laymen, will nourish a strong aversion to methodological discussions. Still, the way many issues are addressed in this book calls for a methodological justification of some sort. In other words, there were two concerns to be heeded. One was to defend the method, style, and assumptions adopted in the book, which are somewhat unorthodox in terms of current norms. The other was to take into account methodology aversion, a feeling that is widespread and often justified. Placing methodological considerations at the end of the book, so that they can be skipped with particular ease, seemed a good way to conciliate the two concerns.

Concerning methodology, three points on which I have worked in the past have a bearing on the way the matter is handled. The first is the methodology of mechanisms, the second the semantic approach to models, and the third the argumentative nature of economics or social science in general. Mechanisms have their habitat first of all in the real world (which explains why we can state our ignorance about them or some of their aspects), but they may also be given a place in models. There, the way in which mechanisms operate can be analyzed in isolation from other influences. Models are first of all imaginary worlds, whose furniture is of the same nature as that of the real world (Giere 1987). Models in this sense are characterized or described by all kinds of means, including sets of equations (mathematical or formal models) but also verbal descriptions or simple geometry. Hypotheses state a relation between some things in models and some things in reality: these things can be mechanisms. Finally, there is a tradition in economics of constructing or developing models, even long chains of models, as components of arguments, especially critical arguments against widespread or dominant views. An implication of that feature is that providing empirical evidence (especially statistical evidence) should be considered always desirable rather than always indispensable.[20]

An important disclaimer is needed at this stage. The relation I suppose is between the methodological views indicated and the way I present and discuss yardstick competition in the different chapters, not between the said views and yardstick competition itself. The importance of the mechanism does not depend on the language employed to talk about it.

## NOTES

1. In this book, the rationale for assessing performance in comparative terms is mainly based on information asymmetry, but that rationale can also be founded on psychological and logical difficulties of reasoning otherwise, even under shared information. See the discussion about the meaning of performance in chapter 2. See also Olsen (2017).
2. I suspect that readers will find bothersome the repeated use in this book of the words jurisdiction and cross-jurisdiction. I share that feeling but I have found no other way to refer indifferently to localities, provinces, regions, and whole countries or their respective governments.
3. Admittedly, a substantial tax increase in one's own city (20 percent in our example) may be perceived as sufficient by itself to revise downward the evaluation of government. As we will see in chapter 2, the coexistence in the same constituency of differently-based assessments does complicate the analysis. For the moment, to make the matter clearer we could suppose that taxation remains constant in the city considered. Then, observation by its inhabitants of a tax increase elsewhere will tend to have a positive effect on their assessment of the incumbent's performance, observation of a decrease elsewhere a negative effect.
4. Thanks to Allers (2014), I have discovered that the mechanism was succinctly present in Parks and Ostrom's (1981) analysis of the performance of police departments in metropolitan areas (see p. 371 of the 1999 reprint).
5. An earlier version was presented in 1984 at the first Villa Colombella Seminar.
6. In these two papers, I did not call my proposed mechanism yardstick competition— although in Salmon (1987b) I did mention the expression incidentally and cite Shleifer's (1985) influential paper on regulation which made it known. Only later, after the publication of Besley and Case (1995), and mainly for convenience, I followed a practice that had become standard and adopted the expression. To avoid the coexistence of a narrow meaning of yardstick competition (Shleifer's) and the broader one I, like most authors, employ (a coexistence discussed in chapter 3), a possibility would be to follow the formulation sometimes used in French, *concurrence par comparaison* (e.g., Auriol 2000). However, that expression can also be misleading, this time by being too comprehensive. Overall, I now think that the case for sticking to yardstick competition is overwhelming. Common understanding of the mechanism, in particular its bottom-up dimension, is now sufficient. For this reason, to avoid the expression "cross-jurisdiction comparisons by citizens," which is cumbersome, we will sometimes refer more succinctly to

"yardstick comparisons," as in Besley (2015). The expression I use in the subtitle of the book—looking across borders—comes from Geys (2006).

7. See in particular Revelli (2002), Vermeir and Heyndels (2006), Bosch and Solé-Ollé (2007), Dubois and Paty (2010), Bianchini and Revelli (2013).

8. See in particular Bordignon, Cerniglia, and Revelli (2003), Solé Ollé (2003), Allers and Elhorst (2005, 2011), Elhorst and Fréret (2009), Rincke (2009), Bartolini and Santolini (2012), Padovano and Petrarca (2014), Delgado, Lago-Peñas and Mayor (2015).

9. See in particular Nannestad and Paldam (1994), Duch and Stevenson (2008), Lewis-Beck and Stegmaier (2013).

10. I treat the expressions "yardstick competition among governments" and "political yardstick competition" as synonyms. The second is more convenient. But, as a matter of principle, I prefer the first for the following reason. Yardstick voting concerns the fate of incumbents but yardstick competition among governments concerns the behavior of governments. The latter is not necessarily the same as the behavior of incumbents. The link between the two is close when the incumbent is a unitary actor who decides the policy of the government (the assumption usually made) and less so but assumedly still present otherwise. I return to that matter in chapter 2, when discussing incentives versus selection, and in chapter 6 when discussing "compound government."

11. When possible, recourse to quasi-experimental methods may mitigate the problem.

12. That reasoning is not specific to yardstick competition. It applies to mobility-based competition as well (Salmon 2015). In both cases, constraints on policy-making are generated by latent competition. At equilibrium, each government seems to pursue its own agenda without paying attention to what is done elsewhere. It knows, however, that, because of their effects under competition (effects on mobility or on votes), some policy decisions should best be not made. In this way, competition is more important than what can be inferred from the observation of the policies that are actually implemented.

13. Similarly, Persson and Tabellini (2000) do not even mention yardstick competition in their discussion of agency (chapter 4). It comes up only as a suggested exercise at the end of a discussion on institutions and accountability (chapter 9).

14. A more radical way (though not really a remedy) to deal with the difficulty is to admit that in many real-world settings yardstick competition will not work (a typical property of mechanisms, incidentally). As far as possible we will try to understand why.

15. The theory of retrospective voting as analyzed by Fiorina (1981) is congruent with that approach, albeit from a mainly empirical perspective. The relationship between accountability and concepts such as representation and responsiveness is analyzed in Przeworski, Stokes, and Manin (1999). It is related to the normative or quasi-normative issues in chapter 9.

16. Alternatively, we can reason inductively in Bayesian terms and suppose that voters update, on the basis of actual performance, their prior beliefs about candidates and platforms.

17. Implicitly so far, we have assumed yardstick competition to take place among governments situated on the same level of governmental systems, among cities for instance. But this is only the horizontal variant of political yardstick competition, which can also be vertical, taking place among governments situated at different tiers. It can also be modeled as relevant among governments whatever

their location across tiers. In this book, the analysis is about the horizontal variety, unless otherwise stated. The vertical case and the all-governments solution are discussed in chapter 8.

18. I did give some attention to the matter already in Salmon (1987b) and then, more extensively, in Salmon (1991, 1997, 2003b, 2006). See also Breton (1996). Some other work related to international yardstick competition is mentioned in chapter 6. The recent contributions of Kayser and Peress (2012), Hansen et al. (2015), and, more ambiguously, Linos (2013) reflect or may announce some recognition in social sciences other than economics.

19. To borrow the title of an important book in which the possibility of yardstick competition is neglected (Acemoglu and Robertson 2012), it may contribute to our understanding of "why nations fail."

20. The purely theoretical point made in Bordignon, Cerniglia, and Revelli (2004) and Besley and Smart (2007) on the possibility of a negative effect of yardstick competition (or of additional information in general) on the welfare of voters illustrates that argumentative function. The contribution is a criticism of the presumption or view that the effect is necessarily positive.

# CHAPTER 2

# A characterization of political yardstick competition

M any aspects of the way I interpret yardstick competition among governments need elaboration. The feature that is most centrally distinctive, compared to other interpretations, is insistence on heterogeneity: I make it concern simultaneously voters, issues, jurisdictions, and politicians. Voters are numerous and diverse not only in their policy preferences and knowledge (as generally conceded) but also in their motivation (as typically overlooked). This is hardly compatible with the assumption of a single representative voter. Policy issues and outcomes are also numerous. Some of them concern many voters, others only a few. In some discussions we will treat the issue or policy dimension considered as if it was the only one, but in general, we will assume it to be one among many. In turn, the jurisdictions involved in cross-jurisdiction comparisons depend on the issues and the voters concerned. Because looking at or being informed about published rankings is one of the ways voters make comparisons across jurisdictions, the number of jurisdictions concerned may be quite large.

We usually refer to *the* incumbent. This applies well to single elected executives like mayors or presidents but the yardstick competition we have in mind may extend to interacting collectives such as governing teams, "political elites," ruling parties, or even regimes. We will return to complex collectives as well as to alternative forms of support. However, like most of the literature, we will generally assume incumbent agents to be forward looking and rational. Because of that assumption, it is convenient for the moment to refer to a single incumbent rather than to the collectives just mentioned. Also like most of the literature, we will generally assume incumbents as well as their challengers to be intrinsically diverse in terms of motivation and competence. However, we will try to avoid dealing with that diversity in the form of dichotomies such as "bad type versus good type" or "competent versus incompetent."

A realistic apprehension of the electorate is not motivated by a methodological concern with realism or the usual misgivings about modeling. It is important if we are to understand yardstick competition as a generally significant and plausible mechanism. For that purpose, we cannot remain in the confined space in which game theoretic models operate—however analytically costly it may be to escape from it. In the first section of this chapter I characterize, without referring to yardstick competition, a type of principal-agent relation between voters and office-holders adapted to the context of elections with large and heterogeneous electorates. The second section is concerned with yardstick competition in that "electoral agency" setting. The characterization is incomplete in the sense that many other aspects of yardstick competition, for instance those related to the existence of several levels of government, are considered in subsequent chapters.

## 2.1. ELECTORAL AGENCY

Voters are not ordinary principals. Their relation with their agent—the incumbent—is quite different from the relation analyzed in ordinary agency theory. This is acknowledged in the theory of political agency but the dissimilarities underlined therein are not those that are the most important when the focus is on large-scale elections. Referring to "electoral agency" rather than to "political agency" is a way to signal the difference.

### 2.1.1. From normal agency to political agency

To single out similarities and dissimilarities with normal agency theory, political agency theory can be summarized as follows. Assumptions made about the nature of the electorate allow that it be reduced to a single representative individual. That individual's vote is forward looking and instrumental: he (assuming masculinity for convenience) uses elections to get policy outcomes congruent with his preferences. His choice is mainly based on past performance (a defining characteristic of agency) rather than on proposals or platforms. In other words, his vote is retrospective. And it is binary: re-elect or oust the incumbent.

How is retrospective voting compatible with the voter being forward looking? One possibility, if candidates are different, is that retrospective voting is used for selection. In Bayesian terms, the voter has the same prior beliefs with regard to the quality of candidates who are not in office. Observation of the incumbent's past performance allows the voter to up-date his beliefs about that particular candidate compared to the expected quality of the others. Another possibility is to assume that the voter adopts, as a *strategy*, the rule of voting out incumbents for bad performance, so as to give them performance-enhancing incentives. The first possibility is the focus of pure selection models, the second of pure moral hazard or incentives models. The most intellectually attractive models are mixed in the sense that they combine the effects of selection and incentives.

According to the literature, and given the single voter assumption, exclusive reliance on incentives encounters two problems. First, the strategy the voter is supposed to adopt requires that he fixes in advance a performance cut-off or threshold. This is perilous when there are exogenous disturbances whose occurrence, magnitude, or impact are known to the incumbent, but not to the voter. If, when the disturbance has occurred, the level of performance that the voter had required beforehand turns out to be too low, the incumbent will limit his or her effort to what is needed to satisfy the threshold; if the required performance was set too high, the incumbent will give up re-election and enjoy short-term benefits at the maximum legally permissible level (Ferejohn 1986).

Second, the rule adopted for sanctioning or rewarding the incumbent may not be credible (in the game-theoretic sense of that word). The reason for that lack of credibility varies across models, depending on the precise way they are constructed.[1] If candidates are assumed to be different, according to Fearon (1999) the voter cannot credibly commit to a rule that would prevent him from focusing "completely on the problem of selection when casting [his] vote" (p. 77). In Besley and Smart (2007), "the voter faces a commitment problem—they cast their votes for re-election after first-period spending decisions have been made. It follows that the equilibrium re-election rule is chosen to select politicians optimally ex post, but it will not provide the efficient degree of ex ante incentives" (p. 759).

As a consequence, more information may have opposite effects on incentives and selection. Suppose that incumbents are divided into two categories: bad types, who profit from information asymmetry to get rents, and good types, who don't.[2] The latter are never tempted to act in a way not congruent with what voters prefer.[3] The bad types are only interested in getting rents. With better-informed voters, some bad-type incumbents, knowing that they will not make it to the second period (after the next election), lose the incentive to pool with (i.e., mimic) the good-type be-havior in the first period (before the next election). They grab maximum rents in the present (this is the bad effect of more information, related to incentives) but they are more likely to be out of office and thus unable to grab rents in the future (this is the good effect of more information, related to selection).

In that political agency setting, ambiguity in the effects of additional information on both the welfare of voters and rents is ascribed to the in-complete character of the incentives given to agents. For Besley and Smart (2007), one reason why "the equilibrium outcomes depart from those as-sociated with an optimal incentive contract for politicians is that feasible contracts are restricted—they are confined to the voter's binary choice of re-election, rather than a general pay-for-performance contract"(p. 759). In addition, "In the standard complete contracts model of Holmstrom (1979), more information is better . . . . With incomplete incentives, an otherwise welfare improving change (more information) may have delete-rious effects on equilibrium behavior that more than offset the direct wel-fare impact. In our model, incentives are incomplete since the threat of not being re-elected is the only mechanism with which the voter may discipline incumbents" (p. 765).[4]

### 2.1.2. From political agency to electoral agency

Why relate electoral agency to large-number electorates as announced? Why refer to size? The idea is simply to stress characteristics of voting that seem intuitive or obvious in the case of large-sized elections whereas when they are supposed to concern voting in general, including in small-scale committees this is only for theoretical purposes and somewhat artificial. The elections I have in mind are those we are familiar with in well-functioning democracies. The minimal size that an electorate must reach to qualify as "large" being only a few hundred, we may assume electorates to be large at all levels of government (localities included).

I assume that a large electorate cannot constitute a collective or unitary actor and relatedly, that the principal-agent relation is not between the electorate and the incumbent but between each voter, acting as a principal, and the incumbent, his or her agent. Voting, especially because it is anony-mous, is an individual and separate act.

In addition to being a principal, each voter is also a sovereign. Voters do not make promises and do not have to justify their votes (also thanks in part to anonymity). It is voter sovereignty in that sense—not the binary character of voting as mentioned in the citation of Besley and Smart (2007) that makes it impossible for voters to make credible commitments.[5] On elections day, whatever happens, voters, enjoying absolute sovereignty, will vote as they please.[6]

Contrary to voters, politicians do make promises. They may even formulate these promises as commitments.[7] There are conceivable systems of representative government in which such commitments would be binding, for instance through mechanisms of imperative mandates or, less directly, permanent revocability. But under prevailing systems of representative democracy incumbents are always free to renege on promises (Manin 1997). And, as is widely observable, incumbents do take advantage of that right. Of course, there may be a specific electoral cost to reneging (specific because distinct from the cost or benefit associated with the policy itself). Some voters feel betrayed and the reputation, trustworthiness, or credibility of the incumbents may suffer. But these ill effects do not always occur, reneging being sometimes interpreted by voters as reflecting statesmanship (Salmon 1993). And in any case the cost—if cost there is— is only one consideration in the rational, forward-looking calculations of incumbents. Performance will often weigh more in these calculations and in voters' reactions than sticking to promises.

That situation may not seem so different from the agents' situation in the main agency theory, at least under realistic interpretations of that theory. There also, agents often calculate whether reneging is more advantageous than keeping promises. However, there is a conceptual difference related to legal obligation or trust. In the main agency theory, promises are made from both sides. The relation is a contractual exchange of commitments. Even when the underlying contract is implicit or incomplete, and transgressions unverifiable (in a technical sense), its provisions can be enforced through mutual trust. By contrast, electoral agency, fundamentally, is not contractual. Referring to contracts, even imperfect ones, is misleading. The fact that the situation of principals (voters) is different in an essential way entails by itself a difference in the situation of agents. Not only legal obligation but also mutual trust as a basis of contracts is excluded.[8] Only unilateral trust can have a sense. Voters may trust their agent, the incumbent, and, as noted, they may feel betrayed. But trusting voters has no meaning. Voters don't betray incumbents. Incumbents consider voters' reactions in terms of pure probability.

We must also note that coordination is not the main theoretical obstacle to the reduction of the electorate to a single "representative" voter. The two characteristics of large electorates just stressed—voting severally and voting sovereignly—do not formally prevent aggregate electoral behavior to be as if coordination had been achieved. To derive that proposition, one can refer to the median voter mechanism or simply assume that all voters are alike.

The real logical obstacle is instrumental voting. It is tempting to assume that, once he is given life, the single voter will vote so that his preferences (with regard to policies or candidates) get satisfied—that is, to assume that he will vote instrumentally. This is to forget, however, that no single voter is really assumed.[9] The reduction of the electorate to a single voter is not total. An essential dimension has escaped: the individual decisions to participate in the vote.[10] Given the insignificance of any individual vote in the case of large-number elections, the motivation of people who bother to vote is puzzling from a rational actor perspective (it is even more puzzling if all voters are assumed to be identical) and, as is well-known, that first puzzle has a bearing on a second one: voting instrumentally.

These puzzles constitute a convenient introduction to a characteristic of electoral agency particularly important to bear in mind for our purpose. Several aspects of heterogeneity in large electorates are widely acknowledged. Voters do not share the same information or interpret it in the same way. They do not have the same policy preferences or priorities. But the puzzles just mentioned suggest that more attention be given to a dimension of heterogeneity generally overlooked in the theoretical literature: voters perceive their role or function as voters in different ways. The implications of that proposition warrant some elaboration. In spite of the insignificance of their vote, many people do vote. The theoretical solutions of that paradox that have been offered (see, e.g., Ansolabehere 2006) are often treated as alternative hypotheses. In reality, we should take on board *all* the solutions proposed. They are fully compatible provided we consider the many voters who compose any large and heterogeneous electorate. Some individuals may think, in spite of the large numbers involved, that their vote could turn out to be pivotal. As a consequence, they consider their vote as instrumental in promoting their preferences—whether these preferences are "egotropic" or "sociotropic" does not matter here. Other voters, even though fully aware of the inconsequential nature of their vote, feel morally, socially, or civically obliged to participate. Many people consider their votes as expressing a retrospective judgment, a ruling, a verdict (Manin 1997).

Voters are heterogeneous in their interpretation of their role, responsibility, or function and that interpretation, we may presume, is reflected in the content of the vote as well as in its motivation. Among the many combinations of motivations and decisions that necessarily exist within large electorates, consider the following two (which may or may not concern a substantial share of the electorate—that does not really matter). Individuals of type A neglect the insignificance of any individual participation and decide to vote prospectively (or perhaps one should say as if prospectively), even strategically (or as if strategically)—as if that contributed significantly to having their policy preferences satisfied. Individuals of type B also know that their votes will not count, but they derive utility from expressing through voting a sentiment, possibly purely retributive, about the incumbent's performance. By assumption the two types are lucid, not victims of any kind of illusion or wishful thinking. Is one more rational than the other? Answering that question is both difficult and unnecessary for our purpose. More to the point, should we exclude one from our assumptions? The view defended here is that we should include both, as well as many others, as producers of the aggregate response of the electorate.

### 2.1.3. Voters and performance: the principle

A question arising at this stage is whether the assumption of strong heterogeneity in voters' motivations and behaviors might not deprive the analysis of any predictive power. Certainly, the electoral response of voters to government action cannot be left completely open or unspecified. This is not only a methodological requirement. It is plausible that in reality, in spite of heterogeneity, the response of voters is not completely unpredictable. The following propositions create minimal restrictions on voters' discretionary behavior.

**Proposition 1.** If a voter considers a policy outcome or government action as reflecting a good (bad) performance on the part of the government, this has either no effect or a positive (negative) one on the probability of his or her supporting the incumbent.

**Proposition 2.** If a voter interprets a change in a policy outcome or government action as reflecting a positive (negative) change in government's performance, this induces either no change or a positive (negative) change in the probability of his or her supporting the incumbent.

Without further discussion, we can assume that the propositions apply without difficulty to all types of voting behavior, including those just mentioned: voting instrumentally or prospectively, or voting as a form of verdict, or satisfying a desire of retribution, etc. Among the questions these propositions do raise, the following two categories need particular attention.

### 2.1.4. Ambiguities in the meaning of governmental performance

The meaning of performance is not as straightforward as is (necessarily) assumed in many discussions. According to dictionaries, performance is about how well or badly something works or how well or badly a job is done or a task carried out. How does that apply to governments? Many tasks or jobs are assigned to government in unconditional terms. In our societies, it is widely agreed that government should ensure that crime and terrorism are deterred, the population kept in good health, the young educated, the elderly and handicapped taken care of, the consumers and the environment protected, the arts and sports encouraged, economic growth fostered, unemployment contained, and so on. This allows many discussions of performance to focus, with no reference to cost-benefit considerations, on how well or badly government carries on these different tasks. Let us accept that for the moment.

In some cases, to be found mostly in domains such as public health and security, we can go even further. The task is not only defined in unconditional terms, independently of cost, but is also expected to produce a perfect outcome. Any instance of incomplete realization is treated as a failure—sometimes to be sanctioned in the form of forced resignation or prosecution of the officials deemed responsible.[11]

However, in most policy areas the implicit definition of jobs assigned to government cannot refer to full realization. Then, there may be no perfectly objective benchmark available to assess government's performance (defined as the degree to which government does its job). Individual voters will have different views about both the definition of the job and its degree of realization—job definitions being distinct from but related to policy preferences. Comparisons over time and over space (across jurisdictions) make these views less uncertain—as noted, this is a second rationale (involving no information asymmetry) for comparative assessments.[12] In this section, I assume comparisons to be made only over time.

Consider governmental policy regarding road casualties and, more precisely, fatalities. The job of government is to prevent fatalities. But the job cannot be defined as making sure that there are none. Thus, the fact that the number is positive cannot be deemed to signal bad performance. Suppose that, in jurisdiction X, the annual figure announced is 4,000. If there are no comparisons over time (assume that the fatality figure is provided for the first time), Proposition 1 applies. Is the performance of government on that issue good or bad? Some insiders may have an informed opinion on the matter from observing directly the way government acts. But assessments by voters can only be based on the difference between announced outcomes and any prior expectations, generally idiosyncratic, that they may have had.[13]

Now, let us allow comparisons over time but not yet over space. Then, it is Proposition 2 which is relevant. Suppose that, about ten years before the current figure, the number of people killed in car accidents in the same jurisdiction was 5,000. Deciding about performance becomes better founded. Incumbents may boast about the change. Should they be believed? As we will see, distinctions must be made within comparisons over time. Some can benefit from outcomes being related to circumstances or events that are recurrent (storms, bad crops, strikes, demonstrations, etc.). Then, the way past incumbents responded to these circumstances provide a kind of (possibly unconscious) benchmark. It allows voters to say with some confidence that the present incumbent has or has not done a good job in that particular instance. Other comparisons cannot rely on such a relatively secure basis. For instance, the underlying source of disturbance in the jurisdiction concerned is an unprecedented shock or a historical and unique trend. The latter is relevant in the case of the car accidents comparisons just discussed. Then reference to the past is prone to be deceptive when not checked or complemented by comparisons over space.

### 2.1.5. Conflicting views among voters

This second category of problems is related to issue multidimensionality. What are exactly the policy outcomes assessed, or their dimensions? As noted, and as will be stressed again, voters must be assumed to be concerned mainly with policy results or outcomes rather than policy instruments. However, it is often the case that policy instruments are also policy outcomes for some categories of voters.

In the political theory of voting and in discussions of electoral accountability, it has often been convenient to distinguish among issues those that enjoy a consensus among voters and those over which voters have divergent positions. The former are generally referred to in political science as valence issues (see, e.g., Fiorina 1981) and in political economy as common-value or non-partisan issues (Besley 2006). Corruption, crime, security, educational results, or economic prosperity are typical instances.

Is the reduction of car accidents a valence issue? Even if it qualifies as one—preferably a non-partisan issue—at the level of political parties or legislators, is it also a valence issue at the level of individual citizens? Everybody is against car accidents but people's feelings may be more mixed with regard to speed and drinking limits or the penalties set for infringing them. In other words, there may be no consensus among citizens on the packages of measures adopted by government to reduce casualties. If this is so, it is somewhat misleading to say that there is a consensus on the policy objective itself. A similar ambiguity may be observed with regard to policies against smoking or even terrorism. The problem is quite general and I doubt that, in reality, there are many issues deemed to be valence issues that would survive a closer inspection of the consensus claimed to exist and thus to justify the label. In fact, assuming issues to be valence issues is above all a matter of convenience. The assumption is one way to simplify the analysis. As such, it will also be made in part of the forthcoming discussion.

The difficulty raised by would-be valence issues is part of a more general problem: how to deal with issue multidimensionality? Let us consider the matter in a domain, public finance, in which the answer seems relatively easy before turning to one, redistribution, in which it is less so.

Most people like reductions in taxation. But some make the link between taxation and public services they approve of. Conversely, as noted, most people are in favor of improvements in education but some make the link with their cost. In the case of small localities, or in systems of direct democracy, the assumption that voters look at combinations of changes in public services and their tax prices is fairly realistic.[14] And it is natural (or even compelling) in models in which the electorate is reduced to a single voter. However, following in particular Hettich and Winer (1988), I will consider it largely true that "the separation of taxes and expenditures is an important characteristic of modern fiscal systems" and in any case, as they do, I will assume (if only for convenience) that "individual taxpayers see no connection between the level of services provided and their own tax burden" (p. 703).

There are at least four additional reasons to make that assumption. First, our focus is on assessments of realized performance rather than on candidate platforms or programs. The links between services and their tax price comes in naturally and openly in the debates over proposals. This is not, or is much less the case, with voters' assessments of past performance.[15] Second, the importance given to accountability is often related to the suspicion that incumbents do not make the relation between outputs and their cost very tight. Between the two, they may get rents (in a broad sense of the term). Alternatively or in addition, they may be biased (or pushed by the bureaucracy or lobbies) toward spending more than voters would decide if they were perfectly informed—the Leviathan bias analyzed by Brennan and Buchanan (1980). Putting pressure only on one side— taxes—independently of the way proceeds are employed is a way to fight that tendency.[16] Third, the claimed allocation of particular tax proceeds to particular expenditures is often illusory because of compensations within public budgets. Fourth, the loss (whatever it consists of) entailed by the separation assumed by Hettich and Winer (1988) may be limited. The fact that an individual does not make the link between an increase in taxation and an increase in some public output is compatible with the two variations having simultaneous effects (one negative, the other positive) on his or her assessment of government. The overall effect might not be so different from what it would have been if we had assumed cost-benefit calculations.

Issues that have a salient redistributive or ideological dimension may seem particularly problematic. They include pure financial redistribution from one part of the population to another but also issues, such as abortion, same-sex marriage, and the death penalty, over which citizens hold strong conflicting views (at one point in time). The treatment we can apply to them is the same as that just discussed: performance assessments are related to the preferences of subsets of the electorate. In retrospect, legalizing abortion and abolishing the death penalty are generally considered major, positive aspects of the performance of, respectively, Valéry Giscard d'Estaing and François Mitterrand, two French presidents. In both cases, opinions on whether the reforms were positive or negative achievements were very divided at the time. Even now, there are still people who deplore them. Thus, one must say that the two reforms signaled a good incumbent performance only or mainly for the subset of the electorate supporting them—a subset evolving over time (and much larger now than then).[17] Similarly, more redistribution improves the incumbent's perceived performance for those who want more redistribution, and it decreases it for those who want less.[18]

## 2.1.6. Incumbents and performance

Even though we may assume that voters do not make the connection between public services and their cost in term of taxation or that voters do not agree on whether a governmental action signals a good or a bad performance, assumptions of that kind cannot be extended to incumbents, to whom we must ascribe an integrated view of the response to their decisions. Let us reason in the spirit of the probabilistic theory of voting. Incumbents are uncertain about the support they may receive from each voter, or category of voters, and how that support will vary as a response to policies or policy outcomes. But we may assume that they assign a probability to individual responses and sum these individual probabilities to get a variation in total expected support.[19]

As a rule, from the incumbents' perspective any action will have positive and negative effects on expected electoral support. In the case of a would-be valence issue such as reducing the number of fatal car accidents, the reduction itself will have a positive effect but many of the instruments available to obtain it will have negative ones. And the reasoning is the same when increased output in one domain is not financed by taxation but, within the budget constraint, by decreased output in another. Better performance in the first domain will tend to increase, while decreased performance in the other will tend to reduce, expected support.

It is tempting to assume that incumbents equate expected electoral costs and benefits at the margin, so as to maximize expected total support. But this would be neglecting an essential ingredient of the agency approach, which is the existence of rents, in a broad sense of the term. As a consequence of that existence, taxes can be reduced for the same output, or output increased for the same taxation, rents being reduced in both cases. Whatever their exact content, by definition rents provide utility to incumbents, who consequently find reducing them costly. Variation in rents, together with support losses and gains, must be included in incumbents' cost-benefit calculations. Leaving aside for the moment the possibility that voters are bad judges of their own welfare, voters have a common interest in rents being as small as possible. One obstacle to that interest being satisfied is information asymmetry.

Other aspects of electoral agency as I interpret it should be noted but, to avoid repetition, will be discussed after taking into account the possibility for voters to make cross-jurisdiction comparisons, a matter I turn to now.

## 2.2. YARDSTICK COMPETITION IN ELECTORAL AGENCY

The way agency was analyzed in the preceding section has two opposite effects on our approach to yardstick competition. The hypothesis that *some* voters engage in cross-jurisdiction comparisons is more credible than the hypothesis that a single representative voter does so. And an implication of the probabilistic voting framework is that the opinion of even a small fraction of the electorate may have an influence on both electoral outcomes and incumbents' decisions. Thus, the intuitive plausibility of an impact of yardstick competition is greater in our electoral agency framework than it would be in the world of single representative voters, or of homogeneous voters, generally assumed in political agency models. On the other hand, the multidimensional heterogeneity of the electorate—a central feature of electoral agency—has an effect on the way that the electorate responds to, or exploits, the possibility of cross-jurisdiction comparisons. Conflicting assessments were already a source of complication in the last section, when no possibility of cross-jurisdiction comparisons was assumed. They also complicate the analysis when that possibility is opened up. For many analytic purposes, that does not matter too much: the view of the sur-roundings in which yardstick completion operates can be somewhat messy or confused without that confusion diminishing the relevance or signif-icance of the mechanism. However, for some analytical purposes, that mechanism must be depicted in a simpler and more precise fashion. Using some additional assumptions, I will derive a simple aggregate function relating support to comparative performance. The additional assumptions are somewhat disturbing, but, to assess their acceptability one will have to take into account the shape given to the function.

### 2.2.1. Voters' comparative assessments

Observation by individual voters of the situation in other jurisdictions may give them a basis to decide whether government is doing a good or a bad job (in a particular policy area or in general). Proposition 1, formulated earlier, then becomes relevant (which, as noted, it was not really when no comparisons were available). Suppose that voter $A$, living and voting in lo-cality $X$, discovers that in most other localities streets are less well paved, less well-lit, and less clean than in $X$. Then $A$ may feel entitled to judge that her government does a good job in that area. Proposition 1 tells us that if that judgment entails a change in the probability that she will support the incumbent, the change will be positive.

However, even in the case of a single individual, things are more uncer-tain, because differences across jurisdictions and changes over time may have conflicting effects on performance assessment. Suppose that $A$ finds streets less well paved, less well-lit, and dirtier both in other jurisdictions compared contemporaneously to locality $X$ (a good point for her govern-ment) and in $X$ itself when comparing the present to the past (a bad point). Whether it is Proposition 1 or Proposition 2 that will weigh more in voter

$A$'s assessment of performance is uncertain. Taking them together we can only say that if they induce a change in $A$'s assessment of government performance in that domain and if that change induces a variation in the probability that $A$ will support the incumbent, the two changes will be in the same direction.

The problem seems even more bothersome at the aggregate level—that is, when considering not one but many voters. An aggregate effect of performance on support cannot be derived mechanically from an effect, even if unambiguous, at the level of individuals. The obstacle has a single cause, albeit one that takes different aspects. We have assumed voters to be numerous, heterogeneous, and (except for Propositions 1 and 2, which are not very demanding) unconstrained in the way they address government performance. This allows that different voters base their assessments on different kinds of observation, or interpret them in different ways.

The implications for cross-jurisdiction comparisons are not really dramatic. The view, generally persuasive, that comparisons must be justified, objective, or well-founded has several sources (I do not contest of course that being justified is preferable to being mistaken). Let me note two. The first is insufficient awareness of the differences between the setting assumed by general agency theory and the electoral context. As we saw, the theory of agency as elaborated originally for the private sector is largely a theory of contracts. In that original habitat, the necessity of some clarity in performance criteria follows from the fact that the remuneration of the agent is related in an automatic or quasi-automatic way to the evaluation of his or her performance. Good and bad performance are rewarded and sanctioned under conditions that are contractually defined in advance—even if this is done only in broad terms (as stressed by the economic theory of contracts itself). The second reason to insist on justification is more sociological, connected not to agency theory but to the deontology of the economic profession. It stems naturally from the concerns of independent individual observers such as statisticians or from neutrality constraints that international organizations must respect. Abiding with deontological norms, these individuals or organizations, when undertaking to evaluate or compare the performance of governments, are obliged to seek objectivity and to justify their results.

In our interpretation of electoral agency—and with it of political yardstick competition—individual voters assess performance as they see fit. The same logic applies to gathering information. To be better informed, individual voters can use any means that they find appropriate. They may seek or follow advice from any source. In particular, they can use comparisons with what obtains in other jurisdictions but only if they have the occasion and feel inclined to do so. For that purpose, they can choose the jurisdictions and the indicators they think appropriate. Let me give two examples.

Example 1: voter A is not interested in what obtains in other jurisdictions. He judges government on the basis of changes over time within the jurisdiction. Voter B, in addition to changes over time in the jurisdiction, takes into account changes over time in other jurisdictions. To return to an example already given, A is content to know that car accidents now kill 4,000 people per year instead of the 5,000 people per year they killed about ten years before. B gives some attention also to the fact that in a neighboring country, over the same period, the number of people killed in car accidents halved. Government's performance in that domain is likely to be judged good by A and bad by B.

Example 2: individuals C and D vote in jurisdiction X, which they know well. For some reason, C happens to also know jurisdiction Y and D happens to also know jurisdiction Z. In the same policy domain, C and D derive from different comparisons the views that, respectively, the performance of X's government is bad and good. To illustrate, we can exploit the study on crime control in Central America published by The Economist (July 12, 2014). It appears from that study that, compared to Guatemala, crime per capita is much higher in Honduras and much lower in Nicaragua. We may imagine that individuals C and D vote in Guatemala and know the crime situation there. In addition, C knows the crime situation in Honduras, D the crime situation in Nicaragua. On the basis of that knowledge, C and D consider the job done by their own government (Guatemala's) at keeping crime under control to be, respectively, good and bad.

How can we deal with the aggregation problem raised by such differences even among voters who share the same concerns or preferences? For statistical studies, there is no serious difficulty. In particular, as I will discuss later, the empirical literature on local finance confirms that a tax increase in jurisdiction X has a negative effect and a tax increase in other jurisdictions a positive effect on voting for (or the popularity of) the incumbent in X.

One should also stress that the effect on performance of any change in the policy outcome concerned (when the initial comparison has no time dimension, as in Proposition 1) or of any additional change in that outcome (when the initial comparisons do have a time dimension, as in Proposition 2) is unambiguous. In our example on crime control, the (static) performance of Guatemala was better than that of Honduras and worse than that of Nicaragua. But reducing crime in Guatemala would improve, ceteris paribus, both the absolute (measured over time) performance and the comparative (measured across countries) performance of that country. Similarly, in our example of car accidents, the reduction over time was from 5,000 to 4,000. Ceteris paribus (nothing changed abroad), an additional reduction of 500, making the outcome 3,500, would have improved the performance of the jurisdiction whatever way it is assessed. Given Proposition 1 and 2, the effect on yardstick voting of these additional improvements is also unambiguous.

Divergence among voters on whether performance is better or worse than elsewhere, or whether it is increasing or decreasing, complicates the electoral cost-benefit calculations of incumbents. In the example just presented, should the fact that the number of car accidents in the jurisdiction has diminished over time induce an election-minded incumbent to relax and even diminish effort in that domain? Or, rather, should the fact that the jurisdiction has done badly compared to others trigger an effort at improving government performance? It is for incumbents to evaluate and decide, and in many parts of this book we can remain unconcerned with the end result of their calculations. Even if the effects of yardstick voting and yardstick competition are ambiguous for us, they are likely to be decidable and important for them. This is all that is necessary for these mechanisms to be politically and economically significant. However, in other parts of our reasoning we need something like Propositions 1 and 2—but applicable at the aggregate level.

### 2.2.2. The comparisons-based support function

The relation needed, at the aggregate level, is between comparative performance (either in a particular policy domain or in general) and expected political support. As we saw, the difficulty is that individual voters' assessments of comparative performance, inasmuch as they are made, are idiosyncratic and often conflicting. As also noted, experts do seek objective, well-founded comparisons. Let us go further and assume that the comparisons they make are correct and yield an evaluation of relative performance which is also correct. Performance evaluated in this way will be called *objective comparative performance*. It takes into account idiosyncratic characteristics of jurisdictions, differential effects of shocks, chance events, differences in natural resources and so on. It can be given any time dimension (long run or short run) and can be measured and formulated in different ways (ordinal or cardinal, static or dynamic, etc.). The following proposition is compatible with the different cases.

**Proposition 3.** If, along some dimension, the objective comparative performance of government is positive (negative), this has either no effect on the electoral support expected by the incumbent or a positive (negative) effect.

Let us return to the car accident illustration. Some voters do not take cross-jurisdiction comparisons into account. They interpret the fact that the number of car accident fatalities has fallen from 5,000 to 4,000 as manifesting a good government's performance. Suppose that this generates an increase of $M$ in the expected vote in favor of incumbent. Suppose now that for the experts, the fact that the number of car accidents has fallen much more rapidly elsewhere signals a negative comparative performance of the country with which we are concerned. It is assumed that experts are always right, thus the objective comparative performance is negative. As a consequence, Proposition 3 tells us, some voters may be less likely to vote for the incumbent. Following the probabilistic voting approach, these diminished probabilities at the individual level have an aggregate effect on the electoral support that the incumbent expects to receive. Suppose that the said effect is an expected support loss of $N$. Altogether, $S$, the variation in total expected support caused by the fall in car accidents is equal to $M - N$. If there is vast majority of voters who do not make or take into account comparisons, the variation will be positive ($S > 0$). However, provided that some voters respond to comparisons, that variation will be smaller than it would have been without yardstick voting.

For some purposes we may go further and assume that objective performance tout court is derived exclusively from objective comparative performance. Experts are entrusted with determining comparative performance, and this by itself, automatically, determines performance tout court. The following proposition, formulated in terms of variation, ensues.

**Proposition 4.** If, along some dimension, the objective performance of government (determined exclusively on the basis of cross-jurisdiction comparisons made by experts) is positive (negative), this has either no effect on the electoral support expected by the incumbent or a positive (negative) effect.

The fact that some or many voters assess performance without taking into account outcomes in other jurisdictions increases the discrepancy between their assessments and what we assume to be reality, but that discrepancy is merged with other causes of ill-perception or noise. In other words, voters' assessments that do not take cross-jurisdictions into account are deemed wrong and are neglected in defining objective performance. Thus, in our car accident example, objective performance becomes clearly negative. Nonetheless, if most voters do not make comparisons, the total vote expected in favor of the incumbent increases, and Proposition 4 is contradicted. That possibility must be understood in the light of two other assumptions, already noted. First, the relationships referred to in Propositions 1–4 should be represented by curves that have an S-shape. Small variations in performance have no or little effect on voting. Second, yardstick voting or competition is a mechanism and as such does not always work or may even have perverse effects. There are many reasons for failure. One of them is voters giving no precedence to comparative performance. The two points are related: a mistaken perception of performance is more likely when the matter is minor and attracts little attention.

### 2.2.3. The S-shaped response of voters to comparative performance

It has been assumed in the preceding discussion that the effect of a variation in comparative performance on support is monotonous: if the effect is not zero, the variation in support is positively related to the variation in comparative performance. But the relation is unlikely to be linear. As illustrated in figure 2.1, one way for it to be non-linear is being S-shaped (being kinked is considered in the next chapter).

The reason for the S-shape is easy to understand. In a given jurisdiction, say $X$, suppose a small variation $p$ (positive or negative) in comparative performance. Very few voters of that jurisdiction perceive the variation, and even fewer voters change their vote as a consequence. The variation $s$ in aggregate support for the incumbent is negligibly small. This is likely to remain true for a range of variations in comparative performance. At one point, however, the effect is no longer negligible. Then, unitary increases in $p$ have increasing effects on support variation $s$: in figure 2.1, the curve becomes steeper. Some people discover $p$ only if it is bigger, only then do conversations and the media focus on it, perceptive voters conscious of $p$ even when small are more likely to change their vote when it is large, and so on. If $p$ is already very large, unitary increases in it have a small effect on $s$. Most people who could be informed about the existence of $p$ are already informed, and those among them who could change their mind with regard

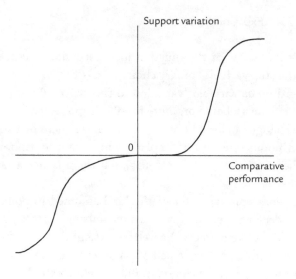

**Figure 2.1**: Comparative performance and support

to supporting the incumbent have already done so. At a certain level of $p$, the curve becomes horizontal because part of the electorate is unconcerned by $p$ whatever its level.[20]

That reasoning seems sensible or even evident. To my surprise, the S-shape has met with some skepticism on the part of several empirically minded colleagues. Let me stress that the relation represented by S-shaped curves concerns the effect on support $s$ of *possible* values of performance variation $p$ in *one single* jurisdiction, not different *actual* combinations of $p$ and $s$ in cross-section studies, or in panels involving several jurisdictions and periods.[21] The curve is meant to answer (for all conceivable values of $p$) questions such as: "What, in jurisdiction $X$, would be support loss or gain $s$ if the variation in comparative performance in that jurisdiction was $p$?" It is a counterfactual relation, similar in this respect to the demand curve implicit when monopolists ask themselves: "What quantity could I sell if I fixed the price at $P$?" Estimation of functions of that type is not easy, as we know,[22] but that is a matter I am not concerned with for the moment (or perhaps in general).

*The hypothesis that the response of the electorate to performance or variations in performance is S-shaped is an essential ingredient of my interpretation of yard-stick competition.* It is only one of its merits that, as noted, it tends to make voters' misperceptions less analytically bothersome. As we will see, what is important is that very good or very bad objective comparative performance is unlikely to remain unperceived by voters, or, alternatively that the fact that it remains unperceived or without consequences is considered puzzling.

## 2.2.4. Explained variable

On the left-hand side of the function just discussed, one does not find any more the step variable "binary choice of re-election" discussed earlier but the continuous variable "variation in the expected number of votes in favor of the incumbent" or, more briefly, "support variation." The nature of the change can be split in two: first, replacement of a step variable with a continuous one; second, replacement of one continuous variable with another. The first change is crucial, but there is also a rationale for the second.

A single representative voter of the kind assumed in political agency models may decide to retain or oust the incumbent. Perfectly coordinated voters may do the same. In the theoretical settings that give the electorate such characteristics, the explained variable can be the binary one: re-election or ousting of the incumbent. But the electorate that we assumed in our characterization of electoral agency is completely different. Voters are numerous and heterogeneous along several dimensions. They decide separately (without coordination). The binary choice facing each individual voter is not to retain or oust the incumbent but to vote or not vote for her. As seen from outside (from the incumbent's perspective in particular) the choice of each voter is apprehended as the probability that he or she will do one or the other. In our analysis, summing these probabilities determines at the aggregate level the expected vote in favor of the incumbent. There is a well-understood relation between that variable and the probability of re-election. Thus, we could as well assume that the summation of individual probabilities determines a probability of re-election of the incumbent. Then, in figure 2.1 the vertical axis would represent that probability or its variation. This would not change dramatically our analysis, the essential implication of the electoral agency setting being that the dependent variable is continuous.

One might claim that this first change (continuous rather than step variable) reflects a diminished ambition for the theory, regarding in particular predictive strength or refutability. Predicting that the incumbent will be ousted is riskier and therefore in a sense stronger than predicting that she will lose some votes or will have a lower probability of being re-elected. When feasible, it might also be more interesting. But, independently of the fact that the electoral agency setting, once adopted, leaves us no choice, there are also advantages to having a continuous dependent variable. One advantage is that it contributes to making the relation "smoother," which in turn has interesting implications for the working of incentives, as we will see.

Why the second change—that is, why variation in expected support rather than variation in the probability of re-election (in both cases continuous variations)? In fact, performance may or may not have a significant effect on support, and variation in support may or may not have a significant effect on re-election prospects. Must the two effects be significant for yardstick competition to work? Not necessarily. The indecisive character of the dependent variable is particularly well suited to the existence in reality of many issues, only one of which is the object of discussion. Suppose that the issue is a relatively secondary one, the rate of an ecological tax, say. Even secondary issues may have a bearing on voting and may also be the object of an analysis in terms of yardstick competition or yardstick voting. For instance, decisions on whether or not to have an ecological tax and on the rate of that tax are typically objects of cross-jurisdiction comparisons made by some subsets of the electorate, often on opposite sides.[23] Even if the voters concerned are few, incumbents are not normally indifferent with regard to the way they respond to policies. Taken together, categorical responses have a significant effect on the prospect of re-election. In that respect, incumbents behave a little like large multi-division firms, attentive to the profitability of all divisions, including those that are small and whose fate is unable to affect significantly the profitability of the firm as a whole. However, regarding each separate issue, incumbents will reason in terms of votes lost or gained, not in terms of re-election or dismissal. If we want to study the effect of yardstick competition when the matter at stake is secondary, it is clear that the appropriate variable is variation in support.

Even when the issue considered is a major one, there is a case for reasoning in terms of votes lost or gained rather than in terms of re-election or dismissal. First, an incumbent may consider the loss of support that would result from bad performance on an issue, even an important one, as costly even if that loss does not increase significantly the probability of dismissal. Insufficient support may prevent the incumbent from engaging in reforms she considers desirable—or, the other way around, it may make necessary reforms she would have preferred to avoid. Bad performance will require counter-measures that are costly along other dimensions: diminished rents or more effort, more clientelism, more spending on propaganda, more cheating, changes in policies concerning other issues, and so on. If we extend our analysis to non-democratic regimes, bad performance may be perceived by dictators as requiring change (in one direction or the other) in the level of repression, which has its own costs (Wintrobe 1998).

Second, although not indispensable, it may be analytically clearer to separate variations in support and variations in the probability of re-election. The impact of a given support loss or gain on the probability of remaining in power will depend on systemic characteristics such as the electoral system or on contingent characteristics such as the initial margin enjoyed by the incumbent. In the empirical work on local finance, taking these characteristics into account has proved helpful for isolating yardstick competition from other causes of policy interaction among jurisdictions. At a more theoretical level, giving systemic characteristics an explicit and independent role will be an essential ingredient of one of the models proposed in chapter 7.

### 2.2.5. Selection and incentives

Political agency models show with precision that additional information could be detrimental to voters. Yardstick competition is an additional channel through which such an effect is possible (see Besley 2006, Besley and Smart 2007, and implicitly Bordignon, Cerniglia, and Revelli 2004). To what extent is the theoretical result relevant in the setting of electoral agency?

Let me insist again on the obvious difference between the two settings. The problems of threshold, coordination, and credibility stressed in political agency models evaporate in the setting of electoral agency. Some voters may have their own, idiosyncratic, threshold, but voters together need not coordinate and need not decide any kind of rule or strategy.[24] Indeed it is exactly because threats and rewards reflect the presence in the behavior of the electorate of non-strategic, or even unintentional, components that they are particularly credible and effective in the eyes of incumbents. The word component is important. Because of voter heterogeneity, the response of aggregate voting to performance has not one but several components. There is no contradiction in supposing the simultaneous co-existence of different attitudes, even when they imply voting differently. Some voters, forward-looking and thinking that there are differences of quality among candidates, will "focus completely on the problem of selection" (Fearon 1999, p. 77). Others, who do not consider selection important or feasible, will be only concerned with sanctioning or rewarding the incumbent. Overall there is a relation between performance and votes and we will focus on it.

To what extent does that apparently major difference between the political agency and the electoral agency settings matter? I am not certain (anymore) that it does very much.[25] All authors are not perfectly clear on the point, but what drives their results, I have realized belatedly, is not the capacity of voters to identify good or bad politicians. The strength of mixed political agency models such as the ones proposed by Banks and Sundaram (1993, 1998), Fearon (1999), Persson and Tabellini (2000), Besley (2006), and Ashworth (2012)—including explicit analyses of yardstick competition by Bordignon, Cerniglia, and Revelli (2004) and Besley and Smart (2007)—lies in the way they describe incumbents, not voters. And the difference between the two settings (electoral versus political agency) is not so large as far as politicians are concerned.

The following story, which leaves aside many complications stressed in the models and does not make explicit all the assumptions it relies on, describes what might happen in an electoral agency setting. Incumbents facing no election behave as they please (they shirk, rest, engage in non-electorally enhancing activities, possibly meritorious ones, etc.). Although I don't like the term, we may call "rent" the utility they derive from that freedom or from its uses (rent is a surplus to conventional remuneration). Incumbents anticipating an election consider the rent they may enjoy in the present (before the election) and the rent they may enjoy in the future (after the election). There is a relation between the two because rent reduces electorally relevant performance. In the present, relinquishing all or some of it increases performance. Increased performance in the present increases expected support at the next election. Increased support at the next election increases the probability of re-election. Thus, if they want to be re-elected, incumbents give up some rent in the present (before the election) to have a better chance of getting some rent in the future (after the election). In other words, they invest in re-election.

In the absence of cross-jurisdiction comparisons, assessments of performance are highly imprecise and uncertain. The return to investing in re-election is low. It is better to enjoy almost maximum rents in the first period (that is, avoid only particularly conspicuous manifestations of rent-consuming) and rely on chance, clientelism, or patronage to be re-elected. When cross-jurisdiction comparisons become available, voters are better able to measure the performance of the incumbent or its variation, and support becomes more responsive to variations in performance. If the policy issue concerned is central (or if we aggregate all issues), variation in support enters a range in which it translates into a significant variation in the probability of re-election. Then, return to investing in re-election becomes significant. Performance improves. The effect of yardstick competition on performance is positive.

Now suppose that governments abroad do a very good job and yardstick competition becomes very demanding. This may be interpreted as a *negative income effect* on our incumbent. Reaching a level of performance that would give a constant chance of being re-elected is costly in terms of for-saken rent in the first period. Our incumbent may respond to that cost either by more or by less investment in re-election. The incentive effect of more intense yardstick competition is ambiguous.

For a selection effect, we must assume differences across politicians (in a way remaining compatible with our assumption that voting is only affected by performance). They may be summarized as differences in "quality" (which may refer to competence, congruence, integrity, etc.). Quality has a positive effect on performance both independently and through elec-toral motivations. Low-quality incumbents find it more difficult than high-quality incumbents to invest so as to compensate for yardstick com-petition. Some of them reduce their investment in re-election (i.e., they shirk more before the election), which increases the probability of their dismissal. Even if they do invest as much as high-quality incumbents, the probability that they are re-elected may be lower. Altogether, the selection effect of elections with yardstick competition may be assumed to increase the average quality of incumbents.

To sum up, yardstick competition will have a negative effect on perfor-mance through incentives when it induces some incumbents to invest less rather than more in re-election without that effect being compensated, through selection or self-selection, by their higher average quality.[26]

A second major difference between political agency models and the set-ting of electoral agency, as we characterized it, is the attention given in the latter but not in the former to the existence of multiple policy issues. As we saw, when there are several issues, and the discussion concerns only one of them, sanctions and rewards are better discussed in terms of con-tinuous, and possibly marginal, variations in support, rather than in terms of re-election or dismissal. The possibility of perverse effects of yardstick competition remains but must be adapted to that situation.

Suppose a secondary policy issue. Selection is irrelevant. As in the above story, the absence of cross-jurisdiction observation means that, in some policy domains, assessments of government performance by voters are highly uncertain, and so investing in them to gain the support of some minorities of voters is usually not worthwhile. Cross-border information on that issue makes performance more assessable and justifies as a con-sequence some effort on the part of incumbents to increase performance as seen by voters and gain the support of some of them. If yardstick com-petition intensifies over that issue, incumbents must devote to it more re-sources to keep in line. They can also decide to devote to it less resources, or even none at all, and redirect their efforts elsewhere. This is plausible with regard to a single secondary issue but, as noted, incumbents are usually attentive to support determined by their performance in each of many different policy domains. If we take all issues together and consider aggregate performance, we are brought back to the situation analyzed in the story just told.

The selection and mixed modeling approaches are certainly fruitful for investigations of some types of circumstances. By and large, their results are robust. The mechanisms they reveal operate also in our more realistic electoral setting. Yet, in this book, as in previous writings, I tend to reason in terms of incentives rather than selection. To some extent, this is a matter of convenience.[27] But it reflects also a focus on policies. Voters do not observe policies (I simplify) but they observe their outcomes and this—thanks to elections and political yardstick competition—has an effect on the policies themselves. Whether that effect is exclusively through incentives or involves also selection does not matter very much. Perverse effects do matter of course.[28] But, once we have acknowledged the possibility of their occurrence (which does not require selection), we do not lose enormously by explaining policies in terms of incentives only. Let me note three additional reasons to favor incentives over selection.

First, the distinction among elected politicians between good and bad types is tricky—the distinction in terms of competence being less so only marginally. Both distinctions are relevant with regard to extreme and relatively exceptional types but questionable in perhaps a majority of cases. In other words, some incumbents are clearly dishonest or inept and some clearly dedicated to the welfare of voters or highly competent. The quality of most, especially when concerned with many policy domains and issues, is unclear and a matter of opinion, even when gauged in retrospect.[29]

One could also observe that, in general, votes are at least in part for or against incumbent political parties rather than incumbent politicians.[30] In the context of yardstick competition, a generalization is even possible from voters and elections to more general relationships involving rulers and ruled—in particular, forms of non-electoral support or acquiescence to political elites or even regimes. It is difficult to extend the good type/bad type or the competent/incompetent distinctions to these collective kinds of incumbents.

Second, following Ross and Nisbett (1991), there is a literature in social psychology and in history claiming that explanations of individual behavior by situation (understood broadly) are generally more correct than explanations by personality (see also Elster 2007, chapter 10). In the theoretical literature on political agency, being a bad or a good type is assumed to be a personal and intrinsic characteristic whereas incentives are part of the situation in which one is placed. Thus, the analysis of Ross and Nisbett

(1991) and Elster (2007) applies. Inasmuch as we accept it, it plays in favor of the incentives approach.[31]

Third, our main reason for stressing incentives rather than selection is related to a more general perspective on competition. Incumbents, even good-type ones if we want to make the distinction, can vary the level and focus of the effort they make. For the welfare of voters, what may count most in incumbents is how they allocate their attention and to what extent they exert themselves. Governmental systems are rigid. There are many "veto players" (Tsebelis 2002) and ways of resisting change. Sclerosis reigns or looms. Benevolent incumbents would like to implement policies they know to be welfare enhancing but often that would require on their part a lot of concentration and energy. Thus, they may turn their minds to other matters, leaving the task of confronting the difficult ones to their successors (see e.g. Howitt and Wintrobe 1995). In such a setting, a major effect of cross-jurisdiction comparisons and yardstick competition is *stimulation*—in the present discussion, this is an additional argument in favor of the incentive approach.

## 2.3.  CONCLUSION

A singularity of this chapter is that about half of it has not been on yardstick competition among governments but on the nature of popular support for incumbents when the electorate or citizenry is assumed to be heterogeneous. I referred to the setting characterized in that way as electoral agency in which the principal-agent relationship underlying the mechanism of yardstick competition has features quite different from those it has in the usual framework of political agency, directly inspired by the framework of agency tout court. One difference is that the whole electorate does not behave as a strategically rational actor, even if some voters do. Another, related, difference is that the relationship between agents and principals is non-contractual by essence, not by lack of credibility: it is an essential characteristic of voters that they commit to nothing. As a consequence of these assumptions, the relation between performance and support, especially as perceived by incumbents, can be directly apprehended at the aggregate level as a weakly increasing curve: the effect of better performance on support is either zero or positive.

When, in the second part of the chapter, cross-jurisdiction comparisons are considered, that curve is supposed to reflect the consequences on support of comparative rather than absolute performance—or, more heroically, performance defined as comparative performance. Heterogeneity increases the intuitive plausibility of yardstick competition being significant, but it also complicates the matter because it allows the coexistence of contradictory assessments, making the aggregate effect uncertain (not so much for incumbents as for us). In that context, two properties ascribed to the support curve are essential: above all its S-shape—thanks to which, when cross-jurisdiction differences are small, confusion, though likely, causes limited damage—but also the fact that the explained variable is support, a continuous variable, rather than, directly, re-election, a step variable.

Finally, I have discussed the trade-off between incentives and selection in the framework of electoral agency. In fact, the results are not changed as much as I thought. What counts most is the motivation of office-holders rather than the nature of the electorate, whereas assumptions about that motivation are more or less the same in the different settings. In particular, the possibility that yardstick competition has perverse effects (a matter I return to in chapter 9) is confirmed whatever the nature of the electorate. Nonetheless, as explained, I have kept my preference for a focus on incentives.

In a sense, all depends on what we expect from yardstick competition. My main interest in it lies in stimulation rather than in more honesty, competence, or congruence. For many countries, the main problem with the problems of society is that too many of them are not addressed with sufficient determination and perseverance, or at all. Often we become conscious of such failings only in retrospect and/or thanks to comparisons with what obtains elsewhere. Hopefully, yardstick competition induces more exertion within governments than there would be in its absence.

## NOTES

1. See some comparisons in Fearon (1999), Besley (2006), Ashworth (2012).
2. See Besley (2006). I focus here on differences in preferences or motivation. Differences in the marginal cost of effort (a form of difference in competence) may have somewhat different implications.
3. They are sometimes called "angels" (Fearon 2011). But being congruent with what voters think they want is not the same as being congruent with their best interest. I will discuss later (mainly in chapter 9) the problem of politicians "pandering" to what voters wrongly take for their interest.
4. Different assumptions lead Belleflamme and Hindriks (2005) to a more optimistic assessment of the effects of yardstick competition.
5. When we reason in game-theoretical terms, impossibility to commit is an obstacle to voters' capacity to provide incumbents with incentives to perform as good agents. This is an instance of a more general idea (full sovereignty, discretion, or

freedom is a weakness not a strength) which is illuminating in some instances but misleading in others.

6. To be exact, it must be noted that the sovereignty of the electorate finds limits in the rule of law—both domestic (reflected in part in the formal constitution) and international. These limits concern the aggregate result of elections. There are also some procedural constraints that concern directly individual voters (vote only once, respect secrecy, etc.).

7. Recently, two French presidents, one from the right (Nicolas Sarkozy) and the other from the left (François Hollande), pledged to quit if the target they set for unemployment was not met at the end of their current mandate.

8. Incumbents' obligations include holding regular and fair elections and stepping down when defeated.

9. The representative voter is not a representative or delegate of the other voters, entrusted to vote in their name. As a consequence, contrary to what Banks and Sunderaman (1998) claim, their model, in which there is a single principal, is not really fit to deal with elections. The fact that it relies on "optimal retention" rather than optimal compensations like most agency models is not sufficient to make it relevant in that setting (assuming that compensations constitute a problem, a matter discussed in chapter 3).

10. The theoretical work on political agency borrows a lot from the way representative agents have been introduced in macroeconomics and business cycle theory in the wake of the rational expectations revolution. But the representative individual who adjusts his or her saving in response to variations in public debt (as suggested by the Ricardian equivalence argument) can be an average emanation of an uncoordinated multitude of rational, forward-looking savers, each deciding the ratio of his or her own consumption or saving. The paradox of instrumental participation in collective decision-making does not arise. *Political* business cycle theory is another matter.

11. Examples in France involving the prosecution and career of top politicians are the infected blood and asbestos scandals. Together with several other high officials, former prime minister Laurent Fabius (in the infected blood case) and former minister and party leader Martine Aubry (in the asbestos case) were charged with manslaughter. Although acquitted in the end, both paid a significant political price. In small localities, the fear of being held responsible and prosecuted for accidents occurring on the territory of the commune is a disincentive to becoming a candidate for the office of mayor. In Athenian politics, strong sanctions in cases of bad outcomes were a disincentive to making oneself available for office. See Manin (1997) and Elster (1999).

12. See Olsen (2017) and the references therein. That comparative evaluation may be justified simply on the basis of absolute evaluation lacking any meaning was already noted in particular by Lazear and Rosen (1981) and by Holmstrom (1982).

13. Voters or more generally citizens do formulate assessments of public services innocent of any reference to comparisons, whether over time or across jurisdictions. These assessments are often puzzling. Let me give an example. In the domain of health and for seventeen industrialized countries, Blendon, Kim, and Benson (2001) compare the ranking proposed by the experts of the World Health Organization (WHO) to the perceptions of citizens. The paper stresses the absence of correlation. For example, 20 percent of Italians against 91 percent of Danes are satisfied with the healthcare system in their country. But among the seventeen countries, Italy and Denmark rank respectively second and sixteenth

with regard to the "overall performance" of the system, eighth and thirteenth with regard to its "overall attainment." Should we really believe the public, as recommended in the study, or the WHO ranking, as the general line of our analysis suggests? For a more general discussion of the relation between information and citizens' perceptions or degrees of satisfaction, see James and Moseley (2014) and the references therein.

14. In Switzerland, both at the federal and cantonal levels, many public investment projects are rejected by votations or referenda because a majority of voters considers them too expensive.

15. Ascribing to voters the capacity to engage in cost-benefit calculations is more demanding than assuming that they react more or less unconsciously to separate variations in taxation and public services.

16. The relationship between "spend more" and "get more" is often problematic—see Revelli (2009) for some evidence.

17. This is a simplification. If some voters are concerned with intrinsic characteristics of the incumbent such as competence or decisiveness, they may simultaneously disagree with policies or their outcomes and adopt a more favorable view of the incumbent because of them (Salmon 1993, Chiu 2002).

18. As Fiorina (1981) writes: "We may very well observe some citizens voting in approval of realized conditions and others voting in disapproval, but all voting retrospectively." And: "retrospective voting can occur on any kind of issue" (pp. 18–19). Grillo and Polo (1993) propose a model of the relationship between accountability and positions in the issue space. See also Persson and Tabellini (2000, pp. 79–81).

19. "I have never understood how one can vote probabilistically," a distinguished scholar objected. But the assumption is not that voters decide to vote probabilistically but that observers, including incumbents and other candidates, assign probabilities to how individual voters (or categories thereof) will vote (Lafay 1993).

20. This paragraph draws on Salmon (1997). I presented figures similar to figure 2.1 (albeit restricted to one quadrant, corresponding to negative performance, as in figure 3.2 of chapter 3) for the first time in a seminar at the University of Siena in 1993 and since then in several papers.

21. S-curves are typically present in the literature on the diffusion of innovations across countries or sub-national jurisdictions, but each curve concerns many jurisdictions and describes an actual, or even observed, process over time. In figure 2.1, presented here, the horizontal axis represents conceivable performance variation, independently of time, and the vertical axis represents the support variation that this conceivable performance variation would cause in that jurisdiction.

22. Even of demand curves in general: see Stigler (1965), especially pp. 213–33.

23. Farmers and truck-drivers against ecologists for instance.

24. Following Fearon (2011), one should say that this is correct only if it can be assumed, first, that fair elections will be regularly held and, second, that incumbents will step down when defeated. In well-functioning democracies, both conditions are satisfied because of a credible threat of coordinated rebellion in case they are not. The threat is credible because not holding a regular election and refusing to step down after being defeated would be "public signals for coordinating rebellion." The matter is different in autocracies and in the case of massive electoral fraud or information manipulation.

25. *Pace* Salmon (2014, 2015).

26. If there are term limits, the following three propositions can be formulated. On average, incumbents who cannot be candidates again behave differently from incumbents who can; incumbents who are re-elected behave differently from incumbents who were elected for the first time; incumbents who face a term limit after having been elected once behave differently from incumbents who face a term limit after having been re-elected—see Banks and Sundaram (1998). Empirical evidence of the first proposition has been used already, in Besley and Case (1995), to isolate the role of yardstick competition in observed interactions among jurisdictions. Differences in behavior are likely to be less significant when incumbent individuals are integrated in long-lived and forward-looking incumbent political parties or teams.

27. Ashworth (2012), who endeavors to demonstrate that the approach is flawed, observes nevertheless that some important contributions still adopt it. Among them he cites Fearon (2011). This is interesting because Fearon (1999) includes perhaps the most articulate and compelling criticism of the pure incentives approach. Ashworth explains the continuing adoption of the pure incentives approach by practical considerations. I argue that convenience in use is only one of its virtues.

28. Other reasons for perverse effects of yardstick competition, possibly more serious than the one discussed here, will be noted in chapter 9.

29. The distinction made in Svolik (2013) is between "bad" and "normal" types of incumbents. A bad type is not interested in being re-elected and takes maximum rents in the present. A "normal type is no angel: if not threatened with a removal from office, he prefers to exploit it rather than behave" (p. 689). Svolik's normal types are Besley's bad ones; Svolik's bad types are absent from Besley's framework and Besley's good types from Svolik's. The societies Besley and Svolik have in mind are discussed again in chapter 9.

30. See Mattozzi and Merlo (2015) for an analysis of why political parties may be responsible for what the authors consider "mediocre" politicians and for references on the measurement of politicians' quality. See also Congleton and Zhang (2013) and the references therein on the relation between the human capital of incumbents and economic performance. My skepticism on that matter may have something to do with the fact that the performance of elected office-holders in France (especially at the national level) has not proved that impressive as a rule although they are generally extremely well qualified on paper.

31. In the afterword inserted in the revised edition of their book, Ross and Nisbett (2011, pp. 247–54) qualify their position by giving more weight to the interaction between personality and situation.

# CHAPTER 3

# Accountability, information, and yardstick competition

We have used sparingly the word "accountability";[1] its meaning had to be made consistent with our main perspective. There is a relation between how we understand political accountability, the information asymmetry faced by voters, and political yardstick competition. This chapter is about that relation. Accountability is discussed in section 3.1. In the case of electoral accountability, a frequent query is whether voters are sufficiently informed and able to process whatever information they get. This is discussed in section 3.2, mostly under the assumption that no information is available about other jurisdictions. The information asymmetry obstacle encountered then by voters takes different forms depending on the domains and issues considered and for some important issues is quite serious. This provides a role for cross-jurisdiction comparisons (and, with them, yardstick political competition) to come to the rescue of accountability. A similar logic underlay the way Lazear and Rosen (1981) and others introduced tournaments or yardstick competition in labor and industrial economics. Section 3.3 stresses a number of points made at the time or later in these domains and exploits their continued relevance for a better understanding of the mechanism when transposed to intergovernmental settings.

## 3.1. ACCOUNTABILITY

The literature on political accountability is large.[2] The following points are particularly relevant for our purpose.

### 3.1.1. Definitions

Accountability is generally defined in terms of agency. It is a feature of a set-up in which agents are accountable to principals for their past or present actions. Accountability must involve responsibility and answerability for the actions. Interpreted broadly, that means that the principals have the right, latitude, or power to assess the actions of the agents in a way that may have consequences for the situation or welfare of the latter.[3]

Our focus is on "downward political accountability," in which the principals are the people or the citizens, or a large subset thereof, and the agents are the incumbents. More grandiosely, the rulers are the agents of the ruled and accountable to them. In democratic societies, downward accountability generally takes the form of electoral accountability, with mass elections as its central mechanism.[4]

A focus on downward political accountability is compatible with incumbents being also accountable in other directions—to the political parties or teams they are members of in particular. When there are several levels of government, an incumbent at an intermediate tier may be accountable to some authority above instead of, or in addition to, the people below.[5] Some of the corresponding links will be discussed later but, regarding their relation with yardstick competition, two differences between these other forms of accountability and downward accountability may be noted now. Voters, or the people, face an information asymmetry obstacle that is not encountered to the same degree by courts, political parties, and lobbies. These organizations have means that are not available to ordinary citizens for investigating the internal machinery of government and assessing its decisions. Consequently, recourse to cross-jurisdiction comparisons causes a smaller increase in the influence of the organizations than the improvement it produces in the capacity of ordinary citizens. Secondly, some distinctive characteristics of mass electorates stressed in chapter 2 under the name of electoral agency become irrelevant when we discuss accountability to these other entities. A mass electorate is not a unitary and even less a strategic actor, as we saw. Its relation with politicians in office is not contractual. But that negative characterization does not generally apply to lobbies or political parties organized to behave as unitary actors and to engage in (implicit) contracts.

An important case is accountability to parliament, which is a form of downward accountability. However, in particular because of the two features just noted, a parliament and a mass electorate do not play their role of principal in the same way. This explains why we will not follow authors such as Benz (2012) when they assume yardstick competition to be based on cross-jurisdiction comparisons indifferently made by voters and legislators. Except when otherwise stated, the framework underlying our discussions is that of a direct relation between an incumbent and, below, ordinary citizens in vast numbers.

### 3.1.2. Accountability and other dimensions of elections

According to the pure accountability perspective, the mechanism of elections has only that single rationale—that is, it exclusively reflects voters' assessments of incumbents' past and present performance. That view is often contrasted with two other pure perspectives. According to one—sometimes called the "mandate view" (Manin, Przeworski, and Stokes 1999)—elections serve to select the policies that will be undertaken in the future. According to the other, referred to as "selection," they serve to select the best candidates (Fearon 1999).

The claim that accountability is driven out as soon as selection becomes relevant is expressed particularly forcefully in Fearon (1999), but it is also present in most papers based on political agency modeling. It is an implication of reasoning in terms of sequential games with a representative voter. We can entertain a liberal view on the matter because, as explained, we do not reason in that way. Our framework is "electoral" rather than "political" agency. The electorate is heterogeneous. Voters have different motivations. Both the dependent variable (variation in expected support) and the explanatory variable we focus on (variation in performance) are continuous aggregates. Thus, our analysis is fully compatible with election results being largely influenced by concerns other than accountability: namely candidates' personality and/or the content of their proposals. It is enough for our purpose that these other concerns do not pretend to explain the behavior of all voters or enough that they make the assessment of past performance count in voters' forward-looking choices of candidates and programs.[6]

Indeed, it cannot be denied that platforms—a mixture of proposed policies and promised outcomes—play an important role in most elections. However, it is also obvious that much of their content is uncertain. That uncertainty has at least five elements: willingness of the winners to respect their promises, internal consistency of the overall platforms, uncertainty of the relationship between policy instruments and policy outcomes, impact of unforeseen or previously unknown circumstances, and, under coalition governments, necessary compromise between coalition members. Voters are more or less aware of these reasons to remain doubtful about candidates' programs and promises. That awareness can, by itself, explain the attention they give to the credentials of the candidates. But their perception of candidates is also uncertain. Many politicians are better at winning elections than at governing once in office. Because voters are aware of the limits of their perception, past performance in office (whether or not that office is the one in competition) is an important selection criterion.[7]

### 3.1.3. Is accountability asymmetric?

The way in which I have just formulated, once again, the effect of performance on support runs against a widely supposed attribute of accountability. Under that interpretation, the consequences of holding an agent (i.e., the incumbent) responsible for something are always negative. One speaks of sanctions, never of rewards. Accountability is considered asymmetric by nature. By contrast, in my approach, assessments of performance may well lead voters to consider that the incumbent has been doing particularly well, which judgment normally leads to an increase in political support—that is, a reward. As accountability is generally discussed, this positive effect does not happen. Why?

Let us consider accountability in ordinary life, outside politics. It is true that it tends to have a disciplining connotation. That feature reflects two frequent characteristics of agency. Agency relations are often built on the understanding that agents will do their jobs, period. This applies to the firemen who save the inhabitants of houses in a fire, the policemen who elucidate crimes, or the pilots who bring planes to a destination. Doing one's job entails no reward. More generally, one may say that agents are the delegates of principals. They are supposed to act as the principals would act if they (the principals) had the same information and were in charge. Again, acting in that way deserves no reward. It is in the nature of the arrangement. Rendering accounts is only about deviations. A second frequent determinant of the asymmetry is related to the time structure of the agency relationship. It is quite usual that an agent is appointed with no indication of time. Or if an obligation of renewal is specified, it is often understood as a formality, possibly satisfied by tacit acquiescence. In other words, retaining the agent in the job is the norm, the default solution, part of the initial arrangement. It is not a reward.

When accountability is discussed in political contexts, these characteristics remain relevant and may be responsible for the asymmetry. The literature on accountability tends to focus on corruption as the main failing to be mitigated or addressed. Because incumbents are supposed to be honest, it is understandable that they are not congratulated or rewarded for not being corrupt. Other failings such as shirking and patronage are perceived in the same way. They should not exist, which means that their absence deserves no reward. In the political agency framework (criticized in chapter 2), elections are a binary choice made by a single voter. Retaining the incumbent in office is the default solution. For a norm-abiding incumbent, re-election is a formality, extending the status quo. Again, it is not to be treated as a reward.

In the setting of mass elections, we cannot reason in this way. Because of heterogeneity in the electorate and because of uncertainty, aggregate support or elections prospects are continuous and stochastic variables. Even under pure accountability (only past performance counts), incumbents are never sure to be re-elected. And uncertainty about the result of elections is even greater if we take into account functions of elections other than accountability. As noted, election outcomes also reflect voters' attention to the programs and personal characteristics of candidates. This gives incumbents an additional reason not to consider the next election as a formality. In such settings, rewards as well as sanctions must be considered as possible results of holding incumbents responsible. This does not imply that they are always equally likely or relevant. And this should not prevent us from focusing for convenience on the negative side of the accountability mechanism, neglecting—albeit without denying—the existence of the other side.

### 3.1.4. Elites

In the context of contemporary democracies with fair elections, one may discuss downward accountability, as we did, under the assumption that the principals are the citizens and the agents are the elected incumbents. That assumption and, associated with it, downward accountability encounter some objections even in that most favorable setting. A major objection is government by the elites.

The view that the elites govern is ambiguous in many respects. It is true that the political personnel are not representative of the whole population, in the sense of sharing with it the same intrinsic characteristics (education, profession, family background, religion or ethnicity, age, gender, etc.). Under a generally accepted interpretation of representative democracy, however, that phenomenon (except recently for gender and ethnicity) is judged perfectly natural (see Manin 1997). Agency and accountability are not really affected.

A different meaning of government by elites is more potentially destructive of our analysis of downward accountability. Elites are said to govern in the sense that public policies serve their interests. The influence of non-elites is claimed to be null. That idea, which is fairly widespread, can be formulated in two main ways. There is a long tradition of glossing completely over government or the state under the implicit assumption that they do not count. They are considered a veil obfuscating the direct relationship between the preferences of the elites and the content of policies. In that case, there are no more principals and agents: the agency relation in a strict sense disappears logically and with it accountability as generally understood.[8]

In the second way to formulate the claim, the existence of government and the state is acknowledged, the agency relation does survive logically, but with the elites as the principals and the state, government, or incumbent as the agent (government is promoted from "veil" to "servant"). If accountability to the elites is deemed perfect, the two formulations (direct relation or relation intermediated by government) come to the same thing. The first is useful in some analytical contexts. As a matter of principle, however, and also for our purpose, the second is preferable. This is so because it respects methodological individualism and does not treat pure categories such as classes or elites as unitary, purposive actors. But it is also preferable because it can easily accommodate the fact that, in our complex societies, elites make up a large and heterogeneous category, with the often-conflicting influences of the various subcategories varying over time and space and across issues.

Indeed, it must be conceded that once their influence is considered in that light, the nature of elites becomes particularly imprecise. Many categories, large or small, influence or distort policies, and they do that through a variety of channels. Some of these categories (billionaires in the United States, graduates of elite universities and schools in Britain and France) can be called elites. Many others (farmers, fishermen, students, taxi drivers), though influential, cannot. Two points should be noted about influence. In many democratic countries (other than the United States), the influence of banks and large business firms is mainly a result of mobility-based competition across open economies. It is related to exit rather than to voice, which explains why even left-wing governments come to terms with them.

The second point is that, in many countries (other than the United Kingdom), the influence of non-elite categories such as students and farmers often operates through the threat of strikes and mass protests rather than through elections. France is a particularly clear case of this.

As the chief executive of the French railways said recently, "France is not like the UK. When there is a problem with the Eurostar in London there is an orderly queue; in France there is a riot."[9] French heads of state or of government, endowed by the constitution with considerable powers when they have a majority in parliament (as is the rule), often seem petrified by the fear of strikes, demonstrations and even revolution. This phenomenon may reflect elites being afraid of the people but also the said "people" not being deprived of any influence. It also confirms that downward accountability does not operate only through elections.

### 3.1.5. Clientelism

Clientelism is a form of accountability but not of the kind that we want to focus on. It does imply that politicians need support from below, in particular in the form of votes. But they get support not through their performance in office (or in relation with their competence and policies) but through the implicit contracts they conclude with separate individuals. The exchange organized by these contracts is between political support or votes and appropriable handouts and goods and services such as jobs, rent-controlled dwellings, and disability pensions.

The mechanism of clientelism is puzzling for at least two reasons: enforcement of implicit contracts and secret ballots. Since there is some clientelism even in countries in which elections are fair, it is clear that both obstacles can be overcome. How exactly is surveyed in particular in Stokes (2009). Let me stress two points. First, it is sufficient for clientelism that handouts change the votes not of all but of some of those they are given to. Then, a weak adherence to a norm of reciprocity may be enough for making handouts electorally profitable. Second, the secret ballot obstacle to clientelism and patronage does not concern party membership. Handouts may thus work indirectly by being used to first boost party membership, which in turn has a positive effect on electoral support.

The effect on performance tends to be negative both directly and because of less performance-based accountability. The case of jobs illustrates the direct link. The fact that some tasks are no longer awarded on the basis of competence reduces the efficiency of the public administration, which in turn reduces the performance of the incumbents. The indirect effect is that clientelism tends to make the voters concerned less responsive, and consequently the incumbents themselves less attentive, to government performance. This is an incentive effect. There may also be a selection effect when clientelism protects "bad" incumbents from the competition of "better" candidates.

### 3.1.6. Accountability and other ingredients of good governance

Good governance is sometimes assumed to depend only on electoral accountability.[10] That view is seriously doubted today. Recent events such as the Arab Spring and its aftermath illustrate both the relevance of forms of accountability other than elections and the limits of electoral accountability. They have added to already existing disillusion about the latter. Observation of cases of good performance in some non-democratic settings and of the ill-effects of the adoption of democracy in others is influencing both public opinion and the scholarly literature. Several recent books reflect the reassessment.[11] A contribution that I find particularly enlightening for our purpose is that of Fukuyama (2011, 2014).

According to that author, the quality of political order has three ingredients: state efficiency, rule of law, and accountability.[12] He provides a fascinating story of the sequential emergence of the three ingredients in different countries. In China the first ingredient to emerge (under the Qin dynasty) was an efficient state. In India and Western Europe, it was the rule of law, which was followed in France with an efficient state. In Britain and the United States, the efficient state came last. Fukuyama simplifies perhaps too much the real historical sequences, and I certainly simplify drastically his analyses. The evolution of the three ingredients was far from monotonic. Efficient governance could be found in Europe as early as the twelfth century: for instance, cities like Bruges, Cologne, Genoa, or Pisa, but also the Norman Kingdom of Sicily under Roger II, England under Henry II, or France under Philip-Augustus (Berman 1983). The rule of law (as a constraint on the sovereign) and downward accountability declined in many places of Europe after the Middle Ages—especially if we consider also cities (a point stressed by Tocqueville 1856, II-3).

For Fukuyama, the sequence explains the problems currently met by many countries. The rule of law and democratic accountability are important to set limits to the tendency of the state to become overpowering or to err in some other way. But prior to any concern about limits, there must be something to limit, in the present case a state enabled to provide with a minimum of competence the services that are needed. One essential feature of such a state is a competent and autonomous bureaucracy. In Fukuyama's sequential analysis, democratic accountability introduced in a country lacking a competent and autonomous bureaucracy will lead to widespread clientelism and patronage. In turn, clientelism and patronage, through the two direct and indirect channels mentioned earlier (incompetent bureaucrats and distracted voters), constitute an obstacle to getting a better performing state.

Still, as Fukuyama himself documents (2014, chapters 8 and 10), Britain and the United States did succeed in getting a better performing state although they had already established downward accountability for some time, as well, for that matter, as rule of law. How did that happen? The story is different in Britain and in the United States, but in both countries some categories of the population located somewhere "below" exerted upward pressure in the direction of reform. This suggests that downward accountability may have a positive as well as a negative effect on state efficiency. Which of the two effects might dominate? As we will argue now, an essential determinant is the nature of the information available "below."

## 3.2. INFORMATION ASYMMETRY AS AN OBSTACLE TO DOWNWARD ACCOUNTABILITY

As noted, both incumbents' actions and their results are difficult to assess from standpoints located outside and below government, in particular from that of ordinary citizens or voters. It is time to examine more closely the degree to which various types of actions and results are concerned. This is important because there is a bias in the literature on accountability, and possibly in accountability itself, toward focusing on the types easy to judge, neglecting others that are not necessarily more opaque but are clearly more fuzzy or controversial.

Corruption is an instance of behavior difficult to detect but easy to judge. One should distinguish between corruption of incumbents and policy against corruption. Corruption (or honesty) of incumbents is special in two ways. Inasmuch as it is apprehended, this is done directly rather than from its consequences. Once established, its interpretation is clear—even if it is up to each voter to decide what importance to give it among the various determinants of his or her vote. Incumbents' policy against corruption is another matter. Like other policies, it is to be judged, indirectly, on its outcome, mainly the observed level of corruption, but also some of the means it uses.

Many authors focus on corruption as the main manifestation or criterion of bad government. That may be because they think that it is the most important failure accountability should address or, perhaps more likely, because it is the most clear-cut. However, honesty is only one of the qualities that voters seek in government. Most other qualities involve information asymmetry in a way that is less simple. To deal with that complexity, voters may rely on the information and interpretations they receive from various sources. There is a relation between sources and issues. With regard to general issues, the main providers of information are the politicians (including incumbents) and the media. With regard to specialized interests, the main providers are interest groups. I will argue that, in both cases, especially if we assume that there is no information obtainable from outside the jurisdiction, the information and interpretation voters get from these sources tend to be biased. Many voters are aware of that tendency. This leads them to use also or principally their direct or almost direct knowledge of outcomes. But, as we saw, this is also problematic.

### 3.2.1. Biased information on general policy issues

Citizens get information about policies concerned with general issues mainly from incumbents, their challengers, and the media. In well-functioning democracies, the informative impact of independent sources located in academia, arm-length agencies, or the judicial system should also be considered.

That politicians in office may not reveal all the information in their possession and may even lie is a definitional feature of the information asymmetry problem in principal-agent contexts. But their challengers are perhaps even more unreliable. As competitors, politicians in the opposition tend to criticize everything incumbents do. Many of the criticisms are unfair. They do include some true information, but extracting it from the flow of biased interpretations is difficult. In addition, only a part of what politicians say is communicated directly to voters. Most of this communication transits through the media. Although in well-functioning democracies that intermediation does mitigate the extraction problem just mentioned, it introduces a bias of its own as discussed later. In settings that are not fully democratic, a typical effect of intermediation is to make the opposition less audible.

In many countries, the media lack independence because of direct or indirect linkages with incumbents. In well-functioning democracies the phenomenon certainly exists but is limited by definition. The main problem then is caused by commercial incentives leading the media to pander to the prior beliefs of their readership or audience (see Gentzkow and Shapiro 2008, Sobbrio 2014 and the references therein). On issues on which they are divided, voters tend to read newspapers, watch television programs, or connect to sites and networks that confirm or reinforce their views. This may increase polarization.

I am even more concerned by another, generally overlooked, effect: pandering may also be damaging when beliefs are common, almost unanimous, rather than divided. There are many historical episodes in which it seems clear *in retrospect* that public opinion went badly, or even catastrophically, astray. Not only did the media let that happen, but in many cases, they were major contributors to collective misjudgment. A similar phenomenon is when public opinion in one country is clearly mistaken as judged from outside, whereas the media within the country contribute heavily to misjudgment.[13]

In well-functioning democracies, there are many independent and trustworthy sources of information. However, for that information to reach ordinary citizens, it must be relayed and reformulated by politicians or by the media, a process subject to the biases just discussed.[14] In authoritarian systems or in systems with incomplete democratic credentials, reliable independent sources are typically lacking.

I have exaggerated somewhat the informational obstacles or biases encountered by citizens with regard to general issues. Recall that, in this section, I am assuming no information from outside. Even then, at least in democracies, many hard, objective facts and statistics would make their way to sizeable numbers of citizens. It is mainly with regard to the interpretation of these facts and to the visibility and weight with which they are endowed that citizens should be assumed to be badly informed.

### 3.2.2. Biased information on citizens' special interests

Information on policies concerning only subsets of the population is channeled in part through interest groups: farmers are informed about changes in subsidies or price support by farmer unions, workers about changes in layoff regulation by labor unions, and so on. To what extent is that channel reliable?

In general, interest or pressure groups are assumed to defend the interests of their members by influence and pressure on politicians. The main channels and means are the provision of information and various kinds of support and endorsement. Pressure also includes sanctions and threats (if only in the form of support reduction). In return, politicians are assumed to favor policy measures groups are interested in.

That view may be correct when groups consist of, or are dominated, by "large members," large business firms in particular (Stigler 1974). In the case of groups consisting exclusively of many small members, labor unions for instance, the view is subject to two objections or questions. The first, notoriously raised by Olson (1965), is how can the tendency to free ride be overcome so that large categories of individuals sharing some interests— that is, interest *categories*—manage to form mobilized or organized interest *groups*. The second, generally overlooked, is why would such groups escape the electoral agency problems discussed at length in chapter 2: indeed, large groups are also divided into ordinary voting members and elected officials—that is, structured along a principal-agent relationship.

As argued in Salmon (1987a), the two objections may be dealt with jointly by giving a group's leader (or leadership team) a central role. I will not summarize that work. The aspect of it which is of interest for our purpose is about information. Within the complex set of goods and services exchanged between politicians or public agencies on one side and the leadership of interest groups on the other, a major category concerns issue framing or manipulation. What is exactly the issue discussed? How is it formulated? What is stressed? What is left out? Group leaders may or may not help focus the attention of group members toward answers to those questions that politicians in office find convenient. Conversely, politicians in office have many ways of enhancing or lessening the mobilization capacity and influence or authority of group leaders: they may or may not help leaders provide ordinary members the selective incentives needed for participation; they may either involve or bypass organized groups when giving satisfaction to interest categories, etc. Reciprocal favors will often succeed in producing convergence on a definition of issues that benefits both sides.

In the absence of cross-jurisdiction comparisons, it is difficult for ordinary members of a group, or, for that matter, of an interest category, to decide whether the emphasis put by the group leaders on some issues, or the neglect of other issues, is warranted and best satisfies their interests. They will be well informed about the group having successfully fought for advantage *A*. But they cannot say whether advantages *B* or *C*, perhaps not even mentioned, could have been obtained instead or as well.

### 3.2.3. Obstacles to assessments of outcomes

Given the difficulties just outlined, voters have good reasons to judge performance mainly on the basis of facts that can be interpreted as policy outcomes. The analysis presented in chapter 2 can be complemented as follows. Let us suppose that voters, or a sizeable subset thereof, do know the facts: a war was lost, unemployment is 10 percent, inflation is 2 percent, VAT has increased by 3 percent, new immigrants make up 3 percent of the population, the country was eliminated at the outset from the World Cup, the city was selected to organize the Olympic Games, etc. Some observed facts point unambiguously, by themselves, so to say, to good or bad governmental performance: something bad happened, officials were observed responding in a chaotic, vacillating, and contradictory way to the event, or, on the contrary, their response was swift and efficient. Even in these cases, unconscious reference to the past, providing norms or prior expectations, may play a role.[15] With regard to many categories of observed facts, however, assessments are more consciously based on comparison with the past. Variable $X$ has increased or decreased, or increased or decreased more than previously. Comparisons over time are quite natural or instinctive. They are also legitimate when the underlying setting is stationary in some sense (including a constant trend for instance). However, the world we live in is definitely not stationary. It goes through a historical process of transformation that is unique and also extraordinarily multifaceted and rapid. Scientific progress and technological inventions are the main drivers of that transformation. They also co-determine the observed data on which comparisons over time can be made. Increases in life expectancy are co-determined by scientific progress and technological innovation as well as by governmental policies. Without cross-jurisdiction comparisons, comparing life expectancy now to what it was at some date in the past says nothing about governmental performance (except perhaps in the case of a decrease).

Comparisons over time may be misleading in both directions. They may make performance look worse than it is in reality. For instance, a negative exogenous shock gets overlooked and the incumbent loses support, which is unfair. The effect of that unfairness on incentives, selection, and ultimately, future performance, is ambiguous.[16] I will tend to stress the second direction. One aspect of the world transformation just stressed is an exogenous tendency toward improved living conditions, at least to date. Comparisons over time that neglect that trend tend to overestimate governmental performance, as noted with regard to life expectancy. Indeed, because the exogenous shock on which we focus our attention is that unique world transformation rather than the accidental or cyclical types implicitly assumed in most of the literature, the bias with which we might be most concerned is toward overestimation rather than underestimation.

## 3.3. YARDSTICK COMPETITION TO THE RESCUE OF ACCOUNTABILITY

Our main interest is about the way yardstick competition operates in the intergovernmental context, but for that purpose it is interesting to return to the way it was supposed to work in its original habitat. Some of the points made in the original setting will then prove important for our interpretation of the transition between the two contexts. A question to which we will give particular attention is mimicking.

### 3.3.1. Tournaments and yardstick competition in their original habitat

The theoretical literature on tournaments in an agency context dates from the early 1980s. The common concern was the determination of optimal contracts between a principal and several agents in a context of information asymmetry. The main points were made within a short period of time by Lazear and Rosen (1981), Holmstrom (1982), Nalebuff and Stiglitz (1983), and Green and Stokey (1983).[17] Shleifer (1985) applied the reasoning to the context of regulation and popularized the expression "yardstick competition." Many contributions followed. The small literature inspired by the seminal article of Knoeber (1989) on tournaments in the production of poultry (see Zheng and Vukina 2007, Tsoulouhas 2015, and the references therein) has clarified and reordered some important distinctions.

Leaving aside hybrids, four different schemes of evaluation and remuneration play a central role in the discussion:

1. Salaries, generally based on monitoring of inputs
2. Compensation (piece rates) tied to outputs without comparisons with other agents
3. Rank-order tournaments, based on ordinal comparisons with other agents
4. Cardinal tournaments based on cardinal comparisons with other agents

The absence of yardstick competition from the list needs some justification. The origin and meaning of the expression are explained in a few words by Shleifer (1985) himself:

> For any given firm, the regulator uses the costs of comparable firms to infer a firm's attainable cost level. Borrowing the term that describes comparison of

private and state-controlled firms, we call this regulatory scheme "yardstick competition." (p. 320)

The formulation used in the conclusion of Shleifer's paper is more general:

> . . . the rewards of a given firm depend on its standing vis-à-vis a shadow firm, constructed from suitably averaging the choices of other firms in the group. Each firm is thus forced to compete with its shadow firm. (p. 326)

The more general formulation—as the close relation Shleifer concedes (p. 320) between his model and the models of Nalebuff and Stiglitz (1983) and, to a lesser extent, Lazear and Rosen (1981)—allows us to consider Shleifer's yardstick competition as a form of contest or tournament and more precisely, a form of cardinal tournament. It is true that the domains are different and the variables involved in Shleifer's "regulatory scheme" and those involved in the agency setting we focus on are not exactly the same.[18] But, as noted by Laffont (1994), a merit of the approach adopted by Shleifer (1985) is that it treats regulation as an agency problem. Following that line, we may say that whether agents are employees or firms, their welfare depends and their efforts focus on the cardinal distance between their output or cost and that of others, which is changed as a consequence. As indicated in chapter 1, I use yardstick competition in a broad sense to cover both rank-order tournaments and remuneration by cardinal comparisons. I refer to the latter as "cardinal tournaments."[19]

Let me return to the list just presented. Suppose that the principal cannot observe inputs. That eliminates scheme 1 from consideration. Scheme 2 (piece rates without comparisons) is widely used. A consideration justifying directly the adoption of scheme 3 is reward indivisibility. For instance, rewards take the form of promotions and only one agent, or a fixed number of agents, can be selected. Then comparative evaluation is necessary, and necessarily made in terms of rank. Another consideration leading to scheme 3 is the inconvenience of measuring output along a cardinal scale. Ranking the performance (output) of agents $A$ and $B$ is easier than attempting to gauge each one individually. Even when measures of output are fully available, it may be difficult to give them a meaning in the absence of a benchmark;[20] both schemes 3 and 4 offer a solution to that problem.

The considerations at the center of the theoretical literature concern the treatment of risk or uncertainty—hereafter referred to as randomness. Again, both schemes 3 and 4 are involved, as well as scheme 2 as a benchmark. Randomness may enter the analysis as follows. $Q_i$, an individual agent's output, has three determinants:

- $E_i$, his or her effort or input
- $N_i$, a random variable specific to his or her production (an "idiosyncratic shock")
- $R$, a random variable common to production by all agents (a "common shock")[21]

If two necessary conditions are satisfied, there might be a case—within the approach focused on randomness—for comparative evaluation and compensation. These two conditions are $R$ being different from zero (that is, the common shock existing) and agents disliking randomness (being "risk-averters"). When these conditions are satisfied, $R$ can be "filtered away" and this, per se, is valuable. However, total randomness does not necessarily decrease because the relative performance of each agent now depends also on the idiosyncratic element in the production of the other agents. In other words, there is a third, often overlooked, necessary condition: the positive effect of getting rid of common randomness must be larger than the negative one of shouldering the idiosyncratic randomness affecting others. This is a serious problem when the number of agents is small but, under standard assumptions about the distribution of randomness, the effect of idiosyncratic randomness in others vanishes when the number of agents becomes larger (the law of large numbers applies). This is obvious in the case of cardinal tournaments: when the group is large, idiosyncratic shocks cancel out and have no effect on peer or group average, whose variation then is a good indicator of common randomness (Holmstrom 1982). Mutatis mutandis, an effect similar in essence obtains for rank-order tournaments among many contestants (Green and Stokey 1983).

Comparisons of the different schemes have been mostly developed in terms of optimality in a context featuring business firms, free choice of contract, and market competition. Many of the points discussed, then, are not really relevant for our purpose. However, the mitigation of information asymmetry—and, in particular, the distinction just described between two types or causes of randomness—is relevant. So are the following points:

(a) Rank-order tournaments use less information than cardinal tournaments, which is a factor of strength or of weakness depending on information availability. Relatedly, rank-order tournaments are less restrictive than cardinal tournaments with regard both to the form of the underlying relation between inputs and rewards and to the distribution function of common randomness. This makes them well suited to non-stationary environments (Green and Stokey 1983).

(b) Heterogeneity among agents in the sense of differences in ability is handled more easily in cardinal tournaments than in rank-order ones. In the case of the latter, remedies must be sought in handicapping or sorting. Otherwise, agents who have a higher chance to win, or to lose, would be disinclined to exert themselves. That problem does not arise to the same degree in cardinal tournaments: all agents, whatever their ability, receive a compensation related to the distance between their own performance and the average performance of peers or of the whole group. The relation between effort and reward is continuous (there is a pay-for-performance incentive).

(c) In rank-order tournaments, whether or not agents have the same ability, equilibrium requires that some randomness, "noise," remains in the relation between effort and output.[22] Otherwise there may be no equilibrium (Lazear and Rosen 1981, O'Keeffe, Viscusi, and Zeckhauser 1984). That problem must be considered together with the opposite consideration that uncertainty may have a negative effect on effort.[23]

(d) Many of the problems encountered by rank-order tournaments vanish or are mitigated when prizes are numerous. Then, the capacity to accommodate heterogeneity and the continuity between effort and reward are comparable in practice to what they are in cardinal tournaments (Knoeber 1989).[24]

### 3.3.2. Transposition

Transposing yardstick competition (understood broadly, including tournaments) from its original habitat to competition among governments is not straightforward. Some of the intellectual obstacles encountered were discussed in Salmon (1987b). A major difference between the two settings is that agents have a common principal in the original but not in the inter-governmental context. This makes yardstick competition among governments quite singular. The mechanism is also singular for reasons that I overlooked or left tacit at the time. These reasons are related to the heterogeneity of mass electorates (stressed in chapter 2), which generates a setting of electoral agency different from the agency relation in its original habitat and from political agency as presented for instance in Besley (2006). In electoral agency, each voter is a principal; each voter is an unbounded sovereign; electorates are not unitary actors but aggregates. This makes electoral agency and, with it, yardstick competition among incumbent politicians, fundamentally *non-contractual.*

The discussion that follows is focused on another consequence of electoral agency conditions, also implicitly implied in the characterization of yardstick competition proposed in chapter 2. Even when cross-jurisdiction comparisons made by voters are ordinal, they recover a cardinal dimension at the aggregate level when apprehended by incumbent politicians. In other words, we often have some aspects of rank-order tournaments at the level of individual voters and of cardinal tournaments at the level of politicians and governments.[25]

Voters get cross-border information in two ways. They may rely on their own observation or on data produced or circulated by public agencies, the media, experts, and other sources. Let us think about the first case. Suppose that the variable in discussion is "success in adapting health care to new conditions." The new conditions referred to are related to progress in scientific and technological knowledge (new medical techniques, new types of equipment, etc.). It constitutes a common shock in the sense discussed previously. Exploiting it requires some governmental input. Country $X$ is less successful than country $Y$ in that matter, but the difference is difficult to measure quantitatively (in particular because of other differences between the two countries). An individual voter would feel unable to express the difference in cardinal terms. At his or her level, only ordinal comparisons make sense. However, as argued in chapter 2 (and illustrated in fig. 2.1), the larger the objective difference even in a vague sense, the larger the number of voters who perceive it or the stronger their response to it, and thus the larger the aggregate support loss in country $X$ and, possibly, support gain in country $Y$. Let me stress two implications. As we saw, one reason Besley and Smart (2007) give for the problems encountered in political agency is the impossibility of "pay-for-performance contracts." I will definitely not use the term contract but an implication of the reasoning just presented is that pay-for-performance incentives are operative and important. Incumbents in both countries will calculate that any amount of additional effort may increase comparison-based support.[26] A second implication of the reasoning is that this effect will occur whether or not the rank order between the two countries changes. In other words, the two incumbents or governments are concerned with *distance,* or variation therein, a characteristic of cardinal, not ordinal, tournaments. Thus, even when cardinal comparisons referring to distance seem excluded at the level of individual citizens, the variable coupled with them at the aggregate level—that is, support variation—is cardinal. Non-cardinality gets bypassed, so to say.

The case just discussed is relatively simple because only two jurisdictions are assumed to be objects of comparisons by voters. It is also relatively extreme because both voters and incumbents are supposed unable to use a cardinal metric for gauging distance. This may be otherwise, depending on the variables concerned. As we will see, the typical assumption concerning yardstick competition made in the empirical study of local taxation is that electoral support reacts to how the level of a tax (or variation thereof) compares to what it is on average in neighboring jurisdictions (i.e., peer average). The comparisons made by individual voters may or may not be exclusively ordinal and they certainly involve different neighboring jurisdictions, but at the aggregate level, because taxation is amenable to cardinal measurement, we have a pure case of cardinal tournament.

This does not imply that pure rank-order tournaments are unimportant at the aggregate level. Many Italians were proud when their country surpassed the United Kingdom in terms of income per capita. If that had not been the case, the Italian government would not have paid something to get that result.[27] As stressed in the general literature on tournaments, one must be attentive to the idiosyncratic component of the performance of others—others' idiosyncratic bad luck or good luck, so to say. The problem may be serious when the comparison is made with one single other. It is rapidly mitigated when the number of others is increased. When comparing the merits of ordinal and cardinal tournaments, there is a natural tendency to assume that the former involves two participants and the latter a larger number (so that peer average is calculated on more than one other participant). As a consequence, the idiosyncratic element in others' achievements is assumed to be a more serious problem for assessing performance in ordinal than in cardinal tournaments. If, for instance, the performance of France in some domain is inferior to that of Germany, there is a real possibility that the cause was Germany being lucky. But if the performance of France is inferior to the average performance of all the other member countries of the European Union, claiming that they were lucky would seem implausible. This is correct as far as it goes. However, because the number of participants is different in the two cases, the comparison is misleading. What should be compared are two ways to assess relative performance in a group of given size, here of France in the EU context: either rank or relation with peer or group average. Then France being below the average or below the median cannot be very different as far as the idiosyncratic element of randomness in others is concerned. The incidence of that element in the EU context is likely to be small in both cases.

The way we have related voting and relative performance has the following implication on rank-order tournaments: for a given jurisdiction, prizes are simply degrees of support, which makes the relation between ranks and prizes weakly increasing. The incumbent can expect to receive a prize if the jurisdiction is seventeenth and a prize if it is eighteenth. The former is the same as the latter (support does not vary) or larger (support increases). The incumbent has an incentive to make the jurisdiction gain a rank.

The possibility that voters pay attention to intermediate positions was already noted in Salmon (1987b, p. 34). However, the comparisons assumed then were based on direct observation or knowledge by voters, with no explicit reliance on published rankings. As a consequence, the number of jurisdictions compared had to remain small. The much-increased publication or circulation of league tables changes the matter.[28] They generally include a large number of jurisdictions. When the scale of a ranking is relatively large, the incentive to gain one rank approximates that provided by a pay-for-performance scheme. Whatever the initial position, losing a few ranks in some of the tables included in the OECD's Program for International Student Assessment (PISA) reports or, less clearly, in the World Bank's *Doing Business* reports may cost some votes and would be better avoided. The publication of the first PISA report generated a "PISA shock" in Germany and the publication of the first *Doing Business* report a less widespread but perhaps even more feverish reaction in France.[29]

### 3.3.3. Mimicking versus outperforming

In the foregoing presentation of yardstick competition, incumbents strive for their jurisdiction to do better than others. This is true both of ordinal and cardinal tournaments (including Shleifer's (1985) yardstick competition). Thus, it might seem puzzling that some of the best contributions on the matter make yardstick competition among governments take the form of *mimicking* and assume the motivation of incumbents to be limited to their jurisdiction not *falling behind* in voters' cross-jurisdiction comparisons.[30] The objective of outperforming others is not mentioned— in fact, I also take this approach in many parts of this book. The reasons for assuming mimicking fall into two categories.

First, the theory of agency developed in both the economics and the political science literature on accountability tend to consider cheating or shirking as the main problem raised by information asymmetry. As noted, accountability is typically discussed in terms of sanctions rather than rewards (it is irrelevant for our discussion that, in a logical sense, they can be interpreted as coming down to the same thing). In the context of agency, economists refer to moral hazard and disciplining. As also noted, that in-terpretation is legitimate in many settings. Jobs must be done. Tasks must be fulfilled without interference from agents' idiosyncratic preferences. Effort must be delivered as required by circumstances. From that perspec-tive, information asymmetry is an obstacle and contractual incentives a substitute for monitoring. Yardstick competition mitigates the obstacle and strengthens the incentives. The performance of others offers a bench-mark valuable for strengthening control and enhancing discipline. For agents, mimicking and not falling behind are important to avert sanctions.

We have seen that yardstick competition as modeled by Shleifer can be considered a special form of cardinal tournament. However, it must be conceded that the pay-for-performance virtue of cardinal tournaments, al-though effective, is less visible in that special form. Instead of competitors being openly rewarded or charged as a function of the difference between their own output and that of others, in the said special form, competitors make automatic and largely intimate (privately known) benefits or losses as a function of the difference between their costs and those born on average by others. Shleifer does stress both the competitive nature of the process and the incentive to outperform others, but these are less apparent than in the case of standard tournaments. The fact that Shleifer's contribution is to the theory of regulation also contributes to its disciplining connotation.

That first interpretation of the emphasis put on mimicking and not falling behind is based on general presuppositions on the nature of agency and accountability. The second interpretation refers to the possibility that incumbents concentrate on "not falling behind" because of a "negative bias" among voters—meaning that voters react more strongly to negative than to positive performance.[31] Figure 3.1, divided in three parts, is a way to present the phenomenon in the setting of comparative voting.[32] $Q$ is variation in a policy output; $X$ is the jurisdiction concerned; $Y$ is another ju-risdiction, or an average, serving as a benchmark. The relative performance of $X$ is simply $Q_X - Q_Y$. It can be positive or negative. $V_X$ is the expected gain or loss of votes for the incumbent in $X$ induced by the relative performance of $X$. The response of voting depends on whether relative performance is positive or negative:

- $V_X = \alpha\,(Q_X - Q_Y)$ when relative performance is positive
- $V_X = \beta\,(Q_X - Q_Y)$ when relative performance is negative

The negativity bias, depicted in figure 3.1a, occurs when $\alpha < \beta$. Figure 3.1b illustrates its extreme version: when $\alpha = 0$, positive comparative perfor-mance has no effect at all.

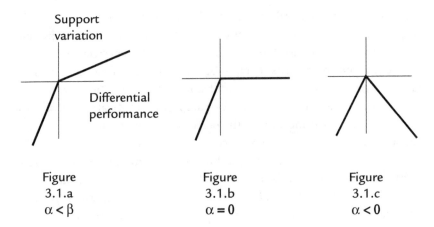

| Figure | Figure | Figure |
|:------:|:------:|:------:|
| 3.1.a | 3.1.b | 3.1.c |
| $\alpha < \beta$ | $\alpha = 0$ | $\alpha < 0$ |

**Figure 3.1**: Negativity bias, total negativity, and divergence aversion

If a performance that is 1 percent lower than a performance elsewhere has a larger effect on votes than a performance that is 1 percent higher, this prioritizes attention to not falling behind. An occasion to have a performance higher than elsewhere might still be seized. That is precluded when $\alpha = 0$. Then, only the fear of falling behind and loosing votes counts.

As discussed so far, mimicking or herding is related to a monotonic vote curve. This makes sense when voters value unambiguously the variable compared: ceteris paribus, more taxes is bad, more growth is good, etc. But many innovations or regulations do not have that property, at least ex ante. For instance, is electricity production based on windmills a good idea? We don't know yet. Nor do voters. Still, political yardstick competition may compel a government to imitate what is done elsewhere. Mimicking and herding then means doing as others do. Divergence, whatever the direction, causes a support loss.[33] Figure 3.1c represents that divergence aversion, corresponding to $\alpha < 0$. As we will see, some of the contributions to the literature on political yardstick competition suggest herding behavior of that kind (see, e.g., Feld, Josselin, and Rocaboy 2002, 2003). The variable object of comparison (public spending, say) can move in any direction provided it does so simultaneously in all jurisdictions. As we will see in chapter 9, herding can be a serious cause of perverse effects of political yardstick competition.

However, it is necessary at this stage to note the existence of an ambiguity in the meaning of mimicking (and herding, for that matter). The word "mimicking" can mean three different things: an objective, a result, and a decided process. Under some assumptions and for some variables (for instance, deciding, with full knowledge of others' decisions, a tax rate instantly effective), these distinctions are unnecessary. But in most circumstances, although generally overlooked, they are important. What we have discussed so far is mimicking or herding as an objective. What we find in much of the empirical literature is mimicking as a result, which may have nothing to do with yardstick competition (it can be due to mobility-based tax competition, for instance). But even if it is related to yardstick competition, it could be the outcome of each incumbent trying to make her jurisdiction do better than, rather than as well as, others in the eyes of her own constituents. The outcomes across jurisdictions would turn out to be close but without an intention of mimicking being the cause of the observed convergence. In that case, the term mimicking is somewhat misleading.

Conversely, mimicking, imitating, or copycatting as a decided process may or may not generate convergence or mimicking as a result and may or may not satisfy mimicking as an objective. Suppose that policy input and output can be distinguished and are related by a production function that is stochastic and has a time dimension. Randomness cannot be eliminated. As we saw previously, a jurisdiction's own (idiosyncratic) element of randomness cannot be filtered away by a focus on relative performance or made insignificant by the law of large numbers. Let us assume that not falling behind is the only objective or concern of incumbents (extreme negativity bias as represented by figure 3.1b). If the incumbent were risk neutral ("randomness blind," so to speak) and could form reliable expectations about the performance of other jurisdictions, she could decide the input in her jurisdiction so as to mimic that performance. We would observe mimicking as a result on average. However, if the incumbent is risk-averse (does not like randomness), mimicking as an objective implies departing from mimicking as a decided process. Each incumbent will try to make her jurisdiction do weakly better than others. As students are sometimes told, limiting one's effort to that which seems just sufficient for not falling behind is a risky strategy. *Because their concern is doing as well as others, incumbents will attempt to make their jurisdiction do better.*

Reducing yardstick competition to mimicking restricts our view of the mechanism and, as noted when mentioning divergence aversion, suggests an indeterminacy that a more dynamic interpretation of competition could perhaps disallow. If each incumbent tries to ensure that her jurisdiction does better than the others, this might preclude the kind of spiral toward bad performance that simple herding could well allow.

A concern with not reducing yardstick competition to mimicking should not prevent us, however, from concentrating when needed on one side of the relationship, namely underperformance. We may do this without

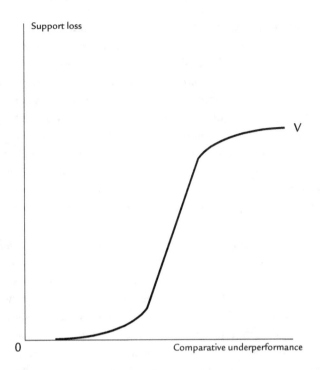

**Figure 3.2**: Underperformance and support loss

assuming that the other side—that is, performing better—is irrelevant. Concentrating on underperformance allows us to use a particularly convenient geometrical representation: in figure 3.2, the horizontal axis measures relative underperformance (or variation therein) and the vertical axis measures (expected) support loss.[34]

## 3.4. CONCLUSION

This chapter was a necessary complement to the characterization of yardstick competition presented in chapter 2. It aimed in particular to integrate that mechanism into the setting of the large literature on the relationship between citizens and office holders. Yardstick competition among governments is meaningful if downward accountability (that is, accountability to citizens) is important, if downward accountability encounters information asymmetry as a serious obstacle, and if cross-jurisdiction comparisons made by citizens contribute to overcome that obstacle. This suggested that three essential ingredients of our reasoning needed some elaboration.

The first is accountability and its limitations (other than those related to information asymmetry). Some attention was given to definitions. We also discussed the usual interpretation of accountability as asymmetric (sanctions rather than rewards). The main idea, however, was that, contrary to other frameworks based on the agency relationship (i.e., Fearon 1999), the one proposed in chapter 2 (basically, electoral agency) gives us the freedom to limit the scope of accountability in various ways without jeopardizing its role or relevance. One aspect of that freedom is that we can treat accountability as fully compatible with other perspectives on democracy, in particular those stressing the choice of policies or the selection of candidates on the basis of personal characteristics. Another aspect is in the way we deal with obstacles to downward accountability, in particular the role of elites and the effects of clientelism. I have argued in this chapter that the influence of elites, whatever they are, may not preclude reasoning in a principal-agent framework with government as agent and citizens, or various categories thereof, as its principals. When accountability takes the form of clientelism, it does limit in several ways the relevance or impact of performance and thus the impact on policy-making of electoral or democratic accountability in the usual sense. But the problem is not equally serious everywhere and in any case the fact that we acknowledge the limits of accountability allows us to take such difficulties with equanimity. The same is true with regard to a third category of objections, those pointing to the importance of ingredients of "good governance" other than accountability—a fashionable theme, notably in the context of development. We can easily admit, without making accountability irrelevant, that the rule of law and especially state efficiency can be, or ought to be, of first importance in the case of many developing countries. All in all, our discussion has left open the possibility stressed in chapter 2 that information asymmetry faced by citizens is a major obstacle to accountability.

The second ingredient concerns that obstacle. Again, there has been no need to claim overwhelming importance. There was no harm for our purpose in admitting that in the case of some, perhaps many, issues, information asymmetry is not really bothersome. In the case of others, however, ordinary citizens are at least potentially in a weak position (in the absence of yardstick information). On this matter, two kinds of issues should be distinguished: general and particular. With regard to the general issues, there is a difference between authoritarian regimes and democracies. In the former, the problem met by citizens is both about access to facts and about their assessment. In democracies, factual information involving policy outcomes is generally available, and the problem is mainly about their interpretation and evaluation. For that, citizens have to rely on the media and on politicians, typically with little possibility of control if comparisons with other jurisdictions are unavailable.

With regard to specialized issues, of interest mainly to some categories of citizens, a major channel of information is through interest groups (farmers, teachers, etc.). In that case, we have argued that it is necessary to acknowledge the distinction between rank and file and leaders and the principal-agent nature of their relation. As I have already argued, many years ago, because of the mobilization logic stressed by Olson (1965) the underlying relation between (large) interest groups and politicians or governments is far more subtle than is generally assumed. Saying that it is also opaque is another way to say that, in their relation with their leaders, ordinary members of large groups face an information asymmetry problem akin to that faced by citizens in their relation with politicians. This reduces the reliability of the information received through that channel.

An elaboration of the third ingredient was also needed because, as we will stress in the chapter 5, yardstick competition is a richer and a more flexible mechanism than implicitly assumed in the empirical work done on it, or more exactly in the way the results of that work are interpreted. In this chapter, it has seemed worthwhile to go back to the original literature, mainly in labor and industrial economics, and to draw from that inquiry important points about the ways yardstick competition could be analyzed when transposed to the political domain. Some distinctions made in the original literature are particularly important for our purpose. Competition may be for rank, that is, along an ordinal scale, or for cardinal distance from an average. In practice, when the number of competitors is large, there is not much difference between the two. Randomness is always essential. It can be common or idiosyncratic. When the latter, it can concern both others and oneself. Again, the number of competitors counts: when it is small, randomness in others should be an important consideration. When the number gets larger, its significance vanishes—outcomes depend only on common shocks and on one's own source of randomness. When yardstick competition is transposed to a political intergovernmental context, the distinctions remain important. Two points have been particularly stressed. One is that ordinal comparisons at the level of individual citizens may lead to competition of a cardinal kind, involving distance, at the level of incumbents. The other is that uncertainty is one reason why in many cases mimicking is an ambiguous way to interpret yardstick competition, a matter to which we will return.

## NOTES

1. This is definitely not because the word accountability has no real equivalent in French (as the word performance has no real equivalent in Italian).
2. See for instance Przeworski, Stokes, and Manin (1999) and Mainwaring (2003).
3. See Elster (1999).
4. I gloss over the question of whether all adult individuals may participate in the elections.
5. Accountability to a higher level of government is a manifestation of upward accountability. So is the accountability of bureaucrats to political office holders. O'Donnell (1998) introduced the concept of horizontal accountability and Mainwaring (2003) that of intrastate accountability, but most of the relations they focus on can also be captured as pertaining to checks and balances (Breton 1996) or the rule of law (Berman 1983, Fukuyama 2011, 2014). Accountability of the cabinet to parliament in parliamentary systems is clearly a manifestation of downward accountability, as noted in the text.
6. Here, we leave aside the case of incumbents who cannot be candidates again because of term limits.
7. Persson and Tabellini (2000, p. 16) reserve the expression "electoral accountability" for models in which voters re-elect only the incumbents who have had a good performance. They call "career models" those in which voters re-elect only the incumbents having a good *expected* performance.
8. The distinction between rulers and ruled is not universal. Some "primitive" societies are relatively egalitarian and democratic. Members make their decisions in common. Thus, everyone is both ruled and co-ruler. In some other societies, decisions in common are also made on an egalitarian basis albeit only by a subset of the population. Let us refer to that subset as "the citizens." Let us also neglect the part of the population typically neglected and refer to the decision-making mechanism in both cases as direct democracy (as is done in many discussions of Athenian democracy). If we assume that citizens delegate some tasks to individuals, we may consider the ensuing relation as one of agency, with citizens as principals and the individuals entrusted with the task as agents. However, it is not of the downward kind. Accountability may arise outside any agency relationship when an ordinary citizen convinces the others to decide something that proves wrong in retrospect. That citizen may be held responsible and even punished for what he or she said.
9. Interview of Guillaume Pepy, Chief Executive Officer of SNCF (the French Railways), in the *Financial Times*, August 17, 2015.
10. An example is this statement by Adsera, Boix, and Payne (2003): "good governance is a function of the extent to which citizens can hold political officials accountable for their actions" (p. 447).
11. See, e.g., North, Wallis, and Weingast (2009).
12. As understood in Fukuyama, rule of law is a constraint on the monarch, to be distinguished from rule by law, which is not, and from accountability, which corresponds more or less to democracy, or what I generally call downward accountability.
13. Instances coming to mind: in France, support for the war in Algeria in the late 1950s; in the United States, support for the second war in Iraq; in Israel,

acquiescence to expanding settlements in the West Bank; almost everywhere until recently, the so-called "war on drugs."

14. Persson, Roland, and Tabellini (1997) argue that one effect of checks and balances is to elicit information that citizens can use.

15. Failure or success in dealing appropriately with natural disasters comes to mind. Public opinion is certainly influenced by standards generated over time. But it may also be influenced by cross-jurisdiction comparisons. In the case of the Katrina catastrophe, Congleton (2006) suggests that citizens in New Orleans may have had recourse to comparisons between bad management in Louisiana and better management in Florida or Mississippi.

16. In the standard contractual theory of agency, treating the agent unfairly bears a cost for the principal. In electoral agency, voters treating incumbents unfairly could be costly to voters, in particular in the long run, via a negative effect on the quality of political personnel. See Elster (1999) for a discussion of the matter in the context of Ancient Greece.

17. See also Baiman and Demski (1980, pp. 195–99).

18. This explains why Shleifer (1985) and yardstick competition are often not mentioned in the literature on incentives in agency settings.

19. The terminology is not completely fixed. Tournaments may be referred to as ordinal or cardinal even when they have both features (Ghosh and Hummel 2015). I gloss over the distinction between peer average and group average, which is negligible when groups reach a reasonable size. When groups are very small, or at the limit when the number of peers is reduced to one, we may assume that peer average imposes itself.

20. A matter we already discussed in chapter 2. Cf. Lazear and Rosen (1981): "it is often impossible to know whether a person's output is satisfactory without comparisons to other persons" (p. 857). See also Olsen (2017).

21. $Q_i = Q_i (E_i, N_i, R)$. The principal observes only $Q_i$. The agent observes $R$ before deciding $E_i$ (see in particular Nalebuff and Stiglitz 1983).

22. In the words of Lazear and Rosen (1981), "contests are feasible only when chance is a significant factor" (note 2, p. 845). See also Nalebuff and Stiglitz (1983, p. 29).

23. Cf. Tsoulouhas (2015): "the higher the total (i.e., common and idiosyncratic) uncertainty, the lower the power of incentives and effort, because uncertainty hampers the strength of the relationship between effort and output" (p. 1227) and "the larger the variance of idiosyncratic uncertainty the lower the effort because the more outcomes depend on luck the less effort the agent will exert" (p. 1230).

24. Multi-prize rank-order tournaments were already discussed in an agency setting, in general briefly, by the founding authors mentioned above. In the study of contests in general, the number of contributions concerned with several prizes is becoming quite large—see Konrad (2009), Sisak (2009), Fu and Lu (2012) and the references therein.

25. This important point was overlooked in Salmon (1987b).

26. Our performance-based vote function is continuous. The dependent variable is variation in the total number of votes the incumbent expects to receive. There is a relation between that quantity and the probability of re-election, and, no doubt, that fact is often in the minds of incumbents when they make their decisions. But, as we argued, the relation may be quite uncertain or distant. Thus, we may consider the number of votes as a kind of *numéraire* (of course, like a unit of money, the utility of a single vote is not independent of quantity). Variations in performance, which at the aggregate level, are also continuous, will cost or earn votes.

If we prefer to assume that politicians have always in mind, in a precise mode, the relation between variations in expected number of votes and variations in the probability of winning, the latter (assumed to be continuous) could directly serve as a *numéraire*.

27. Incorporation of production in the informal sector increased the official figure at the cost of a larger contribution by Italy to the European budget

28. Empirical work on political yardstick competition almost never refers to large-scale rankings or ratings. Revelli (2006) is an exception in the sense that he does take rankings into account. However, he opposes them to yardstick competition. He draws from the introduction in Britain of the so-called national system of social services performance rating the prediction (confirmed statistically) that this will reduce the scope for what he calls yardstick competition (based exclusively on comparisons with neighboring jurisdictions).

29. In the 2013 PISA report, France was clearly distanced by Germany and surpassed also by Poland, two countries which were behind France in 2000. For the first time that triggered some talk of a PISA shock also in France. See *Le Monde*, February 4, 5, 6, 7, and 8, 2014. On the political dimensions of the *Doing Business* reports, see for instance Salmon (2005) and Besley (2015). On the feverish nature of the reaction in France to the first *Doing Business* report, I rely on personal observation. I return to the matter in chapter 6.

30. See, e.g., Heyndels and Vuchelen (1998) and Allers and Ellhorst (2005).

31. In the context of vote-popularity functions, the phenomenon, whose existence and empirical significance are debated, is referred to as a negativity effect or bias by Lau (1985), Soroka (2006), and Olsen (2017) and as a "grievance asymmetry" by Nannestad and Paldam (1997).

32. I draw on the analysis proposed in Dijk (2012, pp. 39–43), itself inspired by Clark and Oswald (1998). In the context of the present discussion, we must replace comparison utility with comparison-induced vote variation and individuals with jurisdictions.

33. That type of behavior is particularly understandable in the case of agents making risky decisions. For an employed agent (or even an independent analyst), being wrong when everybody is wrong is not as consequential as being wrong alone—see, e.g., Scharfstein and Stein (1990). But here (that is, in the text), divergence aversion is located within the electorate—that is, among the principals—rather than in the agent—that is the incumbent—and it is not clear that it is to be explained by risk aversion.

34. The relationship between relative performance and support can be non-linear in two ways, corresponding to figures 2.1 and 3.1. We could combine the two sources of non-linearity by making the S-curve presented in figure 2.1 have a different shape depending on whether the variation in comparative performance is positive or negative. Because of the negativity bias, the portion of the S-curve in the southwest quadrant would be different from the portion in the northeast quadrant (if the former were rotated and brought into the northeast quadrant, it would be situated, for each of its points, higher up than the latter). In fact, figure 2.1 will not be used and the combination just mentioned will not be referred to any more. We will refer exclusively to figure 3.2. To repeat, this does not necessarily mean that we assume a negativity bias: figure 3.2 may also be seen as the southwest quadrant of figure 2.1 rotated by 180 degrees.

# CHAPTER 4

# Yardstick competition and its cousins

Mechanisms in the real world tend to be at work simultaneously. But in scientific inquiry they are often studied in isolation (I return to that difference in the methodological section of the concluding chapter). In many parts of the book, yardstick competition is discussed as if it were an isolated mechanism. This chapter, however, considers some mechanisms interacting with yardstick competition or with which they might but should not be confused.

Two mechanisms are particularly important: mobility-based competition and policy learning.[1] In both cases, there is a large literature on the mechanism itself and practically none on its relationship with yardstick competition. In principle, the distinction between mobility-based competition and yardstick competition is unambiguous. The first is related to what Hirschman (1970) called "exit," the second to what he called "voice." In section 4.1, I discuss some aspects of mobility-based competition before turning to the highly speculative matter of its relationship with yardstick competition. Section 4.2 on policy learning is organized in the same way. However, unlike mobility-based competition, the risk of confusion between policy learning and yardstick competition is very high, so more attention needs to be given to how they can be separated.

In section 4.3, four other mechanisms that also involve cross-jurisdiction information are considered briefly. These are: approval and emulation; incumbents' career concerns; out-of-jurisdiction opinion; and Neo-Austrian institutional competition.[2]

## 4.1. MOBILITY-BASED COMPETITION

As noted, there is a large literature on mobility-based competition (in particular tax competition) and almost none on the way it interacts with yardstick competition—if I am correct, the only theoretical paper about that interaction published so far is Bordignon (2015). In a sense this is quite natural. Yet, a discussion of some aspects of the interaction is necessary, even if it has to remain incomplete and tentative. Among the seven points that follow, the first two—about the distinction between policy-induced mobility and mobility-based competition proper and about the comparative strengths of mobility-based competition and yardstick competition—do not refer to interaction. To varying degrees, the five others do. They concern the locus of interaction, the attitude of immobile voters toward mobility, policy-making autonomy, the exit–voice nexus, and mobility-induced diversity.

### 4.1.1. Policy-induced mobility and mobility-based competition

Mobility-based competition covers a large array of mechanisms and phenomena, which are often discussed in separate bodies of literature. It encompasses in particular Tiebout competition, tax competition, Leviathan taming, welfare competition, and the race to the bottom. At the same time some mechanisms should be kept distinct from mobility-based competition, in particular policy-induced mobility, which may or may not generate or reflect mobility-based competition.

Policy-induced mobility is a simple matter. Suppose that a policy change is decided in jurisdiction $X$. Some agents (households, business firms, investors, factor owners, etc.) may react in ways involving cross-border mobility: the policy change induces them to move into or out of the jurisdiction or deters them from doing so. That formulation covers several phenomena. Following Hirschman (1970), policy-induced moving out is often referred to as *exit*. But policy-induced moving in (entry) and policy-induced mobility deterrence are as important. As a rule, policy-induced mobility will depend on some comparisons with what obtains in other jurisdictions.

Instead of referring to movements (exit and entry) or absence thereof (deterrence), we may reason in terms of statics or comparative statics and define the agents' choice in terms of location. Policies explain in part where agents locate. There is no time dimension here. If policy changes induce changes in location, when or how that effect occurs is irrelevant. In this way, we may avoid the consideration of mobility costs. However, for that to be plausible, it is usually convenient to suppose that some categories of agents are highly mobile and others not at all.

To get to mobility-based competition we must assume some mobility-caused interdependence between the policies adopted in the different jurisdictions. As a consequence of mobility (or location choice), policies adopted in jurisdiction $X$ depend on policies adopted in jurisdiction $Y$ or on average in other jurisdictions. Even then, interdependence may not take the form of competition. This is particularly clear in the case of the Tiebout approach—which is broader than the model of the same name (Tiebout 1956). In the model itself, jurisdictions offer different bundles of goods and services and citizens locate where the bundles satisfy their preferences at the lowest tax price. Historically, the model had three main features. First, it provided an alternative solution to the preference revelation problem. Individuals who vote with their feet reveal their preferences for public goods more reliably, perhaps, than in other ways. However, the intense interest given at the time to preference revelation has vanished. Second, assuming that the number of jurisdictions is large, competition ensures that the tax price associated with each bundle of goods is minimal. Whether such result holds will prove important for our purpose. A third result is spatial sorting according to individual preferences. This generates or enhances spatial heterogeneity, also a matter to which we will return.

Contrary to the model, the Tiebout approach does not require competition. There are many theoretical analyses and also many historical episodes in which policies do induce cross-jurisdiction mobility and lead to spatial sorting according to preferences without reflecting or generating competition, at least directly. Suppose that $X$ is a mainly Catholic and $Y$ a mainly Protestant jurisdiction and that, as a result of some public policies, some Protestants in $X$ move to $Y$ and/or some Catholics in $Y$ move to $X$. It is conceivable that at equilibrium the two governments can be better off. This clearly points to spatial sorting rather than to intergovernmental competition. If we assume more than two jurisdictions, intergovernmental competition may resurface, albeit taking place among Protestant jurisdictions on one side and/or among Catholic jurisdictions on the other. Many of the Protestants (Huguenots) who left France as a result of Louis XIV's ill-considered policies settled in Germany. Mobility-based competition arose not between the French king and the German sovereigns but (to attract the Huguenots) among some of the latter (Brandenburg, Hesse, etc.). It does not seem that Louis XIV wanted the Huguenots to leave France (rather than convert to Catholicism) as a consequence of his policy. From his perspective, the episode is best understood as an instance of involuntary policy-induced mobility—mobility as a side effect, possibly unforeseen, of a policy undertaken for a different objective.

### 4.1.2. Compared strengths of the two competition mechanisms

Is mobility-based competition more plausible than information-based yardstick competition? The view that it is can be derived from a strong version of the rational ignorance hypothesis.[3] Individuals and, even more obviously, business firms contemplating moving out of a jurisdiction have a clear-cut, narrowly defined, incentive to become informed about the state of affairs in the jurisdictions they might move to. In addition, the information needed can be focused on the relatively precise policy dimensions they are concerned with. Short-term financial investors, for instance, need knowledge mainly about interest, exchange, and tax rates and about risk of default. By contrast, individuals for whom the sole utility of information is supposed to be to improve the subjective quality of their vote have no such obvious incentive, whereas, depending on what motivates them to vote (a difficult question anyhow, as we saw), the information about other jurisdictions that they should consider relevant may be quite encompassing.

Incidentally, that argument, which is certainly persuasive from the perspective of traditional economics, also applies to the difference between the information needed by citizens in the context of yardstick competition and the information needed by governments in that of policy learning (a distinction to be discussed later in this chapter). From a strict public choice or traditional economics perspective, the incentive to get informed about out-of-jurisdiction matters is more plausible within governments (i.e., among incumbents and bureaucrats) than within ordinary citizenry. This may be one reason why both mobility-based competition and policy learning are widely perceived as more plausible than yardstick competition.

What seems clearly true in the hypothesis of rational ignorance is that, as a rule, voters or citizens will not pay very much to become informed. Thus, if some knowledge can be obtained only at a significant cost, most voters will rationally abstain from seeking it. Is that argument as compelling as many scholars think?[4] We know that, willingly or not, actively or not, we gather a lot of information on matters in which we have no direct stake. A lot of information flows for free. Far from considering it to be the result of a positive and costly decision, it may be more realistic to say that we do not or often cannot avoid getting it. It is in the air we breathe, so to speak. In addition, we rely on many shortcuts or indirect channels for information—it is seldom the case that we get directly information that changes our opinion on some matter. There is ample empirical evidence that many debates, reports, and positions about important issues may have an immediate and sizeable impact on the views held by many citizens on those issues. Comparisons with what obtains abroad feed naturally into these debates, reports, and positions and thus in the air breathed by ordinary citizens, to continue with the same metaphor. That is sufficient to justify the minimal assumption made throughout this book that what obtains in other jurisdictions has *some* impact on the support that *some* voters are inclined to give to their representatives.

The other side of the comparison is also to be considered. For the larger part of the population, moving to another jurisdiction, and especially moving to another country, as a response to ordinary policies is out of the question. In that case, voice is the only realistic possibility. For our purpose, both forms of competition (mobility/exit and voice) are important. I have defended the relevance of political yardstick competition, but the relevance of mobility-based competition is unquestionable in many domains and contexts, for example with regard to the taxation of business and capital, or among localities within a metropolitan area.

### 4.1.3. The locus of interaction

In democracies and in normal circumstances, individuals do not face a choice between exit and voice. Few citizens wonder whether they will vote against the incumbent or leave the jurisdiction—that is, hesitate between voting in a literal sense and voting with their feet. Most individual citizens do not consider the second action a serious possibility. And those who do, even though they might vote against the incumbent if staying, will in general perceive the matter of their voting as immaterial. Leaving the country and voting against the incumbent are not in the same league, so to speak.[5]

That irrelevance of choice between exit and voice at the individual level is a feature of most migrations, but the choice can be meaningful in some contexts. In non-democratic settings or in exceptional circumstances, using voice may mean joining at some cost an unauthorized or clandestine movement or organization, a decision more straightforward from the perspective of instrumental rationality than simply participating in a large election. One must also concede that notorious individuals, such as politicians, famous writers, and prominent scientists, may also face a plausible choice between voice, in a more literal sense than merely voting, and exit (even though they can sometimes use both in an efficient way by exerting voice from outside the jurisdiction). There is a tendency to focus one's attention on these exceptional cases and overlook the irrelevance of the choice between exit and voice for the much larger category of ordinary citizens. Overlooking the irrelevance may also reflect the tendency (discussed earlier) to treat categories as if they were unitary actors.[6]

Large business firms may have a real choice between trying to influence the content of policies in the jurisdiction by a kind of lobbying (a form of voice) and leaving the jurisdiction in part or completely (a form of exit). To account for the claimed or demonstrated influence of big business (and the "ultra-rich") on policy-making, some US scholars tend to emphasize the first alternative, that is, voice. They may be right as far as the United States is concerned. In the case of most European countries, though, in particular because they are smaller and more open, policy-induced mobility is the dominant source of influence.[7] Whether they belong to the Left or to the Right, incumbents in Europe are mostly concerned with the consequences of their policies on the direction of investment flows and the decisions of business firms about location. Inasmuch as voice exerted by investors and large business firms does count, this is through the implicit or explicit threat of exit. In fact, this is probably also largely the case in the United States at the level of subnational governments.

In general, the two forms of competition are effective simultaneously at the aggregate level. A given policy will induce or deter mobility and at the same time have an effect on political support, in particular through yardstick voting. The constituencies involved tend to be largely separate. For instance, mobility concerns business firms, and voting or yardstick competition concerns citizens.

### 4.1.4. Immobile citizens and mobility

As is widely observable, the attitude of immobile citizens toward policy-favored mobility is currently in a state of flux. Even though some citizens may be harmed in the short run by policies favoring mobility, most of them benefit from these policies in the long run. At any rate, this is what they are told by economists and international organizations, and we may assume that, by and large, through effects on economic growth, this has proved largely true. Economists have also recommended that losers be taken into account and if compensated, that compensation to be as direct as possible (see, e.g., Bhagwati and Srinivasan 1969). But this is more easily said than done, and many losers have remained uncompensated.

That state of affairs has not mattered too much, politically speaking, until recently. As will be explained later in this chapter, inasmuch as citizens compare policies, this is mainly subordinate to a comparison of outcomes. Until recently, comparisons of outcomes have contributed to upholding in the eyes of most citizens the case (made by incumbents and economists) for enhancing markets in general, cross-border mobility in particular, and, by implication, mobility-based competition.

That seems to be changing. The claim formulated most vehemently in the United States and in the United Kingdom that some categories of the population have been "left behind" has attracted the attention of public opinion in other countries. If it were to become clear that this cannot be remedied under current pro-mobility arrangements, a protectionist dynamic could be allowed to replace the liberalization and globalization trend that has been dominant over the last decades. Yardstick comparisons will play an important role in that context. If increased protectionism is perceived as giving good results in some countries, this will encourage citizens in others to press their own government to follow suit. If, on the other hand, some governments (say, in Northern Europe) are observed to both maintain an open economy and prevent subsets of the population from falling behind, this can play in other countries against yielding to protectionist temptations. The question of policy autonomy, to which I turn now, is central in that context.

### 4.1.5. Policy-making autonomy

Indeed, the interaction between the two forms of competition (yardstick and mobility-based) that comes most readily to mind is the erosion of governments' real powers or autonomy brought about by the mobility of goods and services, factors of production, people, and firms—a set of issues extensively discussed today both in the scientific literature and in more mundane surroundings. If mobility-based competition leaves no autonomy to public decision-making at the level of each jurisdiction, no room remains for the evaluation of government performance by citizens. Mobility-based competition will have done the job, albeit in its own way. A trend toward that outcome is prone to be judged in systemic or ideological terms: it tends to be dreaded as a "race to the bottom," if positive values are given to consumer protection, financial and environmental regulation, redistribution, labor standards, and welfare benefits:[8] but it is applauded as the main benefit of decentralization when government is perceived as a potential Leviathan, driven by its bureaucracy and by lobbies, incorrigibly oversized and intrusive (Brennan and Buchanan 1980, or, in different terms, Weingast 1995).

In Salmon (2015), I argue that the loss of autonomy induced by mobility-based competition is generally exaggerated. Both theory and observation tell us that jurisdictions, and thus governments and electorates, keep a substantial degree of policy-making freedom in spite of intense mobility-based competition. I will not reproduce here the theoretical part of the reasoning developed there.[9]

The observation of federal countries such as Canada, Switzerland, and the United States confirms that considerable policy-making power can remain at the regional (i.e., provincial, cantonal, and state) level in spite of intense internal mobility, facilitated in the case of Switzerland by very small distance (see Kirchgässner and Pommerehne 1996, Feld 2007). The same is true at the level of the European Union (including the quasi-member Switzerland). It is difficult for instance to imagine more different policies and political arrangements in all domains than those that endure in the two extremely open economies and societies of Denmark and Switzerland, both countries submitted furthermore to the so-called four freedoms defining the Single Market (free movement of goods, capital, services, and labor). Yet both countries are worldwide models, not only because of their economic success but also as instances of the "good society" (Christoffersen et al. 2014) or ideal "political order" (Pritchett and Woolcock 2004, Fukuyama 2011, 2014).[10] That such comparative success is based on institutional arrangements or blueprints and policies that are so different proves that the complaint that mobility-based competition prevents governments and democratic mechanisms from operating is largely exaggerated.[11] Clearly, because of mobility-based competition, some policies cannot be undertaken by single jurisdictions, except at high cost, but many others can, in particular thanks to compensations operating within policy and institutional packages. The real problem is not so much whether citizens are deprived in part of their capacity to choose or influence choices but rather whether the said packages are those that they would choose if they were better informed. This is where yardstick competition has something to contribute.

### 4.1.6. The exit-voice nexus

We know from Hirschman (1970) that exit and voice are not always mutually reinforcing. In fact, the matter is very complicated. This is perhaps the simplest lesson we can draw from the highly theoretical analysis of

Bordignon (2015), which is focused on the trade-off between incentives and selection. In his model, tax competition is a disciplining device, by itself welfare-enhancing but it may weaken the selection of incumbents which he considers the main benefit of yardstick competition. The outcome is ambiguous, as is generally the case with incentive-selection trade-offs.

Here we will concentrate on the question of whether exit erodes voice— that is, for our purpose, of whether mobility-based competition (or policy-induced mobility) makes yardstick competition less effective. Let us, however, consider briefly the other possibility. One way in which the two mechanisms may reinforce each other was noted in the foregoing discussion: the threat of leaving the jurisdiction constitutes an effective pressure on office-holders. Of course, threats of exit, bordering on blackmail, are not actual exits. Is realized exit weakening or strengthening voice? It is easy to conceive of voice being weakened by exit, but it is also easy to imagine a scenario in which the main effect is strengthening. To elaborate on the idea of the threat, suppose that some members of a category leave the jurisdiction; this makes more credible the threat that others will follow—a threat which in turn reinforces voice.[12] More generally, individuals or firms leaving a jurisdiction can signal underperformance. Conscious of their ignorance (i.e., of facing information asymmetry), citizens treat the phenomenon (or the inverse phenomenon of entry) as a clue for assessing government. One may also observe that, in authoritarian regimes, exit remaining possible offers opponents a safeguard against the repression or retribution their actions may trigger, and consequently, it may increase their resolve to fight the incumbent. Finally, more directly related to yardstick competition, the temporary mobility of individuals (for work or tourism) enhances knowledge of other jurisdictions and facilitates cross-jurisdiction comparisons—a factor that played a role in the transition to democracy in Spain at the end of the Franco dictatorship (Huntington 1991).

One can imagine other ways in which exit may help voice, or mobility further yardstick competition, but for our purpose the opposite effects deserve more attention as they help account for cases in which yardstick competition is ineffective. The seminal insight is in Hirschman (1970). If citizens in a jurisdiction are dissatisfied with the performance of their government and emigration costs are low, while dismissal of that government appears to be uncertain, some citizens will emigrate. If dissatisfaction about government is not equally shared by individuals, it is likely that those who emigrate are more dissatisfied on average than those who decide to stay. This makes life easier for the (badly performing) government and, if the effect is sufficiently strong, annihilates most of the incentives or forces that would lead to policy improvement.[13]

If exit continues, disparities in performance can thus increase without check over long periods of time, even under the assumption of a high level of information. This may happen to independent countries, but subnational jurisdictions are more easily subject to the process than whole countries. Moving out of a province or city is less costly as a rule than moving out of a whole country, and information about what obtains in other jurisdictions at the same level is less costly or easier to come by. Thus, we can expect regional or city decline to be a much more widespread and significant phenomenon and to extend over longer periods of time than the decline of countries as a whole.

What is the effect on the country as a whole? Some of the subnational governments may become permanent under-performers but the consequence will generally be that, progressively, the corresponding jurisdictions will lose population and that their importance in the country as a whole will decrease, while the jurisdictions whose performance is above average will gain population and become relatively more important.[14] From the standpoint of jurisdictions in the first category, mobility undermines the performance competition mechanism. From the standpoint of the country as a whole, whose government might itself be engaged in yardstick competition with the governments of other countries, it is not clear that it does. The same reasoning might be applied to the member countries of the European Union but would then raise even more passionate objections than at the subnational level. Telling a member country that it does not matter if it loses its population provided that this improves the performance of the European Union as a whole is not likely to be accepted with equanimity in the said country or even by foreign observers.[15]

### 4.1.7. Mobility-induced diversity and comparability

Mobility can increase diversity, that is, spatial heterogeneity. The Tiebout mechanism leads to citizen preferences being similar within and different across jurisdictions. In the theory of international (and interregional) trade, under some plausible assumptions about transaction and transportation costs, more integration in the form of fewer obstacles to mobility will lead to an increased specialization of production (as a consequence of differences in factor endowments, of economies of scale, of scope, etc.). In both cases, the spatial diversity that ensues could constitute an obstacle to the comparisons that play so essential a role in our performance competition story.

The problem raised is not as serious as it looks, for several reasons.[16] First, interjurisdictional specialization of production does not extend to the production of non-exchangeable goods and services, both of which can remain quite homogeneous over the whole integrated area (inasmuch as they were homogeneous to start with). Second, we have stressed the variety of the packages of goods, services, and taxes offered by the different jurisdictions to mobile agents. However, many agents (households, small firms, etc.) are not mobile and more likely than mobile agents to exert voice and thus to be those most relevant for yardstick voting and yardstick competition. The main concern of these immobile agents is with outcomes, in particular those related to income and consumption, rather than with policies. The interjurisdictional diversity of citizen preferences with regard to outcomes (i.e., consumption and income) remains limited in spite of the effects of mobility on production. It is even likely to be negatively affected by the increased information flows brought about by integration. Indeed, in the aggregate, the relevant diversity is probably diminishing with increased globalization (as travelers can observe themselves).

Finally, as already argued, citizens should not be deemed completely unable to decide which comparisons are reasonable. To take an example at the local level, inhabitants of suburbs compare the performance of their mayors mostly with what obtains in other suburbs rather than with what is done in the central city, and the inhabitants of central cities engage in comparisons with other central cities rather than with suburbs. Thus, differences between suburbs and central cities are not really an obstacle to the working of our mechanism. The same is largely true of comparisons across countries. In general, European citizens make comparisons among European countries rather than with the United States or India.[17]

## 4.2. POLICY LEARNING

Policy learning is certainly the most important comparison-based mechanism that should be distinguished from yardstick competition.[18] I discuss the pure case first and the way the mechanism may intermix with yardstick competition afterward.

### 4.2.1. The pure case: comparisons by incumbents

Governments observe policies in other jurisdictions and imitate what works (from their standpoint). They may also draw conclusions from the observation of effects they don't like. Voters may or may not be directly involved: that is, in the pure case (the only one considered for the moment) voters do not observe anything in other jurisdictions, but decision-makers may or may not have their support in mind. For instance, governments may imitate policies tried elsewhere that have proved popular in general or with particular constituencies. Alternatively, they may, by observing what their peers are doing, seek the best way not to depend on popular support, how to manipulate public opinion, or how to repress dissent, etc.[19]

Let me note three points.

First, the observation of policy innovations in other jurisdictions is often made at a relatively low, technocratic rather than political, level of government and then brought to the attention of elected office-holders.[20] Independent experts, academics, international organizations, the media, think tanks, organized interest groups and lobbies, etc., may also contribute. As noted, in the setting of local finance and decentralization—that is, when the concerned jurisdictions and governments are subnational— the whole process is often referred to as "laboratory federalism." The use of the term "laboratory" is appropriate because the nature of the process is mainly cognitive, with knowledge as the main good produced and circulated. This explains a difference between that mechanism and yardstick competition with regard to the nature of the jurisdictions from which inspiration is drawn. Distance or unfamiliarity does not affect experts as much as it affects voters. Solutions adopted in distant and unacquainted jurisdictions may be detected and recommended by experts although they are likely to escape the attention of voters.[21]

Second, the observed importance of policy diffusion should not hide the resilience and pervasiveness of policy diversity. To account for the co-existence of diffusion and resilient diversity, one might of course draw from the dynamic nature of diffusion and the static nature of resilience the idea that over time, in each particular domain, policy diffusion and convergence will overcome diversity except when insurmountable and presumably harmful obstacles are encountered—harmful for the societies concerned, that is. Although something like that view may be detected in the positions of some scholars or international organizations, I think that it is largely wrong. Governments may encounter the same problems or pursue the same objectives without necessarily choosing the same solutions or instruments. Comparable achievements in the domains of education, health, security, or economic stability may be obtained under completely different arrangements. I have already cited the book (Christoffersen et al. 2014) in which Denmark and Switzerland are treated as instances of "the good society," albeit in very different ways.

Third, does decentralization favor experimentation as suggested by the laboratory federalism argument? It may not. The main point made in Rose-Ackerman (1980) is a transposition to the context of policy experimentation by decentralized jurisdictions of an argument often made against spending resources on basic research in a small country. That argument relies on the advantage of free riding (or, if one prefers that formulation, on the existence of positive externalities). Whether or not government will experiment with a new policy is the outcome of a comparison between the electoral benefit of the sure solution, consisting in doing nothing now and copying in the future the result of experimentation pursued elsewhere when it is successful, and the electoral benefit and cost of the risky solution, consisting in experimenting. In the absence of yardstick voting, or more generally of any comparisons made across jurisdictions by voters, the outcome of the calculation may often be negative. Experimentation then will not be tempted. A centralized system might produce more of it.

### 4.2.2. On the relation between policy learning and yardstick competition

In the foregoing presentation of policy learning, the observation and assessments of policies elsewhere were exclusively the responsibility of politicians in office, informed by technocrats and experts. Voters were not involved in the comparisons. Once the existence of yardstick competition is acknowledged—this is seldom the case in the literature on policy diffusion[22]—the question of the relation between the two mechanisms arises.

Answering that question is complicated, in particular because the relation between policy outcomes and policy instruments (related to the relation between ends or means or between outputs and inputs) is itself tricky and diverse. Nonetheless, the logic of the two mechanisms suggests a pattern based on division of labor or comparative advantage. I start with a radical version of that pattern. Yardstick competition is founded on information asymmetry, affecting only voters. Policy learning is founded on uncertainty (incomplete information), namely uncertainty about the effects of policies. In the radical version, it concerns only office-holders.[23] Thanks to the observation of outcomes (including innovative outcomes) elsewhere, some voters are more able to assess the performance of their own government. As a consequence, there is more pressure on governments to obtain outcomes that satisfy voters. Thanks to the observation of policy elsewhere, governments reach already pursued outcomes more efficiently.

Observation of other jurisdictions also makes them aware of new feasible outcomes. They may decide to imitate the policies they observe elsewhere, or more generally adopt policies inspired by them. But they may also decide otherwise, either leaving present practice unchanged, or engaging in idiosyncratic experiments. Their motivation may or may not be related to electoral support, which, to repeat, is only influenced by policy outcomes.

This nice division of labor between the two mechanisms is certainly too simple. The difficulty in separating instruments and outcomes, discussed earlier, is an obvious obstacle. Many decision variables that governments (and us, for convenience) would like to treat exclusively as instruments to produce some outcome—for example speed limits to reduce road casualties—have a direct positive or negative effect on the utility of some voters. As such they cannot be excluded from voters' cross-jurisdiction comparisons.[24] This makes more complex the effects on policy adoption of both policy learning and yardstick competition. As stressed several times in this book, complexity may constitute an obstacle for analysis without being a serious difficulty for actors in the real world. In a given context, incumbents will have some views about what variables and what cross-jurisdiction comparisons made by voters may be electorally significant. They will make their decisions accordingly, possibly getting inspiration from what is done elsewhere.

For analytic purposes, we must be less ecumenical. One solution is to deal only with one aspect of the matter. It will often be convenient to assume that voters treat instruments as outcomes. From the standpoint of a municipality, a local tax increase may be considered an instrument, for instance to balance the budget. But, for the purpose of analysis we may assume that the increase is considered a policy outcome by voters (or some subset thereof) and treated as such in the cross-jurisdiction comparisons they make. This, in fact, is the approach adopted in much of the empirical work done in the context of fiscal federalism, including Besley and Case (1995). And this is also an implication of the separation between taxes and expenditures that we defended in chapter 2, with an appeal to the authority of Hettich and Winer (1988).[25]

In that approach, no attention is given to the possibility that some voters wonder whether there was no other instrument for getting an outcome they approve of. How can we take that possibility into account while (despite the problems it raises) maintaining the distinction between instruments and outcomes (in turn central to the distinction between policy learning and yardstick competition)?

Instead of assuming that, in a domain, cross-jurisdiction comparisons made by voters are always exclusively about policy outcomes, let us assume that the comparisons are exclusively about policy outcomes provided they suggest the government doing a good job. If this is not the case, then, in spite of their informational inferiority, voters turn their attention to policies adopted elsewhere. They observe associations or correlations between these policies and outcomes they approve, and they pressurize incumbents to try the policies that seem to work.

To illustrate, suppose that country $Y$ (perhaps China) adopts a market-friendly system and its economy grows more quickly. Country $X$ has a market-unfriendly system and its economy grows slowly. People in $X$ observe the two systems and the two growth rates. They care less about the system than about the growth rate. If the government in $X$ manages to increase the rate of growth of the economy without copying the system adopted in $Y$, this is fine with the people in $X$. If economic growth remains weaker in $X$ than in $Y$, then citizens in $X$ may exert pressure on their government to try the system that seems to deliver the desired outcome. In other words, what people in many parts of the world like about China is not its capitalist or market orientation but the growth rate of its economy. The pressure on their own governments is to get the second, if nothing else, by adopting or trying the first.

I think that this modified pattern is quite robust and can explain many instances of policy diffusion or contagion as well as many instances of its non-occurrence. It also explains in part why the political debate sometimes focuses on obviously instrumental matters and sometimes ignores instrumental choices even when they are quite consequential.

## 4.3. OTHER MECHANISMS

Three of the four mechanisms summarized in the following sections involve cross-jurisdiction comparisons but not of the kind assumed in the setting of mobility-based competition or policy learning. The fourth mechanism might also be confused with yardstick competition, or interact with it, although some of its features make it closer to mobility-based competition.[26]

### 4.3.1. Peer approval and emulation

A reference to that mechanism has been traced to David Hume (who refers to "mutual jealousy").[27] Governments or heads of government want to be well placed in comparisons made by their peers. The motivation may or may not be related to sentiments such as pride, shame, and envy. Support from below, in particular from voters, has no role. Nor has top-down support from some higher authority.[28] The relationship is purely horizontal—peer-to-peer, so to speak.

The mechanism of emulation of peer approval was perhaps particularly important when all office-holders were monarchs but it can still be found operating today. Heads of government meet more and more frequently in all kinds of forums and also communicate electronically. Personal intercourse is enhanced, and thus, possibly, the importance given to peer approval. There is a tendency to rely upon emulation to implement commitments or reach objectives made or fixed in common (in domains such as aid, the environment, military spending, etc.). One should not expect too much from it. The spectacular failure of the so-called Lisbon strategy "for making the EU the world's most competitive economy," adopted by the European Union Council in 2000, is a case in point.[29]

### 4.3.2. Out-of-jurisdiction public opinion

With out-of-jurisdiction public opinion, policies implemented in a jurisdiction are judged by public opinion or subsets thereof located mainly outside that jurisdiction. The jurisdictions concerned can be national (countries) or subnational (communes, regions, provinces, etc.). Let us suppose for the moment that the jurisdictions are countries. Then, the mechanism is part of what has been called "global governance" (see, e.g., Davis et al. 2012).[30] Instead of the approval of peers, or of their own electorate, national governments are supposed to be concerned with the approval of something like world opinion. This is particularly important in domains such as corruption, human rights, human trafficking, biodiversity, etc. Like the preceding mechanism, one should not exaggerate its strength. It is interesting to us mainly because it is close to but distinct from both emulation and yardstick competition.

World opinion may be conveyed and then influence policies in a noncomparative way, as is the case, for instance, when a particular government is singled out and vilified or lauded for the way it treats opponents or refugees. But it may also operate through indicators or rankings (e.g., Transparency International, Doing Business, etc.). In that case, the risk of confusion with my interpretation of yardstick competition looms. The two mechanisms are different, though, because the sets of voters or citizens who compare achievements are themselves different—voters of the jurisdiction in the case of yardstick competition, voters or public opinion mainly outside the jurisdiction in the case of global governance. In one case the channel of influence, consisting in voting or more generally support from below, is straightforward. In the other it is much more complex, diverse, or indirect. It may take, for instance the form of shaming, protest, demonstrations, informal boycott, etc. More effectively, it may involve international organizations and governments, as was the case against apartheid in South Africa. The influence may also be felt through the way it changes public opinion, and thus possibly political support, within the country concerned.

If we turn to the influence of national opinion on policy-making at the subnational level, a simple channel of influence comes to the fore. Public opinion at the national level may force government at that level to impose changes in policy-making at the subnational level. An example in the United States is the intervention of the federal government to uphold individual rights in southern states.

### 4.3.3. Incumbents' career concerns

The expression career concerns is used loosely here and not in the technical sense often adopted in the literature since Holmstrom (1982). Incumbents considered to be responsible for the good performance of the government they lead are rewarded not by increased support from the voters of their jurisdiction (this would be yardstick voting) but by promotion to another job. Who is assessing performance and whereto the promotion? There are several variants of the mechanism. Inasmuch as good performance is interpreted as signaling an intrinsic property of the individual,[31] promotion can be to any kind of job, including in the private sector. However, it seems that the most natural trajectory is to a position at a higher level of government.[32] Political parties, office holders at these other levels of government, and various sets of voters may play a part in the assessments, alternatively or together.

### 4.3.4. Neo-Austrian institutional competition

Because neo-Austrian institutional competition also stresses experimentation and learning, it is expedient to place here a summary of that interesting analysis even though, in fact, it relies on mobility-based competition and does not necessarily involve cross-jurisdiction comparisons.

The neo-Austrian perspective in general stresses ignorance. Market competition is an evolutionary process whose main output is discovery. New methods of doing things, new modes of organization, etc., are tried, and only some survive the selection process, which, in a capitalist economy, is based on competition among firms. Thus, in the background of market competition, there is a competition, more important because related to knowledge, among more abstract items.

When the idea is transposed to the relations among jurisdictions, the duality remains. Competition among jurisdictions is a vector for competition among institutional features. The two, taken together, form a discovery procedure (Vihanto 1992, Vanberg and Kerber 1994). The underlying mechanism is mainly based on the mobility of agents (households, firms, capital, etc.)—with voters having little or no role. Thus, a new institutional feature is tried in a jurisdiction. Thanks to it, the jurisdiction is successful in the competition to attract or retain mobile resources. Eventually, to avoid losing ground, all jurisdictions have adopted the new institutional feature. It has won the institutional competition.

## 4.4. CONCLUSION

As a rule, we may study a mechanism in isolation, abstracted not only from its interaction but even from its coexistence with other mechanisms. If, in this chapter, we have chosen to do otherwise, this is for two reasons. One is the risk of confusion between yardstick competition and other mechanisms; the other is the way yardstick competition is affected by them. The first motivation has led us to review, briefly, a number of mechanisms dependent on the existence of several jurisdictions. We did not discuss how they interact with yardstick competition. Two mechanisms deserved more attention. Mobility-based competition cannot be confused with yardstick competition but interacts with it in ways that can be quite consequential. Probably the main conclusion of our discussion of the way mobility-based competition operates is that it leaves sufficient discretion to governments for yardstick competition among them to remain relevant.

The second mechanism given special attention is policy learning, generally referred to as laboratory federalism in the decentralization literature. In its case, both the risk of confusion and the level of interaction with yardstick competition are important. The main virtue of the solution I have suggested is its simplicity. The main difference between the two mechanisms is who makes the cross-jurisdiction comparisons. In the case of yardstick competition, it is the voters (or citizens); in the case of policy learning, the office-holders and their staff (governments). Information asymmetry is an obstacle for the former. The simplifying assumption suggested, then, is that cross-jurisdiction comparisons made by office-holders can be also about policies whereas cross-jurisdiction comparisons made by voters are normally only about outcomes. This helps identify and separate the two mechanisms, also limiting to a degree their interaction. However, in our simplified story, the interaction reappears when comparatively bad outcomes induce citizens, despite information asymmetry, to turn their attention to policies. In reality the relation between the two mechanisms is certainly much messier. We did not attempt to discuss how they could be disentangled empirically.

## NOTES

1. Policy learning covers what is referred to as diffusion or contagion in many discussions and "laboratory federalism" in the context of decentralization or federalism.
2. I postpone to the next chapter the consideration of expenditure externalities and common exogenous shocks, two sources of policy interdependence that are difficult to disentangle empirically, but not conceptually, from yardstick competition.
3. Throughout this book we do not relate the informational handicap of ordinary citizens or voters to rational ignorance—that is, to the cost of information being higher than the benefit—but interpret it as a manifestation of information asymmetry, that is, of citizens (i.e., principals) being excluded from some of the information available to office-holders (i.e., agents).
4. Time is the main cost involved. But the assumptions made in traditional economics about the cost-benefit balance of time-consuming or time-saving are often misleading when applied to individuals rather than to business firms. Even if costly in terms of time, seeking information can be a pleasant activity per se (as addictive consultation of Google illustrates), and it may be so to a degree varying across cultures. In his *Joyless Economy*, a book quite popular when first published, Scitovsky (1976) compares the attitude of Americans and Europeans with regard to time- or effort-saving devices on motorcars. I am not sure that the comparison is as cogent today—(when recourse to autonomous cars is on the horizon)—as it was in the 1970s—but it is worth citing nonetheless: "Increasingly, American cars have freed the driver the need to know, to do, to think, to exert effort . . . At the same time, European cars have moved in the opposite direction. They have acquired more gears, more gauges, more lights, light as well as horn signals, differential lock, and other such to give the driver more control, more to do. They cater to his desire for challenge and the opportunity to display and exercise his skill" (p. 274).
5. I consider exit in a literal sense, implying crossing some territorial border, and thus neglect the possibility, stressed in Hirschman (1970), that exit may simply consist in keeping in one's private sphere (literally hiding, in the worst case).
6. Hillman (2003), who offers an argument based on private interest in favor of yardstick competition, is not far from treating a category as a unitary actor when

he argues that, because differences in the quality of government tend to be re-flected in the prices of housing, "prospects for personal improvements are better by using comparative observations on government to identify and replace bad government rather than seeking to escape government by choosing to relocate" (p. 573).

7. Threatening exit as a way to make voice more effective is clearly more credible in a European country than in the United States. However, there are reasons for the difference between the United States and European countries other than size and openness. Contrary to citizens of other countries, Americans pay income taxes according to nationality rather than residence. This limits the benefit of exit for the rich in the United States. Financial support provided by individuals to politicians or political parties is more constrained in most European countries than it is in the United States, where business firms may also contribute. This enhances the influence of voice exerted by business firms and rich people in the United States.

8. Race to the bottom has been discussed by law scholars in particular—the expression having been coined, it seems, by Justice Louis Brandeis in 1933. In economics, see in particular Davies and Vladamannati (2013) and Carruthers and Lamoreaux (2016) and the references therein.

9. See Salmon (2015, pp. 87–90) in which the main theoretical arguments are based on or refer to Hochman and Rogers (1969), Epple and Zelenitz (1981), and Oates and Schwab (1988). Let me mention only one point. Typically, mobility-based competition does not take place over single variables but over complex and idiosyncratic packages. Compensations among components are the rule. For instance, rules (concerning work conditions, lay-offs, the environment, etc) that impose a burden on mobile firms that is heavier than the one imposed in other jurisdictions may raise no problem if compensated by a lower direct cost of labor or by less taxation. In Salmon (2006), I developed a similar argument regarding corporate governance.

10. The expression "getting to Denmark," employed by Fukuyama (2011, 2014) in particular, comes from the title of an earlier version of Pritchett and Woolcock (2004)—see Fukuyama (2011, note 25, p. 485).

11. Many studies confirm that point. See for instance Schulze and Ursprung (1999).

12. As a consequence of a feeling of insecurity the number of French Jews emigrating to Israel increased somewhat in 2015. The words used by the French prime minister, Manuel Valls, in commenting on that movement suggest that the prospect of its acceleration played a role in the decision made by the French government to respond to concerns expressed by Jewish organizations and to mobilize military resources for the protection of synagogues and Jewish schools.

13. That formulation falls short of asserting that a government may purposefully induce some categories of citizens to leave the jurisdiction. That possibility is the topic of Mingat and Salmon (1986, 1988) and Glaeser and Shleifer (2005). In both cases, the mayor of a central city increases his or her probability of being re-elected by adopting policies that induce the categories of inhabitants that are the less likely to vote for him or her to move out of the jurisdiction. In Glaeser and Shleifer, the receiving jurisdictions are not considered. The mechanism described is pure policy-induced mobility, not mobility-based competition. In Mingat and Salmon, migration is to suburban jurisdictions within the same metropolitan area (I simplify the issue by neglecting policies aiming to attract or retain). This makes possible the coexistence of competition and interest convergence in a way similar

to that noted in the text with reference to the emigration of the Huguenots to Germany.

14. See Olson (1982, p. 123) for some instances of changes over time of the population ranking of English main cities.

15. The fact that many young Spanish and Greeks emigrated to other European countries as largely a direct or indirect consequence of the policies followed by their own governments was considered catastrophic by most commentators (see, e.g., Borooah 2014).

16. This is a cautious claim. In Bodenstein and Ursprung (2005), increased economic integration makes jurisdictions unambiguously more rather than less comparable and thus facilitates horizontal yardstick competition. See also Sand-Zantman (2004).

17. That European citizens do not make comparisons with what happens outside Europe is a simplification, inappropriate in particular to account for the feeling of "Europessimism" that spread in the European Union in the late 1980s (see chapter 7).

18. In his captivating "history of thought" on interjurisdictional competition, Vaubel (2008) interprets yardstick competition broadly, in a sense that tends to encompass what I call policy learning. This makes the reference to the exit-voice dichotomy ambiguous: many manifestations of policy learning, although they have nothing to do with exit, have also (as I explain in the text) nothing to do with voice.

19. The "battle of Algiers" was "won" by the French army in 1957 with methods (tolerated by the government in Paris) that included recourse to torture and "disappearances." Several South American dictatorships sought the expertise gained in that battle for their own counterinsurgency programs (see Aussaresses 2001, 2008)—a typical "policy learning" episode.

20. An example is the process through which the ambitious environmental regulation adopted in the United States in 1970 inspired similar endeavors in other countries.

21. See Linos (2013). Office-holders and their advisers are likely to be inspired especially by solutions adopted in political or social set-ups that they find similar. As Congleton (2011) explains, during the early Meiji era "many senior Japanese officials found the German experience to be of special interest, because Germany was also in the process of creating a new central government and had only very recently reformed its medieval economic and political institutions. They, like Japan, did so in a setting in which regional nobles had long had significant political authority and in which liberal arguments were increasingly accepted" (p. 501).

22. But see Pacheco (2012), or even, more incidentally, the seminal article of Walker (1969).

23. Obstacles to policy learning by voters are analyzed in particular by Schnellenbach (2008).

24. Some French voters will observe that, contrary to France, Germany has no general speed limit on motorways, which does not prevent it having a lower ratio of casualties per million inhabitants.

25. Breton (1996, 2006) models competition in terms of "Wicksellian connections" between services received and taxes paid, an idea which can also lead to study competition over "efficiency rates," that is more or less in terms of public output divided by public expenditure (Geys 2006). We discuss the matter in chapter 8.

26. Other mechanisms than these four could have been considered. For instance, in Revelli and Tovmo (2007), local elected officials use cross-jurisdiction comparisons to assess the performance of their subordinated administrations. The mechanism is a hybrid, sharing features with both bottom-up and top-down yardstick competition. Top-down yardstick competition is discussed in chapter 8.
27. See citations of Hume in Bernholz, Streit, and Vaubel (1998, p. 5) and Vaubel (2008).
28. However, the variables over which emulation takes place may be influenced by some external, possibly diffused, authority—intellectual or religious in particular.
29. The Lisbon declaration of March 24, 2000 reads: "The Union has today set itself a new strategic goal for the next decade: to become the most competitive and dynamic knowledge-based economy in the world, capable of sustainable economic growth with more and better jobs and greater social cohesion." The implementation mechanism was to consist essentially in peer pressure among heads of state and governments on the occasion of special sessions of their European Council meetings. It is generally agreed that the strategy failed, as declared quasi-officially by the prime minister of Sweden in 2009. As Wyplosz (2010) comments: "Summits of leaders are . . . not where one should expect humility or contrition. Political leaders are not raised to encourage critical comments from each other" (p. 2).
30. Logically, global governance covers not only countries but also subnational jurisdictions. World opinion may be concerned with some policies adopted by the government of Texas or the municipality of Baltimore, not only with those adopted in Washington. I gloss over that complication and suppose that the influence exerted by world opinion is on national governments, not directly on subnational ones.
31. In that context, we must qualify the preference we expressed for moral hazard over selection.
32. To give some examples: from mayor of West Berlin to chancellor of West Germany (Willy Brandt), from governor of California to president of the United States (Ronald Reagan), and from mayor of Florence to prime minister of Italy (Matteo Renzi).

# CHAPTER 5

# The virtue of narrowing: the fiscal federalism setting

T he domain of local finance, decentralization, and fiscal federalism is where yardstick competition among governments started and it is still where it is mostly studied. In this chapter we consider only part of the matter, postponing to chapter 8 aspects involving several levels of government. In other words, our topic in this chapter is horizontal yardstick competition in the setting of fiscal federalism. In that setting, interest in yardstick competition arose from two concerns: dissatisfaction with the existing theory of decentralization and the need to explain observed fiscal interdependence among local or regional governments. These two concerns seem independent but they are not: as suggested already in chapter 1, yardstick competition owes its place in the theory of decentralization to the empirical confirmation of its presence in reality.

The chapter is organized around the distinction between the two concerns but it treats them unequally. In the first, short section, I stress the recognition of (horizontal) yardstick competition as a systemic dimension of decentralized government. In a second, much longer, section, I review informally some of the empirical arguments employed to identify yardstick competition as a mechanism generating spatial policy interdependence. But documenting that something is at work does not imply saying or knowing much about it. That proposition inspires the discussion in the third section. The remarkable achievement of the empirical research surveyed in section 5.2 does not logically produce much information about the mechanism itself. In other words, the mechanism has left a trace in the data but, on the basis of empirical work, remains largely undisclosed. Alternative approaches are briefly discussed in that context.

## 5.1. YARDSTICK COMPETITION AS A SYSTEMIC DIMENSION

A large part of what has been written on decentralized government and federalism is of a systemic nature. In using the term systemic, I am referring to a system (the governmental system in the present case) and the role, place, or function of a particular institution or mechanism in that system. I see the nature of my original contribution entitled "decentralization as an incentive scheme" (Salmon 1987b) as systemic rather than normative or positive.[1] Its purpose was to draw attention to a feature of decentralized government overlooked at the time: the possibility that citizens make comparisons across subnational jurisdictions—precluded by definition when there is no decentralization. With some additional specifications, yardstick voting and yardstick competition can be derived on that basis. They can be important or negligible, their effects good or bad. The systemic point is that their presence is possible and should not be overlooked. As stressed in chapter 1, they are a part, a component, of the system even when they remain latent.

The neglect of that dimension of decentralized governmental systems is not fortuitous. Voters (or citizens, public opinion, the ruled, or more generally the people below) play a major role in political yardstick competition (of the bottom-up variety). This is not the case with two widely followed approaches to decentralization. Being inhospitable to voters, they are also inhospitable to political yardstick competition. In the first—hereafter "the traditional theory of fiscal federalism"—decentralization is associated with spatial heterogeneity. The stronger the territorial or spatial differences among individuals' preferences, needs, or conditions, the larger the scope for decentralized policy-making and, insofar as regions are concerned, federalism. This supposes that there is a necessity for centrally decided policies to be uniform, which in reality there is not. Given the various costs entailed by decentralized government (in terms of externalities, equity, coordination, administration, etc.), the theory compels us to say that if geographical differences were small or could be dealt with reasonably well by the central government, centralization should or would prevail. Something is clearly lacking.[2]

The approach is part of a tradition in economics in which consideration of politics is avoided and office-holders assumed to be benevolent. An oft-cited adjunct to the main theory is the old argument that decentralization brings citizens closer to public decision-making. Its suitability as an adjunct lies in the fact that it requires no political analysis and no spatial differentiation. Still, I have always felt the relevance of the argument quite limited. With some exaggeration and unfairness, I cannot resist saying that the image it suggests is that of small bucolic communes like the one I live in, with public officials next door and one's preferences conveyed while walking one's dog with theirs. The main debate on decentralized government, not to speak of federalism, is about larger jurisdictions. It is not necessary to think of devolution to Utter-Pradesh to consider reduced distance from office-holders a generally dubious proposition and thus a rather unconvincing argument in favor of decentralization. Indeed, whatever the size of a subnational jurisdiction, it is not even clear that citizens get more information or are more interested in being informed about its affairs than about national ones.

A much better argument, also congenial with the reluctance to consider politics, is so-called "laboratory federalism," discussed in chapter 4 under the name of policy learning. One government tries a new policy, and it is observed and possibly adopted by others. Because the traditional theory does not constrain the world to being immobile and benevolent governments to being also omniscient, it can take laboratory federalism on board without difficulty. And that mechanism constitutes a valuable complement to the theory because it is compatible with or even facilitated by spatial homogeneity if that is to be conceded. Whether it can be fully understood without reference to electoral politics is another matter (Rose-Ackerman 1980).

Analyses worked out in the framework of the traditional theory remain valuable for many purposes. To discuss decentralization in systemic terms, however, political economy considerations are needed. The second perspective, which we may call exit-based disciplining of government, is based on such considerations. However, it is a fundamentally *ademocratic* approach to decentralization and federalism. Its main characteristics are distrust of government, trust in markets, and lack of attention to democratic processes. It portrays government as, at least potentially, predatory or the prey of interest groups (including its own bureaucracy). Thus, the main purpose of federalism is to discipline it—to tame the Leviathan. This is achieved by jurisdictions competing among themselves for residents and investment (Brennan and Buchanan 1980). A complementary analysis stresses that the distribution of regulatory competencies among levels must be "market preserving" (Weingast 1995). To stress its distinctive characteristic again, in this general approach the question of whether governments on the different levels are democratic or not is largely irrelevant.

However, it is not only the bad policies that may be eroded by mobility-based competition but also the good ones (the race to the bottom argument) or, at any rate, policies to which the population is strongly attached. As a consequence, in democracies the ademocratic characteristic of the second approach may well turn out to be unsustainable. And even in settings that are not fully democratic, neglecting the possible upward pressure of the people located below might be problematic. For our purpose, however, the main point about that second perspective is that, as with the first, it leaves no room whatsoever for yardstick competition.

Elections are now part of the discussion of decentralization and federalism in a significant number of contributions by economists. However, far fewer stress the accountability dimension of elections. I will not attempt to provide a complete list. Leaving aside my own work and the work directly focused on yardstick competition, let me at least mention (in alphabetic order) Aidt and Dutta (2017), Bardhan (2002), Besley (2006), Breton (1996), Breton, Cassone, and Fraschini (1998), Brosio (1994), Hettich and Winer (1988), Hindriks and Lockwood (2009), Kotsogiannis and Schwager (2008), Persson, Roland, and Tabellini (1997), Persson and Tabellini (2000), Seabright (1996), Tommasi and Weinschelbaum (2007), and Wrede (2006). Not all of these contributions mention, even minimally, political yardstick competition. Still, apprehended together they signal the emergence of a third systemic perspective on decentralization and federalism. By giving an important place to electoral or downward accountability, that perspective offers a propitious setting for a systemic discussion of political yardstick competition. As already stressed, however, economists' attention to political yardstick competition depends above all on empirical results. It is mainly because there has been some success on that front, as we will see now, that we may expect yardstick competition to become more central in the systemic discussion of decentralization and federalism.

## 5.2. YARDSTICK COMPETITION AS AN EMPIRICAL FACT

Empirical work on yardstick competition is part of a research area lying at the intersection of local (subnational) public finance and spatial econometrics.[3] Both domains necessitate specialized expertise. The effort required at their intersection is challenging. The ensuing literature is well informed, technical, innovative, and focused. It has no room for systemic concerns.

The empirical work considered here confirms the presence of yardstick competition at the subnational level. This is its main achievement from our standpoint even though, from a more objective perspective, it is but one result. Existing surveys—e.g., Revelli (2005, 2015)—consider a broader set of mechanisms and findings than the one we are concerned with.[4] And they are more focused on econometric problems than we need be. The following discussion avoids technicalities but shares their focus on identification. What mechanism underlies observed data? To what extent can it be yardstick competition? My purpose here is only to provide an intuitive understanding of the types of reasoning used to answer such questions.

### 5.2.1. Strategic spatial interaction

The starting point of empirical investigations is what seems to be an observed interaction among the values of a single variable (for instance a property tax rate) across neighboring jurisdictions. Neighborhood is a spatial concept;[5] by itself this explains recourse to the tools of spatial econometrics.[6]

A question that could be raised at the outset (although it is typically addressed at a later stage) is whether observed spatial patterns reflect genuine interaction (the value of the considered variable in jurisdiction $X$ being influenced by its value in neighboring jurisdictions, and reciprocally) or only exogenous regional influences or "shocks" unaccounted for. One will speak of spatial dependence in both cases but of spatial strategic interaction only in the first. Establishing spatial dependence is not insignificant[7] but only strategic interaction is of real interest.

Let us assume that somehow, with regard to some fiscal variable, it is confirmed that a given data set reflects not only spatial dependence but also strategic interaction among the values taken by a policy variable across neighboring jurisdictions. Establishing that result in different settings has been a major achievement of research on local finance in recent years. Still, it is natural to want more—that is, to push the identification process further and identify the mechanism accounting for the strategic interaction. Mainly, two mechanisms other than yardstick competition can play that role. One is mobility-based competition, in particular tax competition; the other is expenditure spillovers. Both have been considered in public finance for a long time, although their econometric investigation is more recent.

In mobility-based competition, policies of neighboring jurisdictions interact because they trigger or may trigger cross-border movements (of individuals and firms) that have effects governments care about.[8] Mobility-based competition concerns in particular taxes, public spending, and regulation. As we saw in chapter 4, the cross-jurisdiction comparisons that motivate mobile agents—individual households and business firms—often are not about taxes alone but about combinations of taxes, public services, regulation, and exogenous amenities. However, taking multidimensional comparisons or motivations into account is not feasible under the spatial dependence approach discussed here. The empirical framework generally imposed by the said approach is that of an interaction between the values of a single variable in neighboring jurisdictions. Only a restricted version of mobility-based competition can be analyzed within this framework.

The same methodological limitation applies to the second mechanism, expenditure spillovers. Here, too, there is an interaction among neighboring jurisdictions between the values given to a single variable, in this case a public expenditure item. By definition, the two other mechanisms considered—mobility and yardstick comparisons—are not responsible for the interaction. What remains? Instances come readily to mind when we think of small communes belonging to large metropolitan areas. More expenses devoted to recreational facilities in one commune also provide additional benefits to residents of others nearby. This will lead to strategic expenditure interaction in spending on recreational facilities. A variation in spending on police in one jurisdiction can have an effect on the need for police and thus spending in others. Again, spatial interaction will ensue.[9]

The obstacles to identification are obvious. Many contributions cite the demonstration by Brueckner (2003) that the mechanisms may lead to the same empirical prediction—that is, the same single reduced form equation. Yardstick competition is particularly difficult to isolate. Simplifying somewhat, it competes with tax competition to account for tax interaction and with expenditure spillovers to underlie expenditure interaction.[10]

As noted, it is worthwhile to document and measure interaction, whether or not one also endeavors to find its causal mechanism. Suppose that the counterpart to an average increase in neighboring jurisdictions of 1 percentage point is a 0.5 percentage point increase in the jurisdiction's own tax. That measure is referred to as an interaction effect of 0.5, and indeed, it has exactly that value in Ladd (1992). It was found to be between 0.2 and 0.6 in most subsequent studies of sales, income, corporate, property, capital, motor vehicle, and cigarette taxes as well as total tax revenue in interacting jurisdictions including municipalities, counties, districts, regions, cantons, or states (Allers and Elhorst 2005). Effects of the same order of magnitude are found with regard to expenditure interaction (Allers and Elhorst 2011)—the jurisdictions concerned being more or less the same and the variables studied including total expenditures, social and recreational expenditures, and spending on police.

Before turning to the next step—that is, how yardstick competition has been identified—let me note three points. First, neighborhood enters the analysis as an average of the values of the concerned variable in the neighboring jurisdictions of each jurisdiction. The neighborhood status is generally based on geographical proximity.

Second, the case for using the specific approach of spatial econometrics is implicit in the way the interaction among neighbors is formulated. One feature is reciprocity between the values of a single variable. In time series econometrics, dependence is unidirectional: the value of the variable in consideration at time $t$ influences its value at time $t + 1$. In spatial econometrics its value in location $X$ influences its value in location $Y$ and *reciprocally*. Dependence is bidirectional (and when more than two jurisdictions are involved, multidirectional). Another feature is the idiosyncratic nature of neighborhood. Neighbors do not have the same neighborhood. To illustrate the matter at the level of countries, France and Germany are neighbors but Spain is a neighbor of France and not of Germany, and Poland is a neighbor of Germany and not of France.[11] Thus, neighborhood does not refer to non-idiosyncratic subsets like Europe or South America. These two features taken together contribute a lot to the specificity of spatial econometrics.

Third, the ambiguity of the word mimicking discussed earlier in the general context of yardstick competition is much less bothersome in the narrower setting of local finance or fiscal federalism. In that setting, the variables concerned are decided tax rates or public expenditures, with no reference to uncertainty or time lags intervening between decisions by officials and effects felt by citizens. Consequently, it is convenient and may not be too misleading to refer to strategic interaction as mimicking.[12]

### 5.2.2. Identifying yardstick competition

For determining which of the three interaction mechanisms is at work, the general idea is to exploit the fact that, besides the implication they have in common (spatial interaction), they also have empirical implications specific to each.[13] These specific implications may apply generally or only in particular circumstances, in which case one may benefit from "natural experiments." I will concentrate here on the yardstick competition mechanism.

I will not try to do justice to all the ingenious arguments and sophisticated tools researchers have had recourse to. Besley and Case (1995) remains a good starting point.[14] In that paper, three kinds of empirical evidence are claimed to support the existence of yardstick competition among the governors of the US states. The first is tax interaction: a tax increase of 1 in neighboring states has an effect of 0.2 on a state's own tax. The second finding is the re-election prospect of governors: this is affected negatively by tax increases in the governor's own state but that effect is offset by tax increases in neighboring states. The third finding exploits the existence of term limits: no tax interaction effect subsists for states in which the governor cannot be a candidate again because of term limits. These results are complemented by an informal discussion of why they are inconsistent with mobility-based tax competition (referred to as the Tiebout model).

As far as I know, a direct effect of yardstick competition on the frequency of incumbent defeat has not been sought again since Besley and Case (1995).[15] Nor has a similar three- or four-pronged assault within a single article been attempted.[16] The types of arguments made by Besley and Case are still those mainly used in subsequent contributions, albeit in less ambitious configurations.

The simplest case is that of pure yardstick voting, with the explained variable not incumbent defeat but electoral support. Revelli (2002), Vermeir and Heyndels (2006), and Bosch and Solé-Ollé (2007), concerned with local government respectively in England, Flanders, and Catalonia, provide some evidence in favor of yardstick voting by showing that the negative effect of increased taxation on electoral support to the parties in office is reduced if there is also an increase in neighboring jurisdictions.[17]

Identification of yardstick competition proper has been achieved mainly by revealing the dependence of strategic interaction on electoral arrangements and circumstances. Term limits is a good illustration. We mentioned the result in Besley and Case (1995) that strategic interaction vanishes when governors of US states can no longer run for election because of term limits, an effect found previously by Case (1993). It is also one of the findings in Bordignon, Cernaglia, and Revelli (2003), who refer to it as a reason to believe in the presence of yardstick competition among municipalities in the province of Milan. In their sample, 45 percent of mayors were in their second period in office and could not be candidates again. In the authors' words, "it turns out that local property tax rates are positively spatially auto-correlated only for those jurisdictions where the mayor can run for re-election and the electoral outcome is uncertain, while correlation is absent for those jurisdictions where either the mayor cannot run for re-election because he faces a binding term limit, or where the mayor is backed by a large majority" (p. 201). In their view, these results "definitely suggest that some form of yardstick competition is going on."

Term limits are a relatively uncommon feature of local government;[18] thus, to identify the presence of yardstick competition, the political variables most frequently referred to are the size of the majority in office and the proximity of the next election.[19] These two variables are central to the case for yardstick competition made by Solé Ollé (2003). His study concerns the rates of property, motor vehicle, and business taxes set in a sample of 105 municipalities around Barcelona. Although interaction with neighbors is confirmed, it is significantly less intense when past election margins are larger and in non-election years. Solé Ollé's prudent interpretation of the difference is worth quoting: "The combination of the different results increases confidence in the tax mimicking/yardstick competition hypothesis as underlying strategic tax interaction among Spanish municipalities" (p. 709).

That the size of the majority in office has a significant effect on interaction is also observed by Allers and Elhorst (2005) in their study of the property tax rates set by Dutch municipalities.[20] In addition to that "scientific" argument, they justify the yardstick competition hypothesis by a detailed discussion of why, in the case of property taxation in the Netherlands, it is much more plausible than expenditure spillovers or tax competition as the mechanism underlying tax interaction. Property taxes are small but visible. They are too small to induce expenditure retrenchment or trigger cross-jurisdiction mobility, but their visibility is such that voters place them "among the most resented taxes." Information about them is widely available and used by "consumer lobbies" "to brand municipalities with high tax rates" (p. 496).[21]

Fiva and Rattsø (2007) consider these characteristics of the situation of the property tax in the Netherlands to be also more or less those that prevail in Norway. However, in Norway, the decision to levy the tax as well as set its rate is made at the local level. Thanks to an adaptation of spatial econometrics to discrete choice, the authors feel able to conclude from their empirical analysis that the geographical pattern of the tax does reflect yardstick competition.

The contributions discussed so far are about tax interaction. But yardstick competition has also been discussed in the context of expenditure interaction. In a technically innovative paper, Elhorst and Fréret (2009) exploit data pertaining to welfare spending (on young, elderly, and disabled individuals) in French departments (all except Corsica, Paris, and those overseas). They find "strong evidence" in support of political yardstick competition, as "departments governed by a small political majority mimic neighboring expenditures on welfare to a greater extent than do departments governed by a large one" (p. 948).[22] Bartolini and Santolini (2012) study expenditure interaction among municipalities in the Marche region of central Italy. An interesting aspect of their study is the impact on yardstick competition of a fiscal rule, the "domestic stability pact" (DSP), constraining since 1989 deficits at the subnational levels of government.

Not all municipalities are submitted to DSP. The study shows, first, that yardstick competition is confirmed only when DSP is taken into account in the estimations (yardstick competition would have been undetected otherwise) and second, that only municipalities not submitted to DSP are unambiguously engaging in yardstick competition (reflected by more intense interaction in the year preceding the election).

Particular circumstances are more central in the two contributions I turn to now. Swiss cantons are different with regard to their reliance on direct democracy and the degree of tax autonomy enjoyed by municipal government. For Schaltegger and Küttel (2002), we should expect voters in cantons with more reliance on direct democracy and/or tax autonomy to face less information asymmetry and thus benefit less from yardstick competition. As a consequence, these cantons' policies should reflect less spatial autocorrelation—or, as the authors say, less policy mimicking—than the others. Let me leave aside the impact of fiscal autonomy (which I find puzzling).[23] The main empirical result is that policy mimicking depends on the balance between direct and indirect (representative) democracy, a political variable. Such dependence can hardly be explained by mobility-based competition. It points to yardstick competition as the cause of policy mimicking. Incidentally, it also confirms the link between yardstick competition and the setting in which I have characterized it in this book—that is, *representative* democracy.

The special circumstances exploited in Revelli (2006) are not across space but over time, which makes them function even more clearly as a natural experiment. They concern the United Kingdom, in which the introduction of a system of Social Services Performance Rating (SSPR) was announced in October 2001 and implemented in May 2002. This rating system improves public information about local performance with regard to social services. As a consequence, the relevance of voters' comparisons with neighboring jurisdictions diminishes and with it the main motivation underlying yardstick competition. Inasmuch as spatial auto-correlation reflects yardstick rather than mobility-based competition, it should decrease after the implementation of the SSPR. Revelli estimates and then compares spatial auto-correlation in the provision of social services by English local authorities for the budgetary years 2000/2001 and 2003/2004—that is, before and after the effective introduction of the SSPR. The result is that spatial auto-correlation drops considerably, moving from "significance to insignificance." Under Revelli's narrow interpretation of yardstick competition (to which I will return), that mechanism is, in the area of social services, outcompeted.[24]

There are other contributions that identify yardstick competition as the mechanism underlying spatial interaction deserving of consideration, but let me mention instead some negative or insufficiently significant findings. Foucault, Madies, and Paty (2008) find that spatial expenditure interaction among French municipalities of more than 50,000 inhabitants is not affected by whether or not the years considered are election years, from which they conclude that spatial interaction does not reflect yardstick competition. Edmark and Agren (2008) find strong evidence of strategic interaction in Swedish municipal income taxes but no effect of the size of the majority in power or of whether or not it is an election year. Thus they "find no support for the hypothesis that the tax interaction is driven by electoral concerns." The variable found spatially dependent in Geys (2006) is not taxation or spending but efficiency, defined as the ratio between spending and output, that is, "value for money." The study confirms the existence of spatial interaction among Flemish local governments' efficiency ratings. To identify yardstick competition as the cause of that interaction, it considers its relationship with political variables that influence the probability of reelection (e.g., size of the majority or the coalition). Some relationship in the expected direction is found, albeit not sufficiently significant. Support to the yardstick competition hypothesis is thus considered too weak.[25] In the case of the Swiss cantons, the evidence in favor of mobility-based tax competition is so strong that little remains for yardstick competition to also play a role (Feld and Reulier 2009).

The case of taxation by Walloon municipalities is studied in two separate papers by Gérard and Van Malderen. In one (Gérard and Van Malderen 2012), they find some empirical support for yardstick competition playing a role in tax interaction. But in the other (Van Malderen and Gérard 2013), they find no evidence of yardstick voting. In their view, that negative result also excludes "yardstick competition as a source of tax interactions in the Walloon region, if yardstick voting is a testable hypothesis of yardstick competition" (p. 206).[26]

### 5.2.3. Neighborhood

In most contributions, neighborhood refers to geographical proximity.[27] In general, for each jurisdiction in the data set, the others are divided into two groups: neighbors and non-neighbors.[28] Contiguity (that is, border sharing) is the most frequent criterion. But inverse distance is also used—a compelling solution when the jurisdictions concerned cannot all be contiguous. This is the case in particular when the data set itself is constituted on the basis of a non-spatial criterion such as minimum population. In Solé Ollé (2003), for instance, only those municipalities of the province of Barcelona whose population is over 5,000 inhabitants (excluding Barcelona itself) are considered; in that paper, neighborhood is defined as distance not greater than 20 kilometers.

Most jurisdictions have several neighbors. Following the format of cardinal tournaments analyzed in chapter 3, interaction is modeled as taking place between each jurisdiction and a shadow jurisdiction made up of an average of those defined as its neighbors. One might regret that it is not feasible to consider the interaction between each jurisdiction and each of its neighbors. To some extent, that limitation may be mitigated by the possibility of giving neighbors different weights in the calculation of the average. For instance, weights may reflect differences in the length of borders or in neighbors' population (see, e.g., Lundberg 2014). Many solutions both to the definition of neighborliness and to the calculation of the average are conceivable. They cannot be chosen on the basis of a proper econometric estimation. It is natural that researchers try several solutions and present those that work best.[29] However, complicated combinations will be suspect, especially if not based on theoretical arguments directly related to the mechanism studied. On the whole, parsimony does prevail, with neighborhood generally based on contiguity or simple distance and averages remaining unweighted.

In addition to, or underlying, statistical evidence, two arguments are generally used to justify a focus on geographical neighborhood. First, the common shocks whose influence voters try to take into account by the way of cross-jurisdiction comparisons are particularly likely to have a spatial dimension and concern neighbors. Second, information is spread more easily among neighbors. One reason for that may be that neighbors "belong to the same media market" (Besley and Case 1995, note 9). The relation between belonging to the same media market and yardstick voting is studied on English data by Revelli (2008). His delimitation of local media markets is based on the local networks of the BBC. One formulation of the main result is that the negative effect of a property tax increase on the incumbents' probability of re-election disappears if there is an increase of the same amount among the jurisdictions belonging to the same local media market. Revelli considers the "result to be consistent with the view that voters evaluate their governments based on their comparative tax performance, making use of the information flowing through the local media" (p. 1592).[30]

As noted already in Case, Rosen, and Hines (1993), proximity may refer to similitude and comparability rather than to geography.[31] That this could be the case was already assumed in Salmon (1987b), which included as an example comparisons by some voters of distant medium-sized French cities such as Dijon and Montpellier. It is certain that many voters compare outcomes in jurisdictions they find sufficiently similar whether or not these jurisdictions are also neighbors in a literal sense. The problem is how to explore that possibility in a statistical/econometric framework. Very little work has been done on this so far. Let me formulate three remarks on that.

First, in principle, spatial econometrics in general can be extended to deal with non-geographical proximity. Spatial dependence can take place between "peer institutions," for instance large firms (LeSage 2008), as well as between geographical neighbors. In practice, adapting spatial econometrics to non-geographical contexts is not straightforward—whether in general or when the focus is policy interdependence among governments.

Second, in fact even when neighborhood is defined in geographical terms, a concern with non-geographical proximity, in the form of comparability requirements, is present in most of the contributions just discussed. One way to introduce these requirements consists in excluding jurisdictions whose population is too large or too small: Solé Ollé (2003) and Elhorst and Fréret (2009) exclude Barcelona and Paris respectively; Solé Ollé (2003) and Bordignon, Cerniglia, and Revelli (2003) exclude communes having less than five thousand and four thousand inhabitants respectively, etc.[32] Another way, more indirect, is through control variables, meant to exclude the influence on the targeted findings of dimensions that would distort the comparisons.

Third, non-geographical proximity is probably easier to handle in the study of yardstick voting than it is in the study of yardstick competition proper. If, despite their essential character, we neglect concerns about feed-back effects or endogeneity (discussed later), yardstick voting is a relatively simple mechanism. Detecting its presence comes down to the question: are the votes in a jurisdiction influenced by what is the case or happens in others? Which others? Under the said assumption of non-endogeneity, there do not seem to be serious obstacles to trying various criteria of non-geographical proximity. Yardstick competition proper is another matter: defining dimensions of similarity that make possible the use of spatial econometrics techniques is a major difficulty.

Hayashi and Yamamoto (2017) offer an interesting solution to that difficulty. To study spending interdependence among Japanese municipalities, they exploit the availability of an elaborate categorization of municipalities provided by the central government. In it, municipalities are sorted on the basis of population and activities into 35 groups of "similar entities."

Information on fiscal variables concerning the members of each group is also provided. That information can be used to construct a yardstick or benchmark for each group. Hayashi and Yamamoto compare the effects of neighborhood or similarity drawn from the scheme with different geographical interpretations of neighborhood. It turns out that spending interaction is found only when neighborhood means belonging to the same "group of similar entities," not when it is interpreted geographically. Since the members of each group are dispersed over the whole country, spatial interaction cannot reflect mobility-based competition or expenditure spillovers. The authors ascribe it to yardstick competition for that sole reason.[33]

### 5.2.4. Other issues addressed within the internal discussion

As is normal in economics, the internal discussion has been highly technical, largely motivated by a desire to exploit expanded data sets and experiment with up-to-date econometric tools. Recently, it has also reflected broader interrogations about the orientation of econometrics in general and spatial econometrics in particular (Revelli 2015). Even though questions that look purely technical generally reflect substantial issues, I will only mention here some that can be easily and intuitively understood.

A set of issues immediately coming to mind and mentioned recurrently in the discussion is endogeneity, meaning here the possibility that explanatory variables are not strictly exogenous. For yardstick voting and yardstick competition, this is not a simple possibility: it is central to a framework in which votes are explicitly influenced, for instance, by taxes and taxes, somewhat less directly, decided in view of votes. The best way to deal with it would be to specify a model including the two relations and to estimate them jointly. This is attempted to a degree in Besley and Case (1995). In general, however, the two relations are treated separately. In the study of yardstick voting, instrumental variables are used to deal with the endogeneity of the fiscal variable. For yardstick competition proper, an interaction relation which is silent about voting is specified and only then, as a second logical step, is the effect of some variables related to voting (size of the majority, term limits, etc.) on the empirical estimation considered.

Relatedly, we may return to the puzzling results reported in the two papers co-authored by Gérard and Van Malderen. Let us assume that, effectively, in the same actual setting, tax interaction based on yardstick competition is confirmed (Gérard and Van Malderen 2012) while yardstick voting is not (Van Malderen and Gérard 2013). How is that possible? If "yardstick voting is a testable implication of yardstick competition," to use their formulation, no such combination of results should occur. In fact, yardstick voting is not an implication of yardstick competition for different reasons. Let me mention three.

One possibility, mentioned already in Case, Rosen, and Hines (1993), is that office-holders' decisions are inspired by the belief that relative performance has an effect on votes, whereas in fact it has none: voters do not compare jurisdictions, or comparisons do not change their vote, but office-holders believe or fear the opposite and consequently do engage in policy interaction.

A second possibility points to the relation between taxes and the provision of public services. That relation (which is not tight because of "rents") is assumed away for analytical tractability (or put out of the way by an implicit ceteris paribus clause) in many contributions but nobody really denies its existence. One way to conceive of it would be to suppose that individual voters do make the link between taxation and public services. In chapter 2—like Hettich and Winer (1988) and contrary to Breton (1996)—I assumed that they don't. However, I also assumed that office-holders do. The latter are aware both of the combined effect of taxation and public services on aggregate support and of the relation between taxation and public services through the budget constraint. Suppose that voters do make cross-jurisdiction comparisons and that the mechanism of yardstick voting is at work, albeit in both cases regarding separately taxation and the provision of public services. The objective of budget-constrained office holders will be not to lose more aggregate support as a consequence of the one than they gain as a consequence of the other. If they succeed, it may be the case that we "observe" (detect) tax interaction and expenditure interaction but no variation in support, and thus no yardstick voting.

A third reason is based on a more general apprehension of the multidimensional nature of governmental activities. The issue considered may be one among many. We argued previously that incumbents act like multidivisional business firms or organizations. They pay some attention to all or most issues, even small ones concerning few people, because of their aggregate bearing on support. This makes it possible that a variable could be a detectable object of yardstick competition interaction even though it is too secondary for its variations to be perceptible in the empirical study of voting. For instance, municipalities may interact with regard to their policy in the treatment of waste without differences in that treatment having an observably significant impact on voting.

Other questions have been raised that must be at least mentioned. As discussed in chapter 2, voters may compare either levels or changes in levels. That alternative also applies to the way yardstick voting and yardstick competition are framed. Besley and Case (1995) defend their decision to analyze changes rather than levels on two grounds: large structural differences among jurisdictions, making comparisons difficult, and a need for consistency, which they express as follows: "We also maintain that a model based on agency problems due to asymmetric information about shocks to the cost of providing public services naturally gives way to a specification in which changes in tax matter" (p. 28). But arguments in the opposite direction have been formulated and, in fact, both solutions can be found in the empirical work that we cited. The question has perhaps lost some of its relevance with the availability and exploitation of large panel data sets.

Besley and Case (1995) also discuss whether it is the anticipated or the unanticipated variation of the variable that should be considered. That question is also addressed in Bordignon, Cerniglia, and Revelli (2003) and especially in Allers and Elhorst (2005) and Allers (2012). The idea is simple even though its implementation is not. There are many legitimate reasons for cross-jurisdiction disparities. The argument for taking them explicitly into account—that is, screening them out and thus focusing on the remaining, *unanticipated*, variation—is that "voters should penalize incumbents only for that part of any tax differential for which they are to blame" (Allers and Elhorst 2005, p. 507). But, as noted in Besley and Case (1995), a moot point is whether it is plausible to assume that voters have the capacity (and willingness) to do "regression-based evaluations of incumbents in their heads" implying some knowledge of "the demographic and economic conditions in both their own and neighboring states" (p. 40). Making the assumption in the setting of yardstick competition proper (by opposition to mere yardstick voting) raises technical issues I will not discuss (see Allers and Elhorst 2005) although I agree with Allers (2012) that the matter is important.[34]

Finally, there is an issue I want to mention although I am not convinced of its importance. This is the possibility that yardstick competition could lead to a negative correlation between policy decisions. It is an implication of the theoretical possibility, discussed earlier, that incumbents who feel unable to do comparatively well in the eyes of voters and thus have little chance of being re-elected decide as a consequence to behave badly and grab as much rent as possible in the present. As noted, the said theoretical possibility is developed in Besley (2006), Besley and Smart (2007), and Bordignon, Cerniglia, and Revelli (2004). In an empirical context, the possibility of yardstick competition producing negative autocorrelation is mentioned by Revelli (2005, 2006, 2015). To my knowledge no empirical evidence is cited supporting that perverse mechanism (to be discussed again in chapter 9).

## 5.3. QUERIES

The concern underlying this section is: what relation is there between the empirical findings just discussed and the characterization of yardstick competition presented in chapters 2 and 3? I will consider four questions. Even though the empirical findings are fairly compelling, is it also true of the way they are presented? Is depending on proximity or neighborhood unavoidable? If, as claimed in chapter 2, the relation in a given jurisdiction between comparative performance and support is non-linear, what is the effect on the interpretation of empirical results? To what extent could the main statistical approach be complemented by others?

### 5.3.1. Status of the empirical results

The empirical literature just discussed has achieved something that is both important and limited. *Traces* of the yardstick voting and yardstick competition mechanisms have been found in some data sets. In the case of yardstick voting, electoral results in each jurisdiction have been found to be influenced not only by the variation of a fiscal variable (e.g., a tax rate) in the jurisdiction but also by its variation nearby. This cannot but confirm that some voters are attentive to what happens elsewhere and, when the signs of correlated variations are taken into account, attentive for the purpose of judging incumbents. In the case of yardstick competition proper, the degree to which spatial autocorrelation among neighboring jurisdictions is at work has been found to depend on the electoral prospects of incumbents. That relation is difficult to ascribe to reasons other than yardstick competition—that is, to the fact that incumbents' decisions are influenced, when electorally necessary, by the desire to come out well in voters' cross-jurisdiction comparisons.

Do the results tell us more? At this point I will note some ambivalence in their presentation. On the one hand, authors are generally careful not to claim too much for their findings. I cannot resist citing again the terms used by Bordignon, Cerniglia, and Revelli (2003): their results "definitely suggest that some form of yardstick competition is going on" (p. 201)—see also Solé Ollé's (2003) formulation cited earlier. On the other hand, however, authors tend to suggest too much. Whether or not they formulate explicitly a specific theoretical model before moving to the empirical part of their contributions—that is, to the relations to be estimated—the words they use often reveal that they have such a model in mind and think that it is supported by the findings. That model is typically based on the asymmetric interpretation of agency in general and of yardstick competition and accountability in particular that I have queried in chapters 2 and 3. It may also reflect a belief in the existence of a negativity bias among voters, a matter also discussed earlier.

Let me give some examples of the implicit presuppositions. Contributors exhibit a general tendency to present empirical evidence as showing that voters sanction bad comparative performance. It is not noted that the findings also imply that voters reward good comparative performance. Strategic interaction is interpreted as the consequence of a concern among incumbents with not doing worse than peers in the eyes of voters (i.e., not "falling behind"). The reported evidence could also reflect a concern among incumbents with doing better than others, outperforming them. Similarly, to illustrate findings, only increases in taxation in the jurisdiction and in its neighbors are mentioned although referring to cross-jurisdiction differences in tax reduction (or in mitigating other badly resented policy outcomes) would be as interesting—perhaps even more if unjustified rewards are as or more damaging than unjust punishments.

I must stress that I am not criticizing here the asymmetric interpretation, or of course the empirical results summarized earlier, but only the view that the latter support the former. Yardstick competition can take many forms with which the results of the empirical research are consistent. Some are close to or compatible with the asymmetric interpretation of agency and accountability that researchers have in mind. But others are closer to tournament theory in the spirit of the early literature (e.g., Lazear and Rosen 1981) or even of a dynamic version thereof. It is important for my purpose that empirical results are not associated with only one of the possible forms.

### 5.3.2. Beyond neighborhood

The empirical literature is based on neighborhood or proximity and the instruments it uses are borrowed from spatial econometrics. This makes it dependent on the importance of neighborhood in reality. One may agree with the importance and be bothered by the dependence. Two intuitive a priori reasons for that importance are the likelihood of common regional or local circumstances and the presumption that cross-jurisdiction information is facilitated by proximity. Both are likely to be particularly relevant in the case of small-scale local government, but they may also apply to contexts such as that of US states. There is a third and most compelling reason, relevant ex post: spatial interaction, based on neighborhood, is found empirically significant, as we documented. Probably because it is obvious to empirical researchers, a fourth reason is rarely mentioned: the difficulty if not impossibility of studying econometrically strategic interaction without spatial proximity or, more generally, some partition (based on proximity or similarity) of the whole, studied population. As shown in particular by Manski (1993), the proposition that there is strategic interaction between the undifferentiated members of a whole group, although certainly not tautological in itself, may be difficult to formulate econometrically in a way that is not.

That methodological difficulty concerns yardstick competition proper, not yardstick voting. For the latter, the case for introducing proximity depends on whether it does play a role in reality, not on methodological necessity. An example of the possibility of doing without it is provided by Bianchini and Revelli (2013). There is no mention of geographical proximity in the environmental performance ranking of the one hundred Italian main provincial towns calculated each year by *Legambiente*, a reputable environmental organization (and circulated first via *Il Sole 24 Ore*, an equally respectable newspaper). Bianchini and Revelli find that the position of each town in the said ranking published before a municipal election has a significant effect on the results of that election. In particular, a variation of ten positions entails a variation of about 0.6 percentage points in the electoral outcome. Interestingly for our purpose, the performance registered in the year of election but released after it has no significant effect on the electoral results. This makes clear that voters draw their comparative information mainly from the published *Legambiente* ranking, not directly.

There is no reference to yardstick voting or yardstick competition in Bianchini and Revelli's paper. However, in our interpretation of these two mechanisms, the result just reported does reflect the presence of yardstick voting: voters evaluate comparatively the performance of their municipality and this has an effect on their votes—a sufficient condition for yardstick voting. Revelli (2006), explicitly, and Bianchini and Revelli (2013), implicitly, have a narrower definition of yardstick voting or competition, excluding the idea that voters could get their comparative information from published rankings (especially perhaps those in which proximity plays no role). Because such rankings, at all levels of government, are becoming a major source of the comparative information used by voters, I think that sticking to our interpretation is essential.[35]

Is it legitimate to infer from the evidence of yardstick voting (in our sense) that some form of yardstick competition proper is also at work? Our assumptions about the motivations of politicians make that inference quite natural, as argued in chapter 2. Politicians will be aware of yardstick voting if it is significant. And, in many contexts, they will respond to it in a way that will produce yardstick competition. However, we will see in chapter 7 that various obstacles or disincentives may make incumbents' response insensitive to ascertained yardstick voting. As recurrently stressed in this book, yardstick competition may not work. This may be true even when yardstick voting does.

Let me return to the interesting case studied by Bianchini and Revelli. A 0.6 percentage point variation in electoral outcome for a variation of 10 positions in ranking may seem a small effect. In reality it is impressive since the environment is only one of the issues voters are concerned with. But is it sufficient for incumbents to respond to it by engaging in yardstick competition? Let me recall my analogy, formulated earlier, between the situation of incumbents in a probabilistic voting setting and that of multidivisional firms operating on many markets. In both cases, the job consists of dealing with many issues, and attending the wishes of many constituencies, whatever their size. Thus, small size is not an objection. A more serious problem is that incumbents may decide to concentrate their efforts on other issues than the one under discussion. In multi-issue settings some incumbents may react to voter-sanctioned bad performance on some issue by reducing rather than increasing their input on that issue. For instance, some of the Italian municipalities ranked badly in the latest version of the *Legambiente* index may turn their attention to domains other than the environment.[36] However, some incumbents reacting in that way does not preclude yardstick competition occurring among the others and being significant overall. Because, in that instance, proximity plays no role in yardstick voting, we may suppose that it will also play no role in yardstick competition.

All in all, inferring yardstick competition from established yardstick voting is not unreasonable. The difficulty, with no reference to proximity and no reliance on spatial econometrics, is to document that inference econometrically—and for that purpose to establish econometrically the presence of strategic interaction among the undifferentiated cities. This is one of the reasons why we might consider other approaches to empirical inquiry. Another reason follows from the important point I turn to now.

### 5.3.3. Empirical implications of non-linearity

One of our major points in this book is that the relation between comparative performance and political support in each given jurisdiction (a counterfactual relation similar to demand curves) is non-linear, more precisely S-shaped (or "double S-shaped"), as depicted in figures 2.1. and 4.2. Few, if any, inhabitants of a jurisdiction are likely to notice small differences in performance with other jurisdictions or react to them by changing their vote. However large differences will tend to be noticed by a sizeable number of voters and this will tend to have an effect on aggregate support. This applies to secondary issues as well as to central ones, the meaning of "small," "large," and "sizeable" being different of course in the two cases, and the magnitude of the effect on support reflecting that difference.

Non-linearity of that kind is overlooked in the empirical literature reviewed in this chapter. There are certainly good technical reasons for that disregard. However, it may lead to an underestimation of yardstick voting or even a failure to detect its presence. If a data set includes jurisdictions independently of the degree to which their performance differs from their yardstick (e.g., average of neighbors), yardstick voting could be found to be absent or insignificant, whereas it might be revealed as significant if the data set was segmented so that only jurisdictions whose performance differed from their yardstick above a certain threshold were taken into account.

The implications of non-linearity on yardstick competition proper are more delicate to work out. If incumbents think that voters are inattentive to small differences in performance with other jurisdictions, they will have no incentive not to tolerate them themselves. There will be no observed intentional mimicking of small variations. However, if incumbents know that support from voters may respond, positively or negatively, to large differences, incumbents will try to avoid the negative and generate the positive ones. That will trigger some yardstick competition.

However, it is also possible that no large differences are found. The main implication of the S-shape hypothesis is the enhanced possibility that yardstick competition is undetectable by statistical means (except perhaps experimentation) even though it is important in reality. As stressed already in chapter 1, yardstick competition constrains the decisions of elected office-holders. The combination of the observation of small differences across jurisdictions and no results in the search for yardstick voting and yardstick competition can be fully compatible with the existence of a very strong, albeit hidden, effect of yardstick competition on the decisions of incumbents. I don't know how that problem can be addressed in econometric terms, but it is another reason why alternative approaches could be fruitful.

### 5.3.4. Alternative approaches

In the presence of such impressive a body of empirical research as that reviewed in this chapter, one must certainly be very careful and modest in pointing to or suggesting alternative approaches. Nonetheless, I will mention three directions in which research can be or is already engaged as a complement or alternative to the research reviewed so far.

First, it should be noted that the analysis of strategic interaction and yardstick competition based on spatial econometrics is quite economical in its specification of endogenous variables. For some purposes, it should be less so. In fact, the said analysis considers only one endogenous variable— at once an instrument and an outcome—taking simultaneously different values across jurisdictions. That may be acceptable if the variable is a tax rate or some expenditure. But if we consider variables such as environmental or educational performance (or efficiency, as in Geys 2006), the distinction between outcomes and instruments may recover some importance. So does time. In richer models, some of the many instruments used in reality by governments to engage in strategic interaction would be given a role. For instance, governments might respond to bad comparative performance in a given domain by spending more or changing the allocation of funds in that domain. The effect of these changes on performance would take some time to be felt. Additional information about the content of the response, concerning endogenous variables other than the outcome and including a time dimension, would be helpful for confirming or disconfirming the presence of strategic interaction, especially in settings in which geographical proximity is irrelevant (as is the case in the competition for rank in the *Legambiente* index). Then, as seen previously, electoral variables (and, if they exist, findings of yardstick voting) could provide good reasons to ascribe strategic interaction to yardstick competition.[37]

Second, one obvious alternative or complementary approach is to seek direct information on what incumbents think. Doing that seems appropriate in the present case, and is perhaps becoming less mistrusted in economics than before. So far, however, there is almost no research along that line, an important exception or quasi-exception being Ashworth and Heyndels (1997). Their paper is an econometric study of the opinions of 683 Flemish local politicians about the level of local taxes in their jurisdictions.

The authors assume that voters make cross-jurisdiction comparisons to evaluate their own government's policy. They also assume that incumbents maximize expected votes and are attentive to the political cost of taxation. They find that the opinions of local politicians about the burden of taxation and about how it should change depend on the tax rates in place in neighboring jurisdictions. They interpret that result as "evidence for the existence of 'yardstick opinions' for local property taxes," since "tax policy in neighbouring jurisdictions affects the perceived political cost of one's own tax rates" (p. 499). The "yardstick opinion" mentioned is not exactly yardstick competition (and the relationship between the two is not made very explicit). For our purpose, the paper is important nonetheless because it signals the possibility of an approach to yardstick competition based on direct recording and econometric treatment of incumbents' views on the matter.[38]

Third, an approach different from that adopted in the empirical literature reviewed in this chapter but close to our own reasoning in chapters 2 and 3 consists in neglecting strategic interaction and studying how the inhabitants and government of a given jurisdiction have recourse and react to comparisons with others. Night life consumers in Paris make comparisons with what is available in Berlin and that induces the municipality of Paris to change somewhat its policies. The first OECD report on education achievement caused a PISA shock in the German population, triggering a strong response at various levels of government. French voters are submitted every day to documented claims that France has fallen behind other European countries in terms of growth or that it ranks at the top with regard to public spending. This has contributed to the widespread feeling that politicians in office, as well as their predecessors, are incompetent or don't exert themselves. But this has also triggered some efforts to change policies. Conversely, in Germany, over a long period of time at least, comparative economic success has strengthened the position of the incumbents and induced them to pursue their (in many respects shortsighted) policies.[39]

Several features of that approach must be noted. One is its relation with jurisdiction asymmetry.[40] It is quite common that the inhabitants of jurisdiction $X$ make comparisons with what obtains in jurisdiction $Y$ while the reverse is not true. According to Lewis-Beck, Jérôme, and Jérôme-Speziari (2001), differentials in macroeconomic performance between France and Germany have an effect on voting in France but not in Germany. As a consequence, one might say that there is no clear basis for strategic interaction between the two countries in the domain considered. The absence of reference to interaction is justified then by its absence in reality. In

Hansen, Olsen, and Bech (2015), however, it is shown that the Danes make comparisons with Sweden but whether the Swedes make comparisons with Denmark is not considered. In that case, abstraction from strategic interaction is an aspect of the research strategy of the authors.

Another feature of the approach is to offer an additional way to gauge the degree of confidence that should be given to a cross-jurisdiction comparison of performance. In the mainstream approach, the influence of what happens in other jurisdictions takes the form of a single average. Whether the average is calculated on the basis of one other jurisdiction or of many does not matter. Portugal has only one contiguous neighbor (Spain); France has at least six. If we calculate our peer average not on the basis of contiguous neighborhood but, say, on membership in the European Union, the basis becomes 27. As explained in the last chapter, the problem raised by comparisons with only one other, or only a small number of others, is what I called idiosyncratic randomness in others, which is eliminated by the law of large numbers (and, in fact, quickly when the number of others gets larger). Spain may be lucky or unlucky and comparing Portugal to Spain should take that possibility into account. But it makes no sense to say that on average the members of the European Union other than Portugal are lucky or unlucky. This makes more reliable the comparison of Portugal with the average of other EU members (peer average) or of all EU members (group average).[41] The matter is considered irrelevant or unimportant in the econometric study of interaction among many jurisdictions, and this is probably correct. It should be kept in mind when we consider in depth comparative voting and the policy response to it in a single jurisdiction.[42]

What methods are to be used to follow one or the other of these three directions? They are certainly diverse. Richer models might imply giving up spatial econometrics in its canonical form but this is not sure because econometrics, spatial or not, is evolving rapidly (Revelli 2015). I am incompetent to say more on the matter. Perhaps we should expect most of the evidence to be referred to or produced within the third direction even if that evidence is "soft," relying at best on analytical narratives and case studies.[43]

## 5.4. CONCLUSION

Yardstick competition among subnational governments (governments of cities, regions, etc.) is a possibility that we should now take into account when considering governmental systems. On a conceptual or systemic level, that possibility brings something new into the theory of federalism and decentralization, as I have tried to show in a short section at the beginning of the chapter. The main discussion, however, has concentrated on the arguments and results related to yardstick competition that are found in the empirical literature on fiscal federalism and local finance. In that domain, a drastic simplification of the object studied was possible and has proved very fruitful. Typically, the matter studied consists in the values that a single fiscal variable (a tax rate, say) is observed to take across jurisdictions. Is there some spatial relation between these values? Does that relation reflect a strategic interaction? Might yardstick competition be the cause of the interaction? In the case of yardstick voting, is there an effect on the popularity of incumbents? The simplification of the matter studied does not imply that the work done to answer those questions is also simple. It tends to rely on techniques that are increasingly sophisticated.

A major purpose of this chapter was to provide an informal insight, not into the techniques themselves but into the various ways the arguments concerning yardstick competition have been formulated. The contributions I have examined with that objective in mind deal with different fiscal variables and exploit data sets corresponding to a variety of geographical settings. Some of the findings they report are negative, but the general message seems clear: empirical evidence does support the view that yardstick competition and yardstick voting are operative, play a role, at least sometimes.

What has been achieved is important but also limited. As argued in the third part of the chapter, a *trace* of the mechanism in the empirical data has been documented, but little information of an empirical kind has been provided about the particular form the mechanism can take. That situation reflects the cost incurred by the drastic simplification of the empirical investigation agenda mentioned here. In many contributions, including the most important ones, that cost is masked by the presentation of a theoretical model embodying one form that the mechanism may take. In reality, there is no empirical validation of the specification assumed. Other conceptualizations of the mechanism, including for instance those I propose in this book, could also be compatible with the results. From our perspective, the empirical findings should be welcomed and the theoretical models they are juxtaposed with often glossed over.

Regarding the question of how to investigate empirically the mechanism itself rather than some of its manifestations, I must admit that the remarks and suggestions formulated in the third part of the chapter remain tentative or speculative. They are especially so under a demanding interpretation of what counts as empirical evidence. To what extent is such an interpretation compelling? To get somewhat closer to the working of the mechanism, a solution I adopt in many parts of the book is to focus on the way yardstick comparisons affect policy-making in a single jurisdiction and leave aside strategic interactions involving also others. The empirical support I invoke in that context (see in particular chapter 7) is generally informal.

## NOTES

1. That statement may verge on functionalism, which is generally suspect, but the alternatives—that is, considering the analysis as positive or normative—are even more problematic.
2. "If it occurred that we were in a world without endogenous migrations (i.e., a world in which migrations, whatever their quantitative importance, would not be influenced by the policies of the subcentral authorities) and without other sources of differences in taste, it is not unfair to say that, in its present state, the economic theory of decentralization would be almost bound to predict complete centralization . . . If, in such a world, subcentral government continued to be observed, its existence would then be unexplained" (Salmon 1987b, p. 27).
3. Ashworth and Heyndels (1997), discussed later, is one exception.
4. See also Allers and Elhorst (2005, 2011), Delgado, Lago-Peñas, and Mayor (2015), Santolini (2007).
5. I use the word neighborhood even in contexts in which the word neighborliness might be more appropriate.
6. LeSage (2008) is a relatively reader-friendly introduction to spatial econometrics.
7. Spatial dependence can be checked in a very simple way by inquiring whether something of it survives when neighborhood is defined in terms of alphabetical rather than spatial proximity. This is done in particular in Ladd (1992) and Geys (2006).
8. As we saw in chapter 4, mobility-based competition takes many forms. It is related but should not be reduced to the policy-induced mobility central to Tiebout (1956), the anti-Leviathan function central to Brennan and Buchanan (1980), or the mobility of tax bases central to Brueckner (2003).
9. Because of the single variable limitation, the expenditure spillovers studied cannot include some major cross-jurisdiction external effects. Widely discussed cross-border negative externalities like those generated by French nuclear reactors or German coal-fired power plants are out of reach.
10. Incidentally, it may also be difficult to separate tax competition and expenditure spillovers (the third relationship) because of the budget constraint.
11. Neighborhood can be made to include the contiguous neighbors of the contiguous neighbors (as for instance in Feld and Reulier 2009). This only displaces the argument—in the text replace Spain with Portugal and Poland with Ukraine.
12. This of course assumes that the found correlation is positive, which may not be the case when the underlying mechanism is expenditure spillovers (e.g., more amenities in one jurisdiction inducing fewer in another).
13. In some contributions, there may be a tendency to relate directly observed spatial interaction or mimicking to yardstick competition without further discussion or examination. That tendency was observable in some early contributions. It may also be detected for instance in Dincer, Ellis, and Waddell (2010), but in that case

the variable studied, corruption, may justify the shortcut. With regard to corruption, there is not much scope for ascribing spatial interaction (or contagion) to mobility-based competition or expenditure externalities; as alternatives to yardstick competition, policy learning or even emulation (mechanisms discussed in chapter 4) might be more plausible.

14. Although less convenient, I could have started from Case (1993), which anticipates Besley and Case (1995) along several dimensions, or even from Case, Hines, and Rosen (1988), a working paper in which yardstick competition is more explicitly present than in Case, Rosen, and Hines (1993).

15. Revelli (2008) is an exception.

16. Arguably with the exception of Padovano and Petrarca (2014).

17. In Vermeir and Heyndels (2006), the vote share enjoyed by incumbents is reduced less by an additional 1 percentage point in the local income tax rate than it is increased by an additional percentage point increase in neighboring municipalities. In Bosch and Solé Ollé (2007), "the parties in the government lost 11.5% of the vote when they raised the property tax rate and won 7.5% of the vote when the tax rate was raised by their neighbours" (p. 90). See also Dubois and Paty (2010), and Revelli (2008).

18. With regard to term limits, US governors and Italian mayors remain the main source of inspiration. In their study of interaction among excise taxes in US states, Esteller-Moré and Rizzo (2014) exploit again the existence of term limits for governors. With regard to the excise tax on cigarettes, they find that "only states with non-term-limited governors react (providing evidence of yardstick competition), basically as the election year approaches" (p. 711). The term limits faced by Italian mayors play a role also in Padovano and Petrarca (2014).

19. Rincke (2009) is an exception. To identify yardstick competition between elected boards of school districts on the basis of a difference in the degree of political competition, that degree is not approximated by the size of the majority or the proximity of the next election but by the share of incumbent candidates who were not re-elected in the last election. Districts in which the pressure of political competition, defined in this way, is high are significantly more inclined than the others to adopt innovations tried in neighboring jurisdictions, which confirms in his opinion the role of yardstick competition. On yardstick competition among the bodies governing school districts, see also Hall and Ross (2010).

20. They write: "As the yardstick competition hypothesis predicts, coalitions backed by a large majority mimic neighboring tax rates to a lesser extent than coalitions depending on a small majority. The spatial interaction parameter . . . is 0.22 if the majority is greater than or equal to 75 percent, and 0.41 if not. This difference is statistically significant" (p. 506).

21. Two recent contributions in which the size of the majority in power plays the main role in identifying yardstick competition are Borck, Fossen, and Martin (2015) and Delgado, Lago-Peñas, and Mayor (2015). The variable treated in the first article is public debt rather than the usual taxes or expenditures; one finding is that in Bavaria the spatial interaction coefficient of the municipalities supported by a small majority is significantly larger, "which may indicate that yardstick competition plays a role" (p. 30). The second article focuses on the two main local taxes in Spain, the property tax and the motor vehicle tax; one finding is that "the differences between the estimations that control [and do not control] for majorities are significant, supporting the yardstick competition hypothesis" (p. 365).

22. Again, the main argument refers to the size of the majority, as we saw in the context of tax interaction: "If departments are governed by a political majority in the council of less than or equal to 75 percent, they change their spending on welfare by 17 cents in reaction to a change in spending on welfare of 1 euro by neighboring departments. In contrast, if the departments are governed by a political majority greater than 75 percent, this interaction effect decreases to 3 cents. Both the interaction effect of 17 cents and the difference between these two interaction effects of 14 cents are significant" (p. 948).

23. They write: "Direct democracy as well as fiscal autonomy lead to a tighter link between the preferences of voters and the policy decisions of incumbents which induces less engagement in policy mimicking" (pp. 13–14).

24. The result is confirmed in Revelli (2008) using a different approach. A similar exercise, with a somewhat less dramatic effect, is performed in Terra and Mattos (2017) with regard to the provision of education in Brazil. There also, yardstick competition in its narrow, spatial econometrics sense is squeezed out (only partially in that case) by the introduction of a national performance index.

25. Other negative results are found by Caldeira, Foucault, and Rota-Graziosi (2015) regarding municipal government in Benin and by Baskaran (2014) regarding municipalities close to the former border between East and West Germany. Worryingly for our purpose, Baskaran claims his quasi-experimental study shows that the literature may have overestimated the significance of local tax interaction. A similar negative claim, also justified by reliance on a natural experiment, is formulated by Lyytikäinen (2012) in his study of local property taxation in Finland.

26. They add: "Indeed, if the tax rates of the neighbouring jurisdictions do not influence voters' choices, incumbents do not have to fear an electoral punishment and then mimicking each other is meaningless" (p. 8). They do not discuss explicitly the relation between that proposition and the positive result reported in their other paper. However, the question their formulation suggests is: to what extent is yardstick voting a testable implication of yardstick competition? I will return to the matter later.

27. Neighborhood is often discussed at the level of spatial dependence or strategic interaction (that is, without reference to the underlying mechanism). Here I consider it with yardstick competition in mind.

28. We may neglect here the little-exploited possibility of defining neighborhood in a continuous way.

29. The 20-kilometer threshold mentioned earlier is justified in that way (works best) by Solé Ollé (2003) and Bosch and Solé-Ollé (2007).

30. What we called the idiosyncratic character of neighborhood, particularly clear when the criterion is border-sharing, disappears when the definition of neighborhood becomes belonging to the same local media market. Revelli (2008) compares the results under the two definitions and finds that referring to the media does make the interaction effect stronger.

31. Case, Rosen, and Hines (1993) write: "... *for our purposes, neighborliness does not necessarily connote geographic proximity*. States that are economically and demographically similar may have more effect on each other than two dissimilar states that happen to share a border. Citizens of New York, for example, might find comparisons to Illinois more relevant than those to Vermont" (pp. 286–287). (emphasis in the text).

32. Comparability or non-geographical proximity is addressed directly in Dubois and Paty (2010), who study the relation between the provision of services by French municipalities and electoral results. They compare pure geographical

neighborhood within metropolitan areas and geographical proximity among cities having at least 50,000 inhabitants. In the first case there is no interaction. In the second some is found, and the yardstick voting hypothesis seems also supported.

33. For such ascription to be compelling—especially when voters or elections, or more generally office-holders' motives, are not considered—it must be assumed that only the three mechanisms mentioned can underlie policy interdependence, for instance that a mechanism such as emulation (discussed in chapter 4) is not responsible for the results.

34. Allers (2012) expresses his skepticism in terms similar to those used by Besley and Case (1995) but he regrets the fact and suggests that increased reliance on equalization schemes would mitigate the obstacle met by voters. A rationale for equalization schemes sought in the facilitation of intergovernmental competition was already suggested, in a broader context, by Breton (1987).

35. By referring to yardstick competition in his discussion of the World Bank *Doing Business* rankings, Besley (2015) shows that he shares that interpretation.

36. As we saw, that type of response is modeled in a single-issue context by Besley and Smart (2007) and Bordignon, Cerniglia, and Revelli (2004), but it is more plausible when several issues are assumed. Giving up the fight in one domain does not imply renouncing in general.

37. Although the authors are not concerned with yardstick competition, see Fredriksson, List, and Millimet (2004) for the confirmation that single-variable reasoning is likely to underestimate strategic interaction and for a theoretic and empirical analysis based on the assumption of three policy variables.

38. Neighborhood plays a prominent role in the paper and proves significant ex post. Still, it is not clear why proximity would be a methodological requisite for such treatment: respondents could refer to a national average, for instance.

39. The approach is the same as that discussed in chapter 4 under the name of policy-induced mobility, distinct from mobility-based competition proper. In both cases, the focus is on the effects in a single jurisdiction of its openness and of the situation elsewhere. The strategic interaction is neglected.

40. In fact, jurisdiction asymmetry can also be taken into account in the mainstream, spatial econometrics approach, discussed earlier. See in particular Werck, Heyndels, and Geys (2008).

41. The statistical distribution of outcomes in the other jurisdictions and not only their average may also count. Is it unimportant that a jurisdiction is outperformed by all the other jurisdictions and not only by their average?

42. The number of neighbors plays a role in Reulier and Rocaboy's discussion (2006) of the effect of term limits on yardstick competition.

43. Completely new quantitative methods may also emerge or be borrowed from other domains. The evidence provided in Hansen, Olsen, and Bech (2015) to document the presence of yardstick voting in Denmark is based on a method of "choice experiments" borrowed from marketing. See also Charbonneau and Van Ryzin (2015).

# CHAPTER 6

# The challenge of extending: the international setting

T his chapter is mainly about a puzzle: given all the work done on yardstick competition within countries, that is, among subnational governments, why has there been so little "scientific" work on yardstick competition at the international level, that is, among national governments? Of course, there is no puzzle, or there is a very different one, if there is no yardstick competition among national governments in reality. Some "soft" evidence suggesting that there is, is provided in the first part of this chapter. Assuming there is, I move on to the explanation of why so few scholars have turned their attention to the matter, distinguishing among three categories of obstacles their involvement may have come up against: ideological, sociological, and technical. The last of these is probably the most important. Is the situation changing? A brief survey of the recent literature suggests that it might be. In the last part of the chapter, I return to the problems raised by the variety and complexity of existing governmental systems, a question important in the international setting.

## 6.1. CIRCUMSTANTIAL EVIDENCE

Let me start with an example I gave many years ago in one of my first papers on international yardstick competition. At an exhibition organized in Prague in 1988, visitors were informed that from 1937 to 1985 the number of households per washing-machine had gone down from 102 to 2. According to the correspondent of *Le Monde* (October 28, 1988), the Czechs were more impressed by another observation, put forward by the clandestine opposition: "At the beginning of its existence, Czechoslovakia was one of the most industrialized countries of Europe. Since then, it has fallen behind." It is generally agreed that information about living standards in the West contributed to dissatisfaction among the population of the collectivist regimes of Eastern Europe and eventually to their collapse.[1] The reason why I cite that episode is not its historical importance but the fact that it provides a perfect illustration of a configuration I am particularly interested in: a favorable assessment exclusively based on a comparison over time within the jurisdiction fully reversed by another comparison, also over time, albeit with other jurisdictions. As suggested earlier, unjustified rewards may be at least as serious a problem as unjust punishments, even if there is a tendency to focus on the latter. Of course, this case is also interesting because the countries concerned were not democracies. It shows that comparisons with what obtains elsewhere may be highly relevant also in countries that are not democratic.

The increased importance of international comparisons by citizens is an undervalued aspect of globalization. One reason for their impact is that, along many dimensions, the rate of change can be very high. Some countries are completely transformed in a single generation; others change much more slowly. Countries in the same league at some date no longer are twenty years later. Such relative instability is one of the reasons why the production of comparative information, whether by international organizations, national administrations, and research institutions or by private entities and individuals, has expanded so much. Many people have become concerned with where their country stands comparatively. That greater curiosity or appetite is satisfied in a user-friendly form by the traditional media and through electronic channels. A country's position in a ranking or with regard to an average provides a particularly convenient way to judge its performance. But pair-wise and more direct comparisons are also more important today than in the past. They are facilitated by the international mobility—professional or for leisure—of a large proportion of the population and eased by the rapidly increasing knowledge of English as a lingua franca.

One may also observe that making or citing cross-country comparisons has become a frequent ingredient of public debates. Economic variables (economic growth, unemployment, inflation, deficits, etc.) are particularly prone to be objects of comparison. When relative performance is bad, comparisons with other countries are stressed, normally, by the opposition, when it is good, by the government itself. Whatever their origin and intent, economic comparisons usually make their way toward the center of the political debate.

The situation in non-economic domains is different. There, comparisons are normally of interest to smaller constituencies (a fact which does not necessarily make them irrelevant, as explained earlier) and only occasionally to the general public.

Education, and in particular the impact of PISA is a good (already alluded to) example. The PISA reports, published by the OECD since 2000, include country analyses and rankings of the levels achieved in different domains by 15-year-old students. In most of the countries concerned, the attention given to the PISA reports by the general public has been significant and led to more attention being paid to education in general. But in Germany the effect of the first two PISA reports has been justly labeled a PISA shock. To cite one comment (Fertig 2003), because "on average, German students participating in this standardized test performed considerably below the OECD average and substantially worse than those of other European countries" the first PISA report "induced a public outcry in Germany," it "initiated an intense debate in the media, among politicians and the public on the causes of the results and the consequences to be drawn" (p. 2).[2]

Initially, France performed a little better than Germany and, perhaps for that reason, its PISA rankings attracted less attention. In the PISA report published in December 2010, the rank of Germany was much improved, and in fact had become slightly higher than that of France. The main reason for the relatively disappointing position of France in that ranking was the particularly bad performance of the weaker part of the population of students, not compensated as much as before by the particularly high performance of the stronger part. Given the fact that elitist tendencies and de facto ethnic-cum-spatial segregation were already widely perceived features of the French educational system, the potential for upset in France due to the 2010 report remained relatively modest. However, the 2012 PISA report, published in December 2013, got much more attention, in particular because it showed that the defects pointed out earlier were getting worse. *Le Monde*, a daily newspaper, devoted at least one full page to the matter in each of five consecutive issues (February 4–9, 2014).

What was the reaction of governments?[3] In Germany, a strong policy response, both at the federal level and at that of the Länder, produced, after a lag, a significant improvement (acclaimed under the title "Allemagne: après le choc, la thérapie et le grand bond" in *Le Monde* of December 15, 2010).[4] In France, a concern with reducing elitism in the wake of the PISA reports made its way slowly among specialists (see Dobbins and Martens 2012) and eventually inspired the modest reform of the middle school curriculum defended in 2014–2015—against vehement opposition both from several teacher unions and political opponents but with the approval of the

OECD—by the then French minister of education Najat Vallaud-Belkacem. But new rankings (not only PISA) have led in 2017 to the widely shared view—one may even speak of a quasi-unanimous agreement (except perhaps among teachers)—that more audacious reforms of the primary education system are needed.

There was no PISA shock in the United States even though its rank was near the bottom, even lower than Germany. The explanation proposed in Martens and Niemann (2010, 2013) is based on two observations. First, "US educators" and policymakers learned nothing new from PISA. Awareness of bad performance in education is reflected in the language of policymakers at least since the "Sputnik shock" of 1957. It is particularly salient in *A Nation at Risk: Imperatives for Educational Reforms*, a report published in 1983, and in the justification given for the *No Child Left Behind Act*, enacted in 2002.

Second, the US media paid no attention to the PISA reports. On that point the contrast with Germany is literally stunning. "Of eight major U.S. daily and weekly newspapers,[5] only eight articles over the period of 2001 to 2008 actually covered PISA at all—and of these eight articles only three dealt with the poor results of U.S. students," whereas during the same period the *Süddeutsche Zeitung* alone, for example, published 253 articles (Martens and Niemann 2010, p. 15).

The explanation based on these two observations is convincing as far as it goes but it is too confined to the domain of education. I also invoked earlier pre-existing self-perception as one reason for the absence of a PISA shock in France; however, over the period 2001–2008 there were more than twenty articles related to PISA in *Le Monde* against virtually none in the *New York Times*. There is a difference between no shock and total neglect. Pre-existing awareness can explain the former but not the latter. The contrast in the coverage of the PISA rankings reflects a more general difference between European countries and the United States in the public's appetite for international comparisons of performance.

That difference is tacitly acknowledged by Congleton (2007b) when he observes: "Both ordinary citizens and political elites tend to judge the performance of their own national governments in part by looking at what other governments have achieved. For example, in Europe, newspapers and think tanks often provide statistics that show whether their home country is growing the fastest; is the richest, most egalitarian, most environmentally responsible, or best educated; or has the largest or smallest government, lowest unemployment, smallest deficit, least ethnic discrimination, least corruption, and so forth. This allows voters and national political elites to judge whether their public policies are as good as those of their neighbors" (p. 11).[6]

The foregoing discussion raises a number of questions. Let me mention two. First, inasmuch as our general framework is that of agency, who exactly is the principal and who is the agent? In the simplified mode of reasoning generally adopted in the previous chapters, the principal is the electorate and the agent is the incumbent—that is, an elected person, party, or majority. The illustrations just mentioned suggest a wider interpretation. In the case of Czechoslovakia as well as in the excerpt from Buchanan (1995/96), the agents are collectivist regimes, rather than the particular Communist Party members currently in office; the principals are something like "the people" or "citizens," certainly not "voters." Congleton (2007b) alludes to comparisons by *elites*. How do they fit in our framework? Who was held responsible for the bad quality of education and who responded to the PISA reports in a federal country such as Germany, in which different coalitions alternate at the central and regional levels?

I have argued that international comparisons are perhaps not very natural in the United States, and followed the literature in observing that, in that country, the PISA reports remained generally unheeded. Still, President Obama did point out "that America has been dropping steadily down the international league tables, particularly in mathematics and the sciences" and "that it now ranks 12th in the proportion of its people who graduate from college compared to the first place a generation ago" (*Financial Times*, July 30, 2010). How to interpret that type of declaration? One may argue that politicians would not refer to rankings if many citizens did not also reason, at least to some extent, in these comparative terms. At the same time, it might seem puzzling that an incumbent stresses bad comparative performance. President Obama clearly wanted to persuade some "audience" that education is deteriorating and must be reformed. But did he have in mind voters, legislators, educators, bureaucrats, interest groups, state governments, or the whole nation?[7] Those questions suggest the need, eschewed so far, to acknowledge some of the complexities of compound government.[8]

A second question concerns the relationship between comparative assessments made by voters and yardstick competition. Except perhaps in the case of the response to the PISA shock in Germany, our circumstantial evidence is not directly about yardstick competition, or even yardstick voting. It is about international comparisons of performance made from below (by voters, citizens, the people, etc.) and their reflection in the public debate. The effects on support and then on policy-making are implicit at best. To go further, serious empirical work of the kind surveyed in the last chapter would be welcome. So far, there has been quantitatively little of it.

## 6.2. OBSTACLES

Although this will seem somewhat polemical, it is difficult not to acknowledge the importance, together with technical obstacles, of the ideological biases and of the sociological determinants that explain the limited attention given so far to yardstick competition among governments.

### 6.2.1. Ideological obstacles

A surprisingly high degree of pessimism with regard to the nature of government and to the way democracy works is a central feature of political economy or public choice. This is not only a consequence of assuming that politicians and bureaucrats pursue their own ends and interests. It is also largely a consequence of reasoning deductively and as if there were only one jurisdiction or polity. In the conceptual setting created by that implicit assumption, it seems obvious that it will prove difficult for voters to assess many important policies and their results, especially in the presence of historical change, shocks, and uncertainty. Within that framework, a high degree of pessimism, based on information asymmetry, seems justified: in many policy areas, what could prevent governments from making decisions that are not in the interest of the populations without these populations being able to notice?

The argument developed at length in this book is that acknowledging the existence of several jurisdictions does change the matter. This is true whether that existence is posited in an international setting, the jurisdictions being countries, or in a national setting, the jurisdictions being subnational entities such as regions or communes. However, one must distinguish between pessimism about government and pessimism with regard to democracy. Mobility-based competition among governments, if strong and unhampered, may be deemed sufficient to constrain these governments. It constitutes a generalization of "voting with the feet," which was considered a *substitute* to voting tout court, and as such, it tends to render irrelevant the question of whether a government is democratic or not. Thus, when jurisdictional openness is acknowledged, it is often the case in the literature of political economy and public choice that pessimism about government is mitigated whereas pessimism about democracy is left intact.

Moreover, mobility-based competition is normally perceived as favorable to markets, limiting the possibilities of redistributive policies, and leading to some downsizing of government. From an ideological standpoint, that type of competition is thus well matched with the basic tenets of economic liberalism.

Yardstick competition is another matter. If, because of yardstick competition, voters are better informed and office-holders more accountable to voters, there will be less possibility of discretionary behavior, and thus less governmental or bureaucratic slack and more alignment of public policies with what voters want (Congleton 2007a). May such effects of yardstick competition when it works well (which is not always the case) have a bearing on the system of economic governance? That question does not arise in a significant way in the case of yardstick competition among subnational governments because the economic system is not generally determined at that level. It is mainly at the national level that there is a lively political debate about the size of government and its role in economic affairs.

In practice, we should consider analyses based on competition among governments of the yardstick competition variety as largely neutral with regard to the economic system. Inasmuch as international yardstick competition improves governance, this may affect the degree of reliance on markets in any direction. Indeed, it is the belief that economies work better when they rely more on markets that has prevailed among policy-makers in recent decades. However, a pragmatic approach to the matter is not adopted by all. In the context of an ideological divide framed as "state versus markets," some partisans of markets may fear that any kind of perceived improvement in the accountability of government could have an effect on the economic system in the direction of less reliance on markets.[9] It is less likely that mobility-based competition has such effect because by itself it fosters markets.

There may also be an implicit bias against yardstick competition, to simplify, on the other side of the ideological divide. If governments are supposed to be benevolent and democracy to work fairly well even in an informationally closed and single-government society, this entails that information asymmetry is not considered a serious problem. Then, yardstick competition is irrelevant. If there is an information problem to address, it will be about the revelation of the preferences of the population, not about the informational obstacles encountered by voters in observing or assessing the deeds of office-holders. As we know at least since Tiebout (1956), mobility may help mitigate the revelation problem (if there is one). Yardstick competition cannot. Such a position underlies the attitude of many scholars in domains such as public economics, public finance, and public administration. Inasmuch as some influence on domestic policy-making of what happens abroad is acknowledged, it will be ascribed to inspiration from best practice or peer review among office-holders rather than to a pressure from voters making international comparisons. When voting is considered, the focus will be, under an assumption of perfect information, on the aggregation of preferences and on income distribution.

## 6.2.2. Sociological obstacles

Ideological concerns may thus explain the reluctance of some, but sociological and historical factors are also relevant and account for the abstention of others. Research is necessarily segmented and that intellectual factor of efficiency has a counterpart in the organization of journals, conferences, networks, and careers. Two sources of fragmentation are important for our discussion. Political yardstick competition was introduced in the context of fiscal federalism, decentralization, and public finance (Salmon1987b, Besley and Case 1995) and it has inspired innovative empirical work and theoretical elaborations in the corresponding research areas by scholars generally specialized in these areas. In their work, the variables studied have remained those they are familiar with—mainly taxes, but sometimes also public spending and service delivery—on a particular level of subnational government (regional or local), and in a given country or part of it. There is still much interesting work to do in that research context and little incentive to move out of it.

A second source of fragmentation is an academic and research tradition in which anything international is spun off from the rest, a tradition not yet made obsolete by the growing interest in globalization, and which is as effective in political science as in economics. So, economists and political scientists working on apparently domestic topics tend to neglect any relation of their subject with international constraints and forces and, conversely, specialists of the international are interested in few aspects of the inside of countries. In the case of international economics, putting aside the thriving domains of open macroeconomics and financial markets and regulation, the main links studied are related to the effects of trade and factor mobility on domestic income distribution and the impact of domestic politics (especially lobbying) on the debate on free trade versus protectionism (or mercantilism). These questions are largely unrelated to yardstick competition.

European research in economics and in political science has been, and still is to a large extent, very much influenced by the well-deserved intellectual leadership of US scholarship. The effects of that long-standing influence have been very positive on the whole, but there are a few negative side effects. European researchers should have noticed a long time ago, long before all the current talk about globalization, that a spinning off of the international which is quite tolerable with regard to most issues in a large country such as the United States, is less legitimate and may be seriously misleading when discussing most aspects of small open economies and societies such as those of the European countries. And, more directly related to our concerns in this book, the fact, noted earlier, that yardstick competition between national governments probably does not significantly affect policy-making in the United States may explain that US scholars, first, and then European scholars under their influence have largely disregarded the mechanism in spite of its possible importance outside the United States.

### 6.2.3. Technical obstacles

There is a synergy between the absence of incentives to extend the analysis to a broader setting and a third factor, whose nature is conceptual and technical. The approach that has proved fruitful for identifying empirically yardstick competition between subnational governments in a single country cannot be easily transposed to the study of yardstick competition among national governments. Local taxes in a country are embedded in the set of fiscal arrangements adopted for the country as a whole.[10] This facilitates the comparisons of variations of a single tax (e.g., a property tax) across local jurisdictions. With some exceptions (such as excise taxes on petrol or on cigarettes), comparing a single tax, or its variations, across countries is likely to be misleading because fiscal arrangements, and more generally institutional or systemic arrangements, form clusters that are quite different across countries, with the possibility that various kinds of compensation allow national systems to yield in their own way results that are not so different in the end. It is true, as noted, that yardstick voting and yardstick competition can be formulated in terms of change rather than of levels. This mitigates the difficulty but does not eliminate it when national systems are very different. I have mentioned taxes but the problem is more general. It also affects spending and regulation.

That does not mean that voters will not engage in international comparisons. We have argued that they do, and do so increasingly. But the differences in the two realities (domestic and international) have two important implications. The first relates to the variables assumed to be the objects of cross-jurisdiction comparisons by voters. In the international context, they fall into three main categories. The first consists of topical issues involving regulation. We may include here matters such as divorce, abortion, capital punishment, same-sex marriage, illicit drugs, smoking, speed limits, gender quotas, positive discrimination, immigration, the construction of mosques, and the wearing of head scarfs or burqas. Such issues typically attract the often-passionate attention of large constituencies, with solutions adopted abroad playing a large part in public debates. In most countries, the central rather than the subnational governments are competent and consequently if voters engage in comparisons, this is at the international level.

Admittedly, it may be different in decentralized federations. Inasmuch as regional or provincial governments have the right to legislate on some of these issues, there should be no real difference in the nature and consequences of subnational and international comparisons. So far, however, the literature on the diffusion of legislative innovations across subnational jurisdictions has not—as far as I know and with a few exceptions such as Breton (1996, pp. 235–37), Hugh-Jones (2009), and Pacheco (2012)—given much attention to yardstick competition.

The same remarks apply to a second category of variables consisting in performance or quality in the delivery of services in policy areas like education, health, public transportation, culture, or sports. On these matters, voters, or various subsets thereof, may compare the situation in their own country with what they know of the situation in some others or they may pay attention to the rank of their country in the various comparative statistics made available by the media. Again, there is not much conceptual difference here between the international and the national settings except perhaps that, in many policy areas, there is more relevant information easily accessible for international comparisons than there is to compare the achievements of regional or local governments.

Performance of a macroeconomic kind constitutes a third category. Economic growth or more short-term variations in macroeconomic variables are naturally perceived as concerning above all the national level rather than any subnational one. This is in part because subnational governments have less means to influence these variables than have central governments. But, the main reason is probably the ambiguous bearing on welfare of the values taken by those variables at the subnational level. This is particularly clear in the case of local government. Growth in the number of inhabitants of a city may be a source of pride or envy in some cases but a mixed blessing or a thing to avoid in others. Increased income per head at the local level may reflect "gentrification," without any clear-cut implication with regard to performance.

The second, related, implication of differences between the two contexts (domestic and international) in which yardstick competition among governments takes place concerns the way empirical evidence can be sought. This is probably the most serious problem. The sophisticated techniques (spatial econometrics, in particular) applied to yardstick competition among governments over a single variable like a property tax cannot be easily transposed to empirical assessments of yardstick competition over variables such as economic growth or performance in the delivery of a particular category of services. Several obstacles to such transposition come to mind. Mimicking, which has played such a large role in the empirical literature so far cannot be given the same meaning when the comparisons made by voters are about performance. Mimicking a rate of economic growth, or schoolchildren's level of mathematical skill, is not meaningless, but it is definitely different from mimicking a tax rate. The comparisons made by voters are not dissimilar and have more or less the same kind of influence on their electoral choices, but the way policies can respond to these comparisons are different. In the case of performance, the response may need much time to have an effect and be roundabout rather than direct. Addressing underperformance in one area will lead to increased effort and to adjustments in policies apparently distant from that area. Conversely, the government of a country observed to do better than others in a domain may relax or redirect its efforts to other policy areas.

Leaving aside the response of incumbents, we may seek empirical evidence regarding only the response of voters—that is, yardstick voting. As noted, there is no reason why the reactions of voters to the results of their comparisons would be very different in the international and the domestic contexts.[11] But, in the international setting, we encounter a possible general difficulty—which in fact also affects the empirical study of mimicking. There are large numbers of communes—three thousand, for example, in Bosch and Solé-Ollé (2007)—whereas the number of countries that it would be appropriate to include in a study is small. This may also complicate somewhat (perhaps not much thanks to panel data) the transposition to the international level of the techniques employed to study interaction among subnational jurisdictions.

## 6.3. THE FEW EMPIRICAL RESULTS OBTAINED SO FAR

Until about 2010, the number of writings in which yardstick competition among national governments was mentioned (or referred to under a different name) was not insignificant but few of them included a systematic analysis or an empirical study of the mechanism or its effects.[12] In 2011, I presented at conferences a paper entitled "Yardstick competition among national governments: reflections on a programme that does not exist." Ironically, that coincided with the publication or circulation of several important contributions on the topic that I treated as insufficiently studied.[13] Still, I consider the views I expressed then, and have summarized here, as remaining broadly correct. The obstacles met by the extension to international settings of the work done in the fiscal federalism context are still relevant.

Let me, however, summarize some of the empirical results obtained in the small literature alluded to. Several empirical studies concern yardstick voting rather than yardstick competition proper. An early contribution is the already cited study co-authored by Lewis-Beck, Jérôme, and Jérôme-Speziari (2001) in which it is found that the growth differential between France and Germany has an effect on elections for parliament in France. According to their simple regressions, growth in France being 1 percentage point higher than in Germany increases by 1.4 percent the total vote for the outgoing coalition in France. As noted earlier, no effect is observed in the reverse direction: apparently, German voters pay no attention to growth in France. This is not really surprising. Yet, to predict (with success) the 2013 legislative election in Germany, one of the variables introduced in Kayser and Leininger (2013, 2016), is an average of the growth rates of France, Italy, and the United Kingdom.

The yardstick comparisons influencing voting are also assumed to be made with a single country in Hansen, Olsen, and Bech (2015), also already cited. The method employed is based on the integration of a so-called "choice experiment" (a method originating in marketing) in the 2011 Danish National Election Study. The finding of interest to us is that "voters put substantial weight on how the national economy performs compared to" Sweden (p. 785). The unusual way in which that result is illustrated reflects the method used: "voters require a tax cut of $89 per month to accept Sweden becoming richer than Denmark" (p. 784).[14]

Yardstick voting has also been studied in multi-country rather than bilateral settings. From the work done on a sample of 268 democratic elections between 1978 and 1999, Leigh (2009) derives the proposition that even though their outcomes are more influenced by world growth (which he calls "luck") than by national growth relative to world growth (which he calls "competence"), both do matter. In their influential article, Kayser and Peress (2012) exploit a data set covering 22 OECD countries and 385 elections since 1948. They find that voters hold incumbents more electorally accountable for the domestic than for the international component of growth. Indeed, for a number of democracies, they estimate the effect of "benchmarked growth" to "exceed that of national growth by up to a factor of two."[15]

Yardstick competition proper—that is, as a mechanism underlying strategic interaction—comes out as significant in Redoano (2007) and in Cassette et al. (2013). The work presented in the former is based on a panel of European countries. One result is that interdependence (strategic interaction) among neighboring countries in the setting of public expenditures is greater in election years. This is also true when the variable considered is spending on education. This justifies concluding that the underlying mechanism is yardstick competition in the two cases.[16] In Cassette et al (2013), it is also strategic interaction being more intense in election years that suggests imputing it to yardstick competition.[17] From a study of the discretionary component of fiscal variables in 18 OECD countries over the period 1974–2008, the authors conclude that the yardstick competition explanation of spatial interdependence is empirically supported with regard to the discretionary component of spending but not of tax receipts. Fiscal interactions in Europe are studied also in Hory (2018). Evidence of mimicking and even, more tentatively, of yardstick competition is provided, but interestingly (if confirmed by other studies), under the assumption of a time lag: the behavior mimicked by neighboring governments is that of "last year."

## 6.4. DEALING WITH COMPLEXITY AND DIVERSITY

Our analysis of yardstick competition among national governments is meant to be relevant whatever the particulars of political regimes. However, the worldwide diversity and individual complexity of those regimes raise obvious problems. It is impossible here to analyze and compare in detail the implications of national settings and arrangements on how yardstick competition may work. It is enough to think of the differences between France and Switzerland, two democracies, to realize that the task would be excessively space-consuming. Two questions however cannot be ignored. Both are related to the distinction between agents and principals, or rulers and ruled, when the topic is yardstick competition. The first is about the relevance of the distinction in non-democratic settings and the second about its location when governmental systems are complex.

To study the first question—the relevance of agency relationship outside conventional democracy—let us start at a very general level, leaving aside yardstick competition for the moment. The distinction between rulers and ruled is not always meaningful. As discussed in chapter 3, in some relatively egalitarian "primitive" societies, members make their decisions in common, everyone then being both ruled and co-ruler. As also noted, in some other societies, decisions in common are also made on an egalitarian basis albeit by only a subset of the population, the "citizens," the most famous instance being Athenian democracy. In both cases (neglecting non-citizens), we may speak of direct democracy. In principle, this implies no information asymmetry, no agency relationship, and thus no yardstick competition: citizens decide, and if the outcome of their decision—in particular the ensuing relative performance—turns out to be bad, citizens have nobody but themselves to blame.[18]

That direct democracy blueprint, in its restricted citizenship variant, is interesting inasmuch as the current insistence on ruling by elites or classes comes close to assuming something similar, with the same negative implication on the existence of the agency relationship. I have criticized ruling by elites in chapter 3, when discussing accountability in the context of democracies. In that context, I argued, the state or government cannot be assumed away even when tightly connected to or influenced by some pressure groups or subsets of the population. To what extent is this also true in non-democratic settings? I will insist on three points.

First, the logic of the situation may come close to that of direct democracy limited to a subset of the population, just discussed. If we keep the assumption of common decision-making among the members of that subset but, first, do not specify their mode of decision and, second, assume that they rule exclusively in their own interest, we have an exploitive oligarchy. This is more or less the configuration that North, Wallis, and Weingast (2009) assume to have been widespread if not universal in the past and to be still in force in many parts of the world today. And this is also fairly close to the extreme versions of government by elites that we discussed in the context of contemporary democracies. In both cases, the state or the government, possibly embodied in a chief or a monarch, is deemed unimportant—being only a veil or an obedient servant of the oligarchs, the true rulers. It must be conceded that in the non-democratic setting the state may effectively be non-existent or irrelevant and also that oligarchs are often identifiable and well-armed in order to exploit the rest of the population. Thus, the pure oligarchy story outside contemporary democracies is more plausible than the story of governing by elites within.

For our reasoning, oligarchs who exploit society in their own interest and are accountable to no one except themselves constitute a bothersome obstacle to an analysis in terms of agency and accountability and they can be expected to at least complicate the analysis of yardstick competition. Let me refer to that configuration as the "oligarchic configuration" and oppose to it an alternative labeled the "central actor configuration." In the latter, political decision-making involves explicitly a chief, monarch, state, government, autocrat, or dictator. These central actors have sufficient authority to justify calling them rulers even when closely allied with some elite categories (landowners, say) or acting as their agent. Central actors may declare themselves accountable to no one, except perhaps God, but the claim may always be challenged under some circumstances. Downward accountability is relevant, at least potentially. It is often the case that the same real-world arrangements can be interpreted as corresponding to either one or the other configuration depending on the purpose or object of the discussion. The difference may often be one of emphasis. For our purpose in this book, the central actor configuration is preferable.[19]

Second, downward accountability is more widespread than it would be if depending on the existence of fair elections. As noted earlier, there are other channels through which the ruled can express their views about rulers and exert a pressure on their decisions. They include protests, strikes, demonstrations, boycotts, riots, bombs, and revolutions. The pressure may also come from public opinion.

Indeed, downward accountability is a widespread phenomenon in two ways. One is its presence in real world settings in which there are no elections or no fair elections. Fair elections came relatively late everywhere and are still absent in many countries. Making them a necessary condition for downward accountability would exclude many countries today and would eliminate practically all of them (except perhaps Britain and the United States) until the nineteenth century. In particular there were no elections in France until 1789. Was there no downward accountability in that country until that date? Several decades before—that is, at least since 1750—public opinion was already exerting a considerable upward pressure on policy-making and the selection of political personnel at the top (Ozouf 1988). The second reason why we may assume, with yardstick competition in mind, that downward accountability is quite general or widespread is that it does not have to concern legally all the population. When the franchise is limited to a subset, as was the case almost everywhere, this does not necessarily mean that there is no downward accountability to those who have the right to vote. And potentially at least, the part of the population prevented from voting can make itself heard by other means. Occasionally it does. Anyhow, even if exclusion of a large part of the population is sad, this does not impair in depth the logic of downward accountability or yardstick competition. Before the rise of absolutism in the seventeenth century, the constituencies to which monarchs in Western Europe were or felt accountable included the nobility or gentry but also the inhabitants of cities, non-identifiable as elites but generally fairly literate and sophisticated—not the immense majority of the population made up of peasants, whose uprisings and revolts were severely repressed (see, e.g., Fukuyama 2011, chapter 28).

Third, to a large degree, downward accountability is a continuous variable. I have just mentioned elections and the limits of the franchise. Formal institutions are obviously important and they create a discontinuity. But, especially if we take into account the alternative forms of upward pressure just discussed, at least two other variables also count. One is the degree to which the use of force by the central authority, associated or not with the elites, limits the availability of these alternative forms. I mentioned France before the French Revolution. But in many ways, the French monarchy had become fairly tolerant in the eighteenth century, which of course was not the case of the regimes of Hitler and Stalin. The other variable is the distribution of cognitive characteristics in the overall population. The populations of large cities such as Amsterdam, London, and Paris on the eve of the French Revolution was amazingly literate.[20] These two variables, in particular, co-determine with institutional variables continuous degrees of downward accountability, rather than a binary answer to whether it is present or not.

Let me turn to the second question announced above: where should we draw the line between rulers and ruled, or, preferably here, between agents and principals, in complex political systems? The main difficulty is with legislatures. Are members of parliament to be considered rulers or ruled, principals or agents? Thanks to our focus on yardstick competition, the question, even if complex in general, can be dealt with here as straightforward. The case for yardstick competition relies on the existence of a problem of information asymmetry, which limits the capacity of voters or ordinary citizens to evaluate performance and is possibly mitigated by the yardstick comparisons citizens can engage in. Politicians, whether in the majority or the opposition, or whether in the executive or in the legislative branch, do not qualify as principals. First, they are not hindered, or not hindered to the same degree as are citizens by information asymmetry. And, second, their decisions are themselves relatively opaque and difficult to evaluate by citizens facing information asymmetry. So, for our purpose, legislators must be considered agents of citizens as principals.[21]

That solution does not necessarily complicate the identification of incumbents or weaken the relevance of yardstick voting or support. In many instances, the responsibility for bad or good performance can be attributed without difficulty to incumbents in the executive branch and/or to the majority in the legislature.[22] Sometimes this is more difficult, because of divided government, time lags, etc. Who, for instance, is responsible for the bad performance of Italy with regard to growth, the United States with regard to equality, or India with regard to the fate of women? The fundamental distinction made since the first chapter between yardstick voting and yardstick competition has a counterpart in a distinction between political change and policy change. Even when it is difficult to locate political responsibility and political change, we may often assume that, working in an unanalyzed way, they somehow generate the performance-induced policy changes or policy constraints that are our main concern. The models presented in the next chapter reflect that strategy.

## 6.5. CONCLUSION

The challenge mentioned in the title of the chapter mainly concerns researchers. There is little doubt that there is some yardstick competition among national governments in the real world. Some casual evidence about the pervasiveness of cross-jurisdiction comparisons made by citizens is provided at the beginning of the chapter. Yardstick voting and yardstick competition can be supposed to follow. However, it would be nice to have that presumption more systematically investigated, in particular with standard quantitative techniques. So far there has been little done in that direction. Few researchers have turned their attention to the matter. I have distinguished three categories of obstacles to a greater involvement. Ideological and sociological obstacles play a role although the obstacle that seems the most clear-cut is technical.

The methods that proved successful for studying yardstick competition among local or regional governments in a single country are ill adapted for handling the diversity of national governmental systems. Comparisons of variables like tax rates for example have less meaning across countries than across subnational jurisdictions with a single governmental system. Variables whose comparison at the international level could be more meaningful, related for instance to economic performance or performance in domains such education and healthcare, are difficult to integrate (especially because of time lags) into a quantitative study of yardstick competition.

Yardstick voting seems more amenable to serious empirical investigation than yardstick competition proper, as confirmed by the few studies published so far. However, this is true only if the countries concerned

have relatively similar democratic systems. Otherwise, yardstick competition allows a more universal treatment than does yardstick voting. It
allows neglecting political characteristics so as to consider directly the way
policies respond to differences in performance. That facility inspires part of
the discussion in the next chapter. Whether it could also inspire more conventional empirical approaches remains to be seen. In general, however,
I think that we can trust researchers to find innovative ways to study even
the most difficult questions. This brings us back to ideological bias and the
sociology of the profession, the main condition for some progress being
interest in the topic.

## NOTES

1. Cf. Buchanan (1995/96): "The mere fact that coexisting units of government exist
   and can be observed to do things differently exerts spillover effects on internal
   political actions. As a practical example, even though exit was of some importance, especially in Germany, the *observations* of Western economies, culture,
   and politics by citizens of Central and Eastern Europe were independently critical in effecting the genuine political revolutions that occurred in 1989–91. As
   an additional conceptual experiment, think about how much less vulnerable the
   communist regimes would have been if all of Europe had been under communist
   domination. Or imagine how prospects for the revolution might have fared in a
   world without television" (p. 263).
2. See also Lingens (2005): "The results were considered devastating for Germany,
   since its education systems came at the lower end of average. As soon as the results
   were released in the spring of 2001, many newspapers, politicians, and educators
   had opinions and suggestions for change. When data from PISA-E were released
   in spring 2002, it was a sensation for the press and a scandal for politicians and
   education authorities . . . .The term PISA Shock was used extensively throughout
   German political and educational circles" (p. 329).
3. There is a temptation to simply criticize PISA, and there is a large literature devoted to that task. For a balanced view, see e.g., Duru-Bellat (2011). Countries
   may also decide to opt out, as did South Africa when it retired, for a while, from a
   program comparable to PISA.
4. See Mandel and Süssmuth (2015) for an econometric analysis of popular
   response and the response of authorities at different tiers of the governmental system, all this in the intricate setting of (evolving) German federal
   arrangements.
5. The seven mentioned (note 10) are: *New York Times, Newsweek, International Herald
   Tribune, Washington Post, USA Today, Wall Street Journal*, and *Los Angeles Times*.
6. Even more strongly, Leonard (2005), a strong British supporter of European
   integration, wrote:

   > Europeans . . . are asking tougher questions of their own governments.
   > Commentators . . . have missed the revolutionary effect that European integration
   > has had on our national political debates. Because of the European Union, national
   > governments [are] being held to account in an entirely new way: their performance is

compared with that of their neighbours. Day after day, even Eurosceptic newspapers like the Daily Mail [are] showing that British tax-payers [are] paying above the European average. Increasingly, this "European average" pits EU governments against each other in terms of their ability to deliver key services, and gives a touchstone against which citizens can judge their national government's competence. When a survey showed that fewer Germans reached the top scores for literacy than in twelve of the fifteen European Union states, the government was forced to respond immediately with an investment programme totalling 4 billion euro to support all-day schooling. Tony Blair has made a commitment to raising spending on all public services to the European average. President Chirac has pledged to reduce the rate of corporation tax to "la moyenne européenne" within five years (p. 94).

We may accept Leonard's description of the phenomenon without being as sure as he is that the European Union is mainly responsible for it.

7. The audience targeted by some references to the international rank of the country is not the electorate but the legislature in Case, Rosen, and Hines (1993).

8. It is in such a setting, also, that the interesting contribution of Linos (2013) should be situated.

9. For a strongly liberal (pro-market) perspective in which political yardstick competition is nonetheless given a positive role, see Bernholz, Streit, and Vaubel (1998). They write: "While the possibility of exit protects minorities, the increased scope for interjurisdictional comparisons facilitates the control of governments by democratic majorities" (p. 5).

10. I neglect the case of decentralized federations in which regions have significantly different fiscal systems.

11. The discussion of the difference between comparisons of performance and comparisons of a change in a single tax remains relevant, however. As we will emphasize later in this chapter and even more in the next one, performance often reflects public policies over long periods, involving not only the present incumbents but also their predecessors, who might now be in the opposition.

12. The list includes Breton (1996), Lewis-Beck, Jérôme, and Jérôme-Speziari (2001), Breton and Ursprung (2002), Sand-Zantman (2004), Pitlik (2007), Redoano (2007), Cassette and Paty (2008), Devereux, Lockwood, and Redoano (2008), Kammas (2011), Leigh (2009), and Duch and Stevenson (2008). One may add Buchanan (1995/96), Bernholz, Streit, and Vaubel (1998), Leonard (2005), and Congleton (2007b), cited earlier.

13. Kayser and Peress (2012), Cassette et al. (2013), Hansen, Olsen, and Bech (2015), Mandel and Süssmuth (2015), Dassonneville and Hooghe (2015), Kayser and Leininger (2013, 2016), and Hory (2018), in particular, include empirical work.

14. It is also found that voters display a negativity bias: their only concern is Denmark "not falling behind" Sweden.

15. A more informal argument used by Kayser and Peress (2012) in favor of what we call yardstick voting is that incumbents were not punished for the ill-effects of the recession of 2008–09. They write: "If there were a single period in the last half-century in which voters should have uniformly punished their governments, one would expect it to be the great recession of 2008–09. Surprisingly, relative to their performance in the preceding election, the executive's party lost vote share in only 9 of 16 elections" (p. 661). I am not sure that the argument would remain valid if we allowed for a longer delay in voters' response (which indeed might not be completely over). One reason might be that the governments' response to the 2008–09 crisis (saving the financial system in particular and rescuing banks) was largely collective and coordinated, giving as a consequence discontented voters

a reason for incriminating the whole international set of incumbents without trying to differentiate among them.

16. The absence of yardstick competition in Redoano (2014) is signaled by a small difference with Redoano (2007) in the title.

17. An argument already used in Elhorst and Fréret (2009) as we saw.

18. In practice, the matter is more complicated. If we assume that citizens delegate some tasks to individuals, we may consider the ensuing relation as one of agency, with citizens as principals and the individuals entrusted with the task as agents. In that case, however, it is not clear whether agency should be considered bottom-up or top-down and accountability downward or upward. If, for instance, the said individual is an ambassador, the agency should be seen as top-down—akin to the agency relation, between political office-holders and bureaucrats, studied by Revelli and Tovmo (2007). If the individual is a magistrate in charge of deciding and implementing policies along many dimensions, the relation becomes more like the bottom-up agency relation central under representative government. In other words, the distinction between representative and direct democracy is relatively clear with regard to law-making but much less so with regard to agency. As noted, accountability can also arise outside any agency relationship when an ordinary citizen convinces the others to decide collectively something that proves wrong in retrospect. That citizen may be held responsible and even punished for what he or she said.

19. In Fukuyama (2011), a book spanning several thousand years and a large and heterogeneous spatial territory, what I call the central actor configuration largely dominates. One of the exceptions was "oligarchic dominance" in Hungary, discussed in chapter 25 of that book.

20. Cf. Bell (2001): "In Paris, by the end of the old regime, over 90 percent of men and 80 percent of women could read" (p. 84). The figures for Amsterdam and London are similar (Houston 2002).

21. As we saw in chapter 3, information asymmetry between ordinary members and leaders is also an important feature of unions and other interest groups. This is also true of political parties.

22. In the empirical work on interaction among subnational governments (chapter 5), municipal majorities are often treated as policy-making incumbents.

## CHAPTER 7

# Two heuristic models

This chapter presents revised versions of two models that I have often used since conceiving them several years ago. They are heuristic in the sense that, although they may stimulate thinking, they do not display the features supposedly required from models (but see chapter 9). I could as well have called them geometrical models, which would have reflected the appetite for geometrical reasoning that I acquired when studying international trade in the style of James Meade and Harry Johnson, but that might have made them even more objectionable.[1]

The first model is a counterfactual exercise about the way governments allocate their attention, effort, or resources among three uses: getting support from special interests, getting support from policies that satisfy common interests (economic growth in particular), and engaging in activities having no effect on support. The allocation is compared in two hypothetical states of the world, one in which the jurisdiction is informationally closed in the sense that there are no cross-jurisdiction comparisons by voters and the other in which the jurisdiction is informationally very open in the sense that the comparisons are compelling. A number of empirical predictions can be derived (or suggested) when it is assumed that openness has degrees and that its absence has remedies (checks and balances and federalism in particular). Hypotheses can also be derived or suggested from the bearing of yardstick competition on activities that are not support-enhancing but still valuable, in particular in the domain of international political relations.

The second model is about the effect of underperformance on policy-making. The reasoning is based on an interaction between two determinants of the effect: the degree to which citizens engage in and

respond to cross-jurisdiction comparisons and the degree to which governmental policies are constrained or change as a result of citizen's response.
The reasoning inspires a list of reasons why, in blatant cases of underperformance, yardstick competition may still not work.

It must be conceded that our focus on underperformance entails
neglecting a large part of the effects of yardstick competition and thus
underestimating the significance of the mechanism. For instance, the
fact that the comparative performance of a country in the economic domain is *above* average may have many interesting effects, some of them
quite substantial. It may allow the government to misbehave along other
dimensions—human rights, corruption, nepotism, etc. More positively, its
effect may be to allow the government to engage in policies that do not
increase electoral support although, according to some criteria, they have
some merits.

However, the decision to concentrate on underperformance is not only
for convenience. Because yardstick competition involves matters of information, perception, and issue salience, common sense suggests that underperformance tends to attract more attention than its opposite (Soroka
2006) and even that, often, only serious underperformance will be noticed
or have a significant political impact. There are also reasons more directly
related to the perspective that we have adopted. We are not interested
in popularity per se but in policy change, actual or potential, and, obviously, policy change is more likely to be triggered by bad than by good
performance. It must also be recalled that we characterized the yardstick
competition mechanism as a kind of security device, intervening as a substitute or complement to mechanisms that do not do their job properly.
This makes it more relevant almost by definition when performance is bad
rather than good.

## 7.1. FIRST MODEL: YARDSTICK COMPETITION AND THE ALLOCATION OF EFFORT

I try first to present the basic framework as simply and with as little
algebra and geometry as possible. I then introduce the absence or presence of yardstick comparisons as an exogenous element and compare its
effects on how governments or incumbents allocate their efforts. The
remaining of the section is derivative in different ways: constitutional
remedies, empirical predictions, and an application to international political relations.

### 7.1.1. The framework

The government is constrained by its access to a fixed resource $R_T$. It divides that resource into three different uses:

- promoting a macroeconomic goal such as economic growth ($R_Y$)
- transactions with special interest groups or categories ($R_G$)
- discretionary use ($R_U$)

Thus:

$$R_T = R_Y + R_G + R_U. \tag{1}$$

In association with the use of unspecified fixed resources, fit only for that purpose, employing $R_Y$ produces a macroeconomic outcome $Y$:

$$Y = Y\,(R_Y). \tag{2}$$

Under similar conditions, $G$ is the net level of support to special interest groups or categories achieved by employing $R_G$, that is:

$$G = G\,(R_G). \tag{3}$$

Both $Y$ and $G$ yield electoral support $S$:

$$S = S(Y, G). \tag{4}$$

Office-holders are not interested in $Y$ or $G$ per se but they want to remain in power. This requires a level of electoral support $S^*$. $R_U$ is the only use of the resource from which the government derives utility, other than remaining in power. The objective of the government is to maximize $R_U$ under the constraint:

$$S = S^* \tag{5}$$

The way the maximization works is represented geometrically in figure 7.1.[2] The variables are measured (starting from O) along the four axes delineating the four quadrants. The budgetary constraint (1) shows up in the SW quadrant in the form of triangle OMM′. The relations (2) between $R_Y$ and $Y$ and (3) between $R_G$ and $G$ are represented, respectively, by curve OF in the NW quadrant and curve OV in the SE quadrant. Their

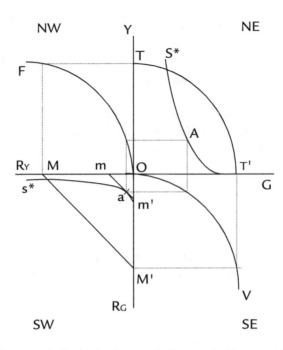

**Figure 7.1**: Allocation of effort in the absence of with no yardstick competition

shape reflects the usual assumption of decreasing marginal productivity of the variable factor. If the government kept no part of the resource for uses other than those two, any distribution between them would be represented by a point along MM' in the SW quadrant and would yield a combination of G and Y along the production-possibilities frontier TT' in the NE quadrant. However, as noted, the government maximizes $R_U$ and needs only a level of support $S^*$—represented by curve $S^*$ also in the NE quadrant.

That level of support can be also expressed in terms of inputs in the SW quadrant—that is, by curve $s^*$ (derived graphically from $S^*$). The distribution of R that maximizes $R_U$ under the constraint $s^*$ can be analyzed in that quadrant. It is represented by tangency point $a$ (that is, on a 45-degree line as close to the origin O as possible under the constraint of having a point in common with $s^*$). From that point $a$, one can in turn derive geometrically point A on the $S^*$ curve in the NE quadrant.

### 7.1.2. Differential information asymmetry

The information situation of citizens is reflected in the position and shape of support curve $S^*$. Information asymmetry means that citizens do not observe curves OF and OV. If they did, $S^*$ would be tangent to the frontier HH', its counterpart $s^*$ tangent to line MM' and thus no room left for $R_U$. As usual, the first consequence of information asymmetry is to generate an informational rent, here in the form of $R_U$.

The second consequence is a bias in the distribution of government resources between the two support-enhancing activities. In the absence of information about what obtains abroad, and given the nature of historical change discussed earlier, curve $S^*$ is almost vertical and the government devotes very little resource to $Y$ (that is, $R_Y$ is very small). Voters are uncertain about governmental efforts and competence with regard to both $Y$ and $G$ but they are more uncertain with regard to $Y$. Thus, variations in $Y$ have less impact on support than have variations in $G$. For a marginal variation in the resource to have the same effect in terms of support, whether the resource is spent on $Y$ or on $G$ (condition of interior equilibrium), one must be very close to the horizontal axis in the NE quadrant, or to the vertical axis in the SW quadrant—that is, the government must have devoted almost no resources to $Y$. In other words, as discussed in the context of multi-tasking by Holmstrom and Milgrom (1991), the less measurable task is sacrificed.

We could push the reasoning further and assume $S^*$ to be perfectly vertical and $s^*$ horizontal. That would reflect the assumption that variations in macroeconomic performance have absolutely no effect on support and, consequently, that absolutely no resources are devoted to that objective. In that case, equilibrium would be reflected by point $A$ being located on OT' and point $a$ being located on OM'. The information asymmetry assumption implies that some resource $R_U$ would remain to be employed discretionarily ($S^*$ cutting the horizontal axis before T'). This is the universe underlying a large part of traditional public choice thinking, in particular that which focuses on rent-seeking. In that universe, office-holders transact with interest groups, which constitute a subset of interest categories, and keep some resources for their own discretionary uses. As a consequence, worthy general interest objectives are sacrificed. This view justifies distrust in government and all the usual normative or prescriptive implications of that distrust.

When it is acknowledged that citizens compare policy outcomes in their country with what obtains abroad, the information asymmetry problem they face is mitigated. The improvement is larger where the problem was the most serious, that is with regard to common rather than special interest issues. To save on space, let me describe in words the change to be made in figure 7.1. The production function curves OF and OV, and consequently the production-possibilities frontier TT' are unaffected. The support curve

$S^*$ is now less vertical if not almost horizontal. Its counterpart $s^*$ in the SW quadrant reflects the change in such a way that the tangency point $a$ is on a 45-degree line more distant from the origin—which means a decrease in $R_U$—and at a position on that line reflecting an increase in $R_Y$. The effect on $R_G$ is ambiguous.

However, as an extreme case, one could imagine that growth performance, assessed by comparison with some foreign or international yardstick, would be so compelling that support curve $S^*$ would become horizontal and its counterpart $s^*$ vertical. $R_G$ then would be equal to 0: transactions with interest categories would be fully abandoned. The model, which belongs to statics, is not well fit to deal with that case. Still, we will see that the possibility that yardstick competition over growth becomes excessively compelling may explain some features of the arrangements observable in the real world.

### 7.1.3. Constitutional remedies

I did not know Holmstrom and Milgrom's (1991) analysis of multi-tasking when I developed the model from which the exposition in the text is derived.[3] With some changes in the interpretation of the variables, figure 7.1 could serve nonetheless as a geometrical treatment of their main point. For instance, a schoolteacher's job could include two tasks, one (noted $G$) consisting of teaching basic skills (reading, spelling, counting), the other (noted $Y$) of "socializing" children. It is much easier to measure what has been achieved with regard to the first task than it is regarding the second. Alternatively, an academic assumed to teach and do research might be promoted or paid according to his or her performance in terms of research publications ($G$) with much less uncertainty than in terms of what can be known of his or her teaching ($Y$). Because the principals can more easily measure and thus reward $G$, there is a tendency on the part of the agent to sacrifice $Y$, that is to devote to it little effort or resource (small $R_Y$).

Hence, the idea—if complementarities allow—of separating the two tasks, that is, of assigning each to a different job (and thus person). This is one of the solutions suggested by Holmstrom and Milgrom. In fact, in Salmon (1991), the introduction of constitutional or quasi-constitutional constraints and arrangements also corresponds to that idea. When, in an informationally closed society, the matter is the tendency to sacrifice macroeconomic performance, the constraints and arrangements in force at a constitutional level may be called checks and balances. They include separation of powers, meta-rules limiting government intervention in the economy, independent central bank, federalism or decentralization—that is, in the last case, the transfer to subnational governments of some of the powers originally given to central government. Consequently, "government" must be reinterpreted as "the executive branch of the central government." Even if it were doing nothing, some levels of macroeconomic performance and of transactions with interest categories would obtain— the latter involving then the sub-central governments and the legislative branch. Federalism is particularly important: the yardstick competition between governments that would by assumption be impossible at the level of the central government would then take place at subnational (i.e., regional and local) levels.

I will not reproduce here the change in the geometry used then to express these possibilities (see Salmon 1991). Let me just indicate the general idea. Both curves OV and OF now start at a distance from the origin and are flatter. The production possibilities frontier TT' is closer to the origin, reflecting the cost of checks and balances, but government (that is, the executive branch) gets less rent or discretionary resources and is possibly induced to devote relatively more effort to macroeconomic performance compared to transactions with interest categories.

The problem, in an informationally very open society, might be the reverse one—consisting in the risk that the political dominance of macroeconomic performance generated by yardstick competition leads to an excessive reduction of the attention given to special interest groups or categories. In Salmon (1991), the quasi-constitutional constraint suggested then is a "ratchet rule": give more to interest categories if the country ranks well in terms of macroeconomic performance and safeguard at all costs what has been given except if it becomes clear to all that this prevents a macroeconomic performance equal to what obtains abroad. In geometrical terms, it corresponds to obliging government to choose the intersection between the horizontal or quasi-horizontal support curve and the frontier—that is, to give up any informational rent. In later work (Salmon 2003b), I suggest a different constitutional solution to the same possible bias. It consists in decentralizing to subnational governments policies targeted to special interest categories, so that the concern of the central government with macroeconomic performance does not lead to their elimination.

An objection must be mentioned at this stage. In the industrial or labor-economics context Holmstrom and Milgrom (1991) are concerned with, it is natural that a principal, at some meta-level, redesigns jobs and reassigns tasks. However, it is not natural in the setting we are concerned with. Rather heroic assumptions on the relationship between constitutional and infra-constitutional decision-making are needed. Functionalism looms, as it does in fact in any theory of constitutional design inspired by the economic theory of incentives. Let me gloss in part over the difficulty and formulate the matter as follows. In the absence of the meta-rules or quasi-constitutional arrangements just mentioned, citizens would not forever remain unaware of the biases incurred. In democratic settings, one might speculate that, sooner or later, some candidates or parties would put the issue near the center of the electoral debate. As a consequence, eventually, something in the direction suggested by the model would be done to mitigate at least some of the effects deemed harmful.

### 7.1.4. Empirical predictions

A number of empirical predictions were suggested in Salmon (1991). To summarize, let us say that when one moves (transversally and/or over time) toward more openness to information from abroad, the model (complemented by the quasi-constitutional remedies just discussed) suggests three consequences: checks and balances become less relevant, transactions with special interest categories more entrenched, and rates of economic growth more aligned. With regard to the first two consequences, the tentative evidence provided at the time has not fared too badly.[4] With regard to the third, it has.

Investigating that failure reveals an aspect of the yardstick competition mechanism that makes it more complex than assumed so far. In Salmon (1991), it was pointed out that the economic growth of the six founding member countries of the European Community over the period 1967–87 was almost perfectly aligned. On average GNP was multiplied by 1.81 with none of the six countries differing from it by more than 0.08. The claim based on these figures was modest. It was argued that because the said countries "should be as sensitive to comparisons of macroeconomic performance as one can reasonably hope for in this imperfect world," if their performance had diverged, this would have been "certainly annoying for our model" (pp. 178–79). If we repeat that exercise for the period 1990–2015, GNP per capita at purchasing parity was multiplied by 2.43 on average, but the figures for the Netherlands and Italy were, respectively, 0.20 above and 0.41 below that number. Therefore, to be consistent over time, we must concede that these results are "annoying for our model." At the same time, they suggest a way in which the reasoning should be complemented.

Let us look more closely at the cases of France and Italy. The relative underperformance of the Italian economy is clear from the figures just cited. In the case of France, there has been no decline in absolute terms, but the relative decline since 1981 and especially since 1990 has been significant. Income per capita moved from 10 percent above to 5 percent below the OECD average (Morrisson 2015). In 2002 France and Germany had more or less the same GDP per head; in 2016, it was 17 percent higher in Germany than in France (*The Economist*, March 4, 2017). Thus, it is clear that yardstick competition has not prevented Italy and France from falling behind. However, and this is the aspect of yardstick competition on which we must insist at this stage, in both countries falling behind has progressively become a major issue in the political debate among political parties and candidates, reflecting the fact that cross-jurisdiction comparisons of economic performance have gained a prominent place in the reflections of many voters. The generalized awareness of underperformance has generated a lot of political instability (taking different forms in France and in Italy because of the specificities of their political systems).

One might say that yardstick voting is confirmed even though yardstick competition proper is or seems inoperative. Why? In the terminology of our model, the answer must be sought in the transactions with interest categories rather than in checks and balances (of little importance at least in France). In Salmon (1991), as a corollary of the ratchet rule mentioned above, a second meta-rule was suggested: "if it is demonstrated (for instance by rapid majority rotation) that the level of transactions with interest categories prevents the country from achieving macroeconomic performance equal to what obtains abroad, then, and only then, can these transactions be reduced somewhat" (p. 177). This would necessarily take time. Morrisson (2015) is quite pessimistic (even more for France than for Italy) about the likelihood that the process of economic decline will be reversed or even stopped. If we take yardstick voting and competition into account (which he does not), we can be more optimistic than he is with regard to the likelihood that a process of catching up will eventually take place.

### 7.1.5. Yardstick competition and international political relations

The implication of the model we want to focus on is international leadership. But, before turning to it, we must note that yardstick competition (independently of the model) may have other implications on international political relations. To give one instance, it may add something to the explanation of international rivalry. Cross-border contests between incumbent governments can easily be misinterpreted as competition among countries, which then seem to be engaged in zero-sum games although economic theory suggests that they are not. Both the theory of international trade and macroeconomics suggest that an exogenous increase in income per head in country A should be welcome in country B, but we can observe that this is not always the case. Politicians in country B will not always remain shy of invoking economic competition or even "economic war" to comment the fact. Of course, this can be partly justified or explained by some of the qualifications formulated in economic theory, by the persistence of mercantilist fallacies, or by relative-income psychological motivations. However, one should also consider the possibility that the attitude follows from the situation of cross-border rivalry in which politicians in office rather than ordinary inhabitants are placed. Indeed, yardstick competition implies that incumbents and citizens are objectively in different positions with regard to the performance of other countries.

The theory of leadership or hegemony we are interested in owes much to Kindleberger (1976). According to that author, the international economic order can be achieved only if one country plays the role of a leader or "stabilizer." The proposition has been extended, beyond economic matters, to international order in general and to international regimes and institutions (Keohane 1984). The view that, in a setting of anarchy (that is, when there is no overarching authority), the hegemony or leadership of a single country can impose order and stability is hardly new. But it is usually associated with the idea that the hegemon or leader exploits the others. Kindleberger's analysis is inspired by the idea, stressed in Olson (1965), that the reverse may well be more important. For collective action to take place, it may be necessary that the small exploit the large.

The reasoning is simple. International order is largely a non-excludable public good. Each country has an incentive to free ride and the effect may be that the good is not produced. A country sufficiently large to reap a large part of the benefit of the public good may ensure that the good gets produced. For that purpose, it can force the other countries to contribute or it can let them free ride - "coercive leadership" or "benevolent leadership" in the terminology proposed by Snidal (1985a, 1985b). The said other countries will always welcome the latter, but they can also welcome the former when their forced contribution is less than the benefit they derive from the public good—that is, from international order.

The crucial point for Kindleberger (1976), Keohane (1984), and our own analysis is whether the large country is willing to fulfill the leadership role. The question arises not only when leadership is benevolent but also when it is coercive provided it entails a net cost of provision for the large country. Nevertheless, to simplify, let us assume that leadership is benevolent. The model offers one way to discuss the matter (see Salmon 1992). The following assumptions are necessary for that purpose:

- international leadership of the benevolent kind consumes resources—that is, in our model, part of $R$
- it is not support-enhancing
- the incumbent maximizes $R_U$ under the constraint of reaching $S^*$, as analyzed in the model
- the incumbent may derive from leadership (and its positive effect on international order) some utility; in other words, spending on leadership is one of the possible uses of $R_U$
- only countries that are large can play the role of leaders, large however being relative to the public good or setting considered (world order, European Union, Eurozone, OPEC, Mercator, etc.) and leadership being possibly exercised not by only one but, collectively, by a small number of countries

Under these assumptions, variations in $R_U$ may cause variations in the same direction in the willingness to exert leadership and on the likelihood that leadership will take place. Kindleberger and Keohane are mainly concerned with the erosion of the leadership of the United States. According to Salmon (1992) "if there has been an erosion of American leadership, this is mainly because the macroeconomic performance of some other countries has eroded the freedom of the American government to engage in non-support enhancing activities in general and in those involved in leadership in particular" (p. 378).

In Salmon (1992), however, the case mainly discussed was the new role that Germany could play in the European Union in the wake of German reunification and other changes in the central and eastern parts of Europe. Those events were making Germany both larger and more central. As an application of the views defended by Kindleberger, it was argued in the paper that a German hegemony should be welcome rather than feared. But as an application of the model it was also argued that it was unlikely, intense yardstick competition among the member countries of the European Union leaving little room to incumbents for spending resources on activities that were not support enhancing.

Has the prediction been confirmed? As noted earlier, yardstick competition since then did not work as predicted. We mentioned the relative underperformance of France and Italy. The relative success of Germany is also well documented. It could have given its government the resources to engage in non-support-enhancing activities and then play a leadership role of the benevolent kind. The German government responded differently. It did play a leadership role in a sense but mostly not, I think, in the sense discussed earlier in the tradition of Kindleberger, implying exploitation of the leader. The German incumbent government behaved as if its dominant concern was support by its voters—even more of it than was strictly necessary. In the terms of our model, the relative performance advantage enjoyed by Germany was employed to reach a support curve $S$ to the right of $S^*$ rather than to increase $R_U$ and engage in activities such as leadership that had no direct electoral benefit.[5] As a consequence, the public good of European Union and Eurozone stability was produced to an insufficient degree, allowing the widespread feeling of skepticism about Europe that developed in the 2010s.[6]

## 7.2. SECOND MODEL: THE IMPACT OF COMPARATIVE UNDERPERFORMANCE

To what extent are governments constrained by citizens' cross-country comparisons? The reasoning that follows distinguishes between two sets of factors. The first is related to the availability of the relevant information and the attention the population gives it. The second concerns the political set-up. The strength of the constraint introduced by the yardstick comparisons will depend on how much discontent a performance gap would generate in the population and to what degree that discontent translates into effective pressure on incumbents. We discuss the matter first in general terms and then as a list of reasons why yardstick competition may not work.

### 7.2.1. The framework

The framework can be presented succinctly by reference to figure 7.2. I turn to some comments afterward. In figure 7.2., the variables represented along the two axes are more or less those indicated in figure 3.2. Here, they are called underperformance and discontent. Underperformance is supposed to be objective. At the same time, it is supposed to be comparative or relative in the sense that it relies on what obtains in other jurisdictions as a yardstick. One may suppose that it was established by competent experts with the help of meaningful international comparisons (meaningful in the sense of taking into account specifics such as natural resources, natural disasters, etc.). Thus, one may indifferently speak of underperformance or relative underperformance.

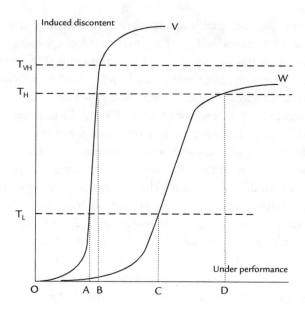

**Figure 7.2**: Tolerable underperformance

Curve OV indicates, for a given country or jurisdiction, what would be the effect of underperformance on citizens' discontent. It reflects both the extent to which citizens would be able and willing to use cross-jurisdiction comparisons so as to perceive underperformance and the effect of that perceived underperformance on their aggregate level of discontent. The S-shape of the curve was explained in chapter 2. Curve OW, which concerns another country or setting, lies at the right of curve OV and has less slope because all or some of these relations are looser (to yield the same level of discontent, more underperformance is needed).

Will citizens' discontent induce a policy change? We make the rough assumption that some level of discontent would be considered politically intolerable and thus would trigger a policy change. And we assume that the said level—that is, tolerance limit or threshold—is an indicator of an important characteristic of the political regime or set-up. We will call that characteristic "discontent sensitivity" or "responsiveness." For a given country and a given category of policy issues, the said indicator is expressed in figure 7.2. as a horizontal line. Three of these lines are drawn, representing three tolerance thresholds, noted $T_L$ (for a *low* level of tolerance), $T_H$ (for a *high* level) and $T_{VH}$ (for a *very high* level), corresponding respectively to high, low, and very low discontent sensitivity or responsiveness.[7]

Intersections between the horizontal lines and curves OV and OW indicate the maximum underperformance politically tolerable without policy change. Four values of that maximum are represented on the horizontal axis. Point $A$ corresponds to a combination of the factors mentioned making the yardstick mechanism work well and point $D$ to a combination making it work poorly. The mechanism does not work at all when there is no intersection. In figure 7.2 this occurs when the level of information and the discontent effect correspond to curve OW and the political situation to horizontal line $T_{VH}$. Point $B$ reflects a situation in which policy-making is not very responsive whereas even a small underperformance causes much discontent. As a result of the first characteristic, only a relatively high level of discontent would trigger policy change, but, as a result of the second characteristic, that high level of discontent could be brought about by a degree of underperformance that is relatively small. Point $C$ corresponds to a situation in which office-holding is very responsive but in which the attention the population gives to underperformance is mediocre. A small degree of discontent would trigger a policy response but underperformance would have to be relatively important to cause even that degree of discontent.[8]

### 7.2.2. Discussion

In past presentations of the diagram or variants thereof (e.g., here in chapters 2 and 3), I was not always consistent in labeling the vertical axis. In fact, it is rather indifferent for our purpose whether the variable measured on that axis is dissatisfaction, discontent or support loss. This is largely because the underlying relations are assumed to be monotonic: variations along the horizontal axis have either no effect on the variable measured on the vertical axis or an effect always in the same direction. Thus, more underperformance either has no effect on discontent or increases it. More discontent either has no effect on support or increases support loss. Thus, overall, more underperformance either has no effect on support loss or increases it. As explained in chapter 2, this must be understood in probabilistic terms. The aggregate effects of an increase in underperformance can be summed up as single numbers—that is, an increase in the expected degree of aggregate discontent or an increase in expected support loss. I refer to discontent because it is more intuitive and seemingly less dependent on a probabilistic framework than political support. It also appears more versatile—that is, more capable of fitting comfortably with all kinds of societies, regimes, and circumstances.[9]

In Salmon (1997), the stress was put on differences between political regimes—in the case of democracies, between electoral systems. A given level of discontent, it was argued, will not have the same effect under a system of majority rule allowing rapid changeover in office of competing political parties and making, thus, office-holding highly contestable and under proportional representation systems in which voters cannot but with great difficulty get rid of rulers whom they do not like. In the first case, I argued, we have maximum democracy according to the already cited Popperian definition of democracy as a system "in which we can get rid of bad rulers without bloodshed." Accordingly, in Salmon (1997) horizontal lines like those in figure 7.2 were meant to correspond to different political regimes (including electoral regimes in the case of democracies). Moving upward along the vertical axis, four regimes were distinguished and referred to as high contestability, partitocracy, authoritarian, and totalitarian. Because of their electoral systems, Britain and Italy illustrated high contestability and partitocracy respectively.[10]

In the context of this model at least, I have come to think that it is better to refer only to the degree to which policies respond to discontent or support loss (whether actual or potential)—that is, to give up any characterization of the constitutional or electoral regime beyond the characteristic suggested by the responsiveness indicator itself. I also abstain from referring to political change, understood as the replacement of the incumbent. The relationship between these political characteristics and responsiveness would require a much more elaborate analysis than the simple classification I used in Salmon (1997).[11]

As explained at the outset (chapter 1), if we are essentially interested in policy change and only indirectly or instrumentally in political change, this is first of all because our domain is political economy rather than political science. But there are more interesting reasons to gloss over political change. One is that the underperformance analyzed does not necessarily concern a highly important and salient issue such as, for instance, economic growth. Suppose that the horizontal axis refers to a policy dimension with low salience or only capable of attracting the attention of a small number of voters. Even under the assumptions of probabilistic voting and intense political competition—implying that every voter counts—it is implausible that office holders would be thrown out if they crossed the tolerance threshold regarding underperformance along that dimension. However, because secondary issues apprehended together do count politically (e.g., in electoral terms), under the said assumptions it is reasonable to expect that *on average* office-holders will change their policies so as not to cross the said threshold.

Another reason is the possibility already noted that much time is needed for underperformance to reach the tolerance threshold and/or for reforms to have a significantly positive effect on performance. This in turn has two implications. First, accountability is blurred: underperformance has been building up under different administrations or party coalitions so that the whole political personnel are in a sense responsible for it. This may strengthen some anti-establishment movement but not to the point of making credible a replacement both of the incumbents and the candidates of the opposition who were in office earlier.[12] Political change, then, as sanction or retribution, is often unfair and incomplete although, as a threat, it can still constitute an incentive. Second, although policy changes aiming at improving performance are immediately necessary to satisfy voters, their actual effects on performance are often observable only later, at a time when the present incumbents might not be in office any more. As noted, the first PISA report was a shock in Germany in 2000–02. It did impose a change of policies (complicated by federalist assignments of responsibilities), and that change did produce after a lag of about ten years the significant improvement acclaimed internationally. In the meanwhile, different coalitions had alternated to govern the country at the federal level.

Finally, it must be stressed that political change often fails to trigger policy change. We mentioned earlier relative economic decline in France and Italy. In both countries public opinion was well aware of the phenomenon. In France, that awareness explains in part the striking fact that the outgoing majority lost eight out of the nine legislative elections that took place from 1981 to 2017 (it won only in 2007). In the French semi-presidential system, who is in power depends on who wins the legislative election.[13] Thus, in France, retrospective voting or the "rascals out" mechanism seemed to work almost to perfection under the majority voting system, generating a changeover in power of the same two parties at each election (except one) until 2017, when for the first time voters eliminated both. Nonetheless, policy change of the magnitude needed to alleviate relative decline did not occur. It is too early at the time of writing to say whether that discrepancy will disappear as a consequence of the 2017 elections, based like the others on majority voting, but which brought a drastic political personnel renewal.

### 7.2.3.  A checklist of reasons for ineffectiveness

Some empirical implications of yardstick competition among national governments have already been discussed in the context of the first model. For instance, empirical support was mentioned for the proposition that the more the economy of a country is open—and thus presumably the more its government is constrained by yardstick competition over macroeconomic variables such as growth—the more the country relies on, or tolerates, corporatist arrangements and the less it needs checks and balances. One could also add that government is likely to be larger.

Here, we focus on a single aspect of the mechanism, tolerance of underperformance, as illustrated in figure 7.2. Some variables already alluded to are now interpreted as obstacles to the working of the political yardstick competition mechanism at the level of national governments. We take as a starting point or benchmark the proposition that, thanks to the mechanism, the relative underperformance of a country should be limited, and thus convergence from below to the average should prevail—that is, *if there were not some obstacles, in need of identification, to the efficacy of the mechanism.* In other words, serious and enduring underperformance constitutes a *puzzle* that needs to be investigated, the inquiry being organized around the question: Given the possibility of yardstick competition, why, in the case of this particular country and particular issue, do we observe substantial and persistent underperformance? That question might inspire an econometric treatment, but we will remain content here to develop it as a checklist. As suggested when discussing figure 7.2, ineffectiveness— that is, large tolerable underperformance—typically requires a conjunction of obstacles related to the form and position of the S-shape curve and obstacles related to the position of the tolerance horizontal lines. Let us first simply list some categories of obstacles.

(1) Are there significant physical or quasi-physical obstacles, imposed by the rulers, to the availability of cross-border information? Many authoritarian regimes use coercion to limit access. Democracies do not, in general. So far, the net effect of technical progress has been a reduction in the rulers' capacity to control cross-border information flows, but it is not certain that this will not change in the future.

(2) Do the rulers succeed in biasing information in other ways (influence on television channels or newspapers, propaganda, manipulation of statistics, etc.)? This is standard practice in authoritarian regimes and does happen occasionally also in democracies.

(3) Are there non-political (e.g., cultural, linguistic, religious, spatial) obstacles that prevent the public from gathering or recording information about the situation abroad? It has been claimed that some ideologies and religions (Islam in particular) may have caused obstacles of that kind (see Buruma and Margalit 2004, Glazer 2009, Paldam 2009, but see Bellaigue 2017). As discussed in chapter 6, a lack of interest or curiosity regarding developments abroad may also be a

cultural characteristic that is natural among the people of a large and rich country such as the United States.

(4) Is relative underperformance objectively ambiguous and thus difficult to assess? For instance, income per head and economic growth may be conflicting economic indicators, as was the case of the United Kingdom after the Second World War. Or, underperformance may be masked because it also affects neighboring countries, as has been the case, over some periods of time, in Africa, Latin America, and Europe.

(5) Are different personal preferences and interests (e.g., age, attitudes toward inequality, environmental concerns, preference for leisure) entailing different opinions on the question of whether a well-perceived level of relative performance is or is not relevant?

(6) Are there reasons for the whole population or a majority of the electorate to simultaneously be well aware of underperformance and not want the policy changes that would alleviate it? This is the main explanation of some cases of persistent regional underperformance suggested in Salmon (2010).[14] The effect is typically augmented by the tendency of many discontented inhabitants to leave the jurisdiction—an instance of *exit* undermining *voice* as discussed in Hirschman (1970) and here in chapter 4.

(7) More generally, would the incumbents lose more support than they would gain if they undertook to change policies so as to increase performance?[15]

(8) Do permanent features of the political system (autocracy, electoral system, veto players, clientelism, etc.) tend to make policy-making generally or structurally irresponsive to popular dissatisfaction?

(9) Does the current political configuration (e.g., salience of a religious or ethnic issue, absence of credible opposition, popularity of the leader) tend to make policy-making contingently irresponsive to popular dissatisfaction stemming from perceived underperformance?

The first six possibilities underlie, in figure 7.2, the shape and position of curve OW, whereas the last three concern the position of the horizontal threshold lines $T_H$ and $T_{VH}$. The list is tentative. Its purpose is only to illustrate the kind of inquiry which could be made for a given country or category of countries. For a given country, several of these possibilities should be analyzed as operating together, as suggested in the model.

The strategy we have in mind is in a sense similar to that underlying two articles published in the December 2010 issue of the *Journal of Economic*

*Literature.* Their titles are: "Why isn't Mexico rich?" (Hanson 2010) and "Why have economic reforms in Mexico not generated growth?" (Keohe and Ruhl 2010). As these titles suggest, in both cases the analysis starts from a puzzle.[16] On many grounds, one would expect Mexico to have become rich, but it has not. Given the thorough and apparently meritorious market-oriented reforms implemented in the late 1980s and early 1990s under the influence of the best experts (including one of the authors of the second article), isn't it puzzling that Mexican growth has remained so relatively feeble?[17]

The explanations provided in the articles do not refer to yardstick competition, or, for that matter, to any political variable.[18] They point to weaknesses such as insufficient protection provided to creditors (in particular because of faulty bankruptcy procedures), perverse inducements in favor of the informal sector, rigidities in the labor market and ineffectiveness of public education—the latter mainly responsible if we follow Hanushek and Woessmann (2010).

From our perspective, the question is why have these weaknesses not been addressed so as to improve growth? And, more precisely, why has not the pressure from yardstick competition been sufficiently strong to impose reforms in these matters? This brings us back to our checklist, which, we may suggest, should be added to, or merged with, the list of possibilities discussed in these articles.

Obstacles to the working of yardstick competition included in that checklist may or may not be serious depending on country characteristics and other circumstances. Obviously, I am definitely not suggesting that they are so serious that, as a general proposition, yardstick comparisons cannot have any effect on government performance. Such a proposition, however, is implied in the following opinion expressed by Fukuyama (2015) about the relation between citizen information and government performance:

> The theory that there should be a correlation between the increased availability of information about government performance and the quality of final government outputs rests on a number of heroic assumptions—that citizens will care about poor government performance (as opposed to being content to benefit from practices like ethnic-based patronage); that they are capable of organizing politically to put pressure on the government; that the country's political institutions are ones that accurately transmit grassroots sentiment to politicians in ways that make the latter accountable; and finally, that the government actually has the capacity to perform as citizens demand. (pp. 16–17)

As explained at length in chapters 2 and 3, we need no heroic assumptions of the kind mentioned by Fukuyama. Thus, not all but some citizens must "care about poor government performance"; even unorganized citizens and their "inaccurately" transmitted "grassroots sentiment" do have, in particular through elections, some influence on government behavior and performance; and governments do have some inclination and capacity to respond positively to some citizens' demands. As it is formulated here, Fukuyama's criticism targets a straw man and, ironically, lacks realism.

## 7.3. CONCLUSION

I called heuristic the two models presented in this chapter but I could also have called them vintage, since their mode of presentation was already obsolete when I conceived them. My justification, if there is one, is postponed to chapter 9. The two models have another feature in common: strategic interaction is largely glossed over and the focus is placed on how a jurisdiction responds to its citizens observing what happens elsewhere. In the first model the direct effect is to reorient priorities toward policy objectives of general interest rather than focused on interest categories. In the second model, there should be a limit to underperformance. In addition to the main message that each tries to convey, the implications, propositions, or distinctions derived from them offer a convenient introduction to questions that should have been discussed in any case. For instance, the fact that economic growth in a country exposed to yardstick competition is durably inferior to that of its neighbors suggests that the content of public debates or the possibility that the gap is in a sense voluntary, two matters important in themselves, should be considered.

## NOTES

1. See, for instance, Meade (1952), Johnson (1973).
2. The model is inspired by the specific-factors model of Jones (1971) and figure 7.1 by the diagram Caves and Jones (1985) use to present it.
3. Earlier versions of Salmon (1991) were presented in various seminars and conferences (Villa Colombella Seminar, European Public Choice Society, Journées de Microéconomie Appliquée) in 1988–89.
4. I will not attempt to update the little rank correlation exercise that showed a positive relationship between openness and various indicators of "corporatism" available at the time (Salmon 1991).

5. Not only true leadership but also long-term domestic tasks such as maintaining infrastructure have tended for a long time to be sacrificed in Germany. At a time of negative or very low long-term interest rates on German government bonds, it seems particularly puzzling that infrastructure has been starved of investment for so many years. See e.g., Guy Chasan, "Cracks appear in Germany's cash starved infrastructure," *The Financial Times,* August 4, 2017.

6. The historical reasons why Germans were generally reluctant to see their country become a hegemon or a leader are well known, but the sheer relative size of that country and its economic performance since reunification could not but give it that role de facto. The obstacle to a joint leadership involving also France and/ or Italy was the bad relative performance of these two countries. The query formulated in the text is about the nature of the leadership and of the convictions that inspire it. Since we assume that the choice is discretionary, the personal characteristics and inclinations of the individuals in office are decisive.

7. Thresholds of that kind are usually associated with the requirement that voters coordinate their votes (Ferejohn 1986). This is not necessary if we assume that discontent leads only to a decrease (of a magnitude varying across individual voters) in the probability that they will support the incumbents. See Fearon (2011).

8. B is to the left of C in the diagram but as we will see this could easily be the other way around.

9. Although quite intriguing, I neglect the public administration literature on the determinants of dissatisfaction (see James and Moseley 2014 and the references therein).

10. As the diagram was drawn, that difference between the two countries was outweighed by a difference in sensitivity to cross-border comparisons (that is, by a difference between the respective S-shaped curves), Italy being more open to cross-border comparisons than Britain. If we transpose the argument made then to figure 7.2, this would put Britain at the intersection of line $T_L$ and curve OW, making $C$, on the horizontal axis, the limit of tolerable underperformance, whereas Italy would stand at the intersection of line $T_H$ and curve OV, with tolerance for underperformance at $B$—that is, much smaller. In the light of experience since 1997, one may now find the outweighing result much too optimistic as far as Italy is concerned. The order of the horizontal lines and of the S-shaped curves of the two countries might still illustrate basic differences between them, but their aggregate effect on the horizontal axis would now make Italy more rather than less tolerant of underperformance than Britain ($B$ and $C$ remaining the labels for Italy and Britain, $B$ would now be to the right of $C$).

11. According to *The Economist* (passim.), the Chinese regime is *responsive* but not *accountable*.

12. At least, that was the case before the French elections of 2017 and Italian elections of 2018 (one should perhaps add the presidential election of 2016 in the United States).

13. In the French semi-presidential system, if there is a contradiction between the outcomes of a presidential and a legislative election, the latter prevails, with the prime minister (supported by the legislature) instead of the president fulfilling almost all of the functions imparted to the executive branch.

14. The basic idea is simple: underperformance is correctly perceived and generates discontent but no pressure for change ensues. Contrary to what the inhabitants say, they prefer the status quo to any realistic alternative (for instance autonomy or independence). In these cases, the basic framework of information asymmetry

between office-holders and citizens—or even the distinction between rulers and ruled, agents and principals—although still ostensible, is in reality irrelevant or inconsequential. The situation would not be different if the characteristics of direct democracy were openly operative.

15. That formulation allows us to include cases of domination of society by a social class or so-called elites without compelling us to gloss over the role of government and renounce methodological individualism—as seems to be the case for instance in Acemoglu and Robinson (2005). See chapters 3 and 6 for an elaboration of that argument.

16. Hanushek and Woesmann (2010) also start their analysis from a puzzle about growth in Latin America.

17. Curiously, Kehoe and Ruhl (2010), who spend a lot of time comparing the growth of income per head and of productivity in China and Mexico, argue in the end that the comparison is not really justified. The conditions for rapid catch-up growth are not the same in the two countries because the income per head of Mexico is still much higher than that of China. Thus, negative characteristics that do not cause too much harm for China at the present stage of its development do hamper growth in a country like Mexico, whose productivity is less distant from the productivity level of the more economically advanced country. The ambiguities displayed in the article illustrate the difficulties mentioned in point 4 of our checklist

18. With one exception, Hanson (2010) noting that "in 2006, it was in part disillusionment with the economy that brought Mexico within a hair's breadth of electing a populist president who campaigned on reversing earlier liberalization" (p. 988).

# CHAPTER 8

# Vertical interactions

T he organization of this chapter is very simple. I consider first some changes that must be made in the analysis of horizontal yardstick competition among governments when these governments are part of a governmental system in which there are other tiers. I turn afterward to vertical competition—that is, competition between governments situated on different levels of the system. Finally, I discuss vertical interactions and yardstick competition in the context of the European Union.

## 8.1. HORIZONTAL YARDSTICK COMPETITION IN MULTILEVEL SETTINGS

In this section I assume that yardstick competition remains purely horizontal in the sense that the competing governments are at the same tier of the governmental system, for instance competition among municipalities or competition among regional governments. However, the existence of other tiers is acknowledged, and this complicates the analysis in two ways. One is shared outcome responsibility, the other split principals.

### 8.1.1. Shared responsibility for outcomes

The traditional approach to the division of responsibilities across tiers may or may not entail serious problems for yardstick competition. It does not when the division is assumed to be about well-defined classes of public outputs and when tax revenues are assumed to cover expenditures at each tier. Central governments are in charge of defense or macroeconomic conditions; municipalities of maintaining streets, roads, gardens, and public amenities on the communal territory; regional governments are possibly in charge of education or health care, and so on. Voters can compare macroeconomic outcomes across countries, public amenities across towns and cities, and education or health care conditions across regions. They also can make cross-jurisdiction comparisons of taxes or tax rates,[1]

However, the traditional approach opens the door to serious complications when it acknowledges the existence of grants or transfers and thus of what has been called "vertical fiscal unbalance": governments at one tier spend more than they tax and the gap is filled by grants or transfers received from governments at another tier—the most common case being that of transfers from central to sub-central governments. The usual justification for such arrangements is that governments at some tier have a comparative advantage in taxation and governments at another tier in providing some categories of public goods. What is generally seen as the main drawback, compared to a more transparent system in which governments on each level would have to rely on their own taxes or tax rates, is reduced accountability and distorted incentives. There is a large literature on that matter (see, e.g., Ahmad and Searle 2006, Ambrosiano and Bordignon 2015, Boadway 2015). Vertical fiscal unbalance may certainly complicate the task of voters who want to make cross-jurisdiction comparisons. Still, as we will see, in some respects it can also make their task easier.

Vertical fiscal unbalance can be seen as a form of partial or incomplete decentralization, the focus on fiscal variables being convenient for representing in a tractable way other, more complex, manifestations of the phenomenon. The complexity should not be overlooked, however. It is possibly greater in unitary states than in federations, although in the latter complexity may characterize at a lower tier the relations between regional governments and municipalities, for instance. An instance of complexity, studied in Breton and Salmon (2009), concerns the implementation of environmental rules. Enactment, monitoring, and enforcement of those rules are tasks—each divided into very different activities—that are typically distributed or fragmented all over the governmental system. For instance, monitoring may rely on inspectors but also on external actors such as environmental associations; or, instead of or in addition to coercion, enforcement may call for the provision of information and other forms of assistance. Governments at different jurisdictional tiers are not equally equipped to engage in these different activities. In the short or medium term, their comparative advantage depends on general and long-lasting systemic arrangements largely unrelated to specific domains such as the environment. There are three main categories of limits to the capacity of a government at a given tier to contribute in a given way to the implementation of environmental rules. The limits may stem from the law and the general architecture of the governmental system (who is authorized to do what? and with what means?), from insufficient organizational or processing resources (in particular, the absence of trained, field personnel), and from the size of its financial resources (or constraints on their use). Thus, French regions, contrary to the state or to municipalities, have almost no enactment power and scanty processing capacity. However, they have financial resources that can be employed discretionarily. Thus, the main way in which French regions contribute to the implementation of environmental rules and objectives is through financial support.[2]

Although they do refer to efficiency in a setting of vertical competition, Breton and Salmon (2009) are mainly concerned with the positive analysis of why, in the policy domain studied but also in other domains, responsibility is almost unavoidably shared among several jurisdictional tiers—a matter already addressed in Breton (1996). From a more openly normative perspective, Joanis (2014) also studies vertical complementarity among different tiers of government, in his case with regard to the provision of a local public good. His main point is that partial decentralization is desirable only if the benefits of complementarity outweigh the costs of reduced accountability. That result is derived from a political agency model in which "a central government and a local government compete for the support of the same voters (though in separate elections) by each contributing to the good" (p. 36). That formulation, which has illustrious antecedents, will be discussed later.[3]

How do citizens cope with shared governmental responsibilities? Brosio (2007) offers an interesting solution, in the form of an index of decentralization we will refer to as the Brosio Index. The idea, quite original, is formulated as follows:

> In a completely centralized system of government the probability of reelection of the central government depends on the level of provision of both national and local goods, while in a completely decentralized system, the central government is electorally responsible only for the provision of national goods. The degree of decentralization can thus be inferred from the impact of the provision of local goods on the re-election prospects of the central government. (Brosio 2007, p. 183)

The index itself compares the coefficients of impact on electoral support, *for the central government*, from the provision level of two public services, one (D, say defense) clearly centralized, the other (H, say health care) partially decentralized. If the impact coefficient of H is zero (i.e., if variations in H have no impact on support at the central level), H can be said to be fully decentralized. If the impact coefficients of H and D are equal, H can be said to be fully centralized. In between, the more apart the two coefficients, the more H is decentralized.

One might object to such reliance on the subjective views of voters. However, the usual, supposedly objective, assessments of decentralization miss something important that the Brosio Index captures. The views of voters are important to elected office holders and thus the Brosio Index does signal objectively important feedback effects on the reality of decentralization as measured by other means. One such effect is stressed in Brosio and Jimenez (2015). If partial decentralization essentially means vertical fiscal imbalance—here the central government supporting financially the production of H through a grant—the higher the Brosio Index, the greater the incentive for the central government to make sure that voters are satisfied with H and thus the greater the incentive to maintain or increase that grant. This is seen by Brosio and Jimenez as one solution to the problem of commitment by the central government to continue financing decentralized spending through grants, a matter quite important in unitary states.

However, if we assume (as justified later) that a state being unitary implies that the tasks can be reassigned by the central government alone, the effect of a high Brosio Index could also be to affect negatively the level of decentralization as measured by conventional means. The fear of voters becoming dissatisfied with H might induce the central government to become more involved in the organization and production aspects of H and, if need be, rather than maintain or increase grants, recentralize a number of the activities that had been assigned to the local governments. In other words, the commitment discussed in Brosio and Jimenez is conditional on the good behavior of decentralized governments—which suggests something like implicit contracting.

Brosio defines his index independently of horizontal yardstick competition (which he discusses separately). The index refers only to incumbents at the central level. I will make three remarks on yardstick competition in the context of the present discussion. First, in the case of a grant allocated fairly, cross-jurisdiction comparisons made by voters should help them to disentangle the influence of the central government and that of the junior ones on observed outcomes. Suppose that the central government reduces overall transfers, or transfers in a given domain. For voters at the sub-central level these variations in grants generate a shock whose magnitude they cannot observe or assess. When the grants are reduced, some local governments will increase their own taxes while others will reduce provision levels; few will manage to keep both categories constant. By assuming a common shock, voters may infer from cross-jurisdictions differences an assessment of the effort made by their elected local governments. Second, if financial transfers are tailor-made and can be influenced by lobbying from the local governments, voters may include in a positive way the ability to obtain transfers in their assessment of the performance of local incumbents (see Boarnet and Glazer 2002, Bordignon, Gamalerio, and Turati 2013). Getting subsidies is considered one of the merits of a good governor or mayor. When this is the case, voters can engage in cross-jurisdiction comparisons (of outcomes) without taking grants explicitly into account. Third, grants from central governments are often supposed to have a redistributive function. In economics, the matter is generally discussed in purely empirical terms or from a normative perspective, with no reference to political economy (e.g., Boadway 2015). From a political economy or systemic perspective, an objective of equalization (through grants or a redistribution formula) could be to create what has been called in another context a level playing field, making competition among local governments more relevant. Breton (1987) insists on that objective of equalization, which he calls the promotion of "competitive equality" (p. 311). [4]

### 8.1.2. Split principals

In the principal-agent relationship assumed so far, the incumbents are the agents of only the voters. But, we noted in chapter 4 (in the context of what we called career concerns), that performance may not be assessed only by voters and/or, if judged good, may be rewarded not by re-election but by promotion to a better job. We considered the mechanisms involved then as close to but distinct from yardstick competition as characterized in chapter 2. We return now to the matter, this time in the context of a multi-tier government. One of the possibilities opened in that setting is that office-holders at one subnational tier of the jurisdictional system are the agents both of voters and of some authority at a higher tier. This can be referred to as a hybrid version of yardstick competition: a mixture of top-down and bottom-up horizontal yardstick competition.[5] It is helpful to start with the simpler case of pure top-down horizontal yardstick competition even though it is not yardstick competition in our sense.

In the pure case of top-down horizontal yardstick competition, the whole governmental system is seen as a single organization controlled from the top. Mayors, governors of regions and provinces—or local party leaders if the ruling party is the main locus of power—are unelected officials. They are given some autonomy and are rewarded or punished according to the relative performance of the governments or jurisdictions they are in charge of. Thus, they are in a situation of horizontal yardstick competition, but the performance comparisons are made from above—by other unelected officials at a higher subnational tier or by the political rulers themselves at the top. The reward may be a promotion to a more important jurisdiction at the same or a higher tier. But it may also simply consist of being confirmed in the same job. As analyzed in particular by Maskin, Qian, and Xu (2000) and Xu (2011), that organization of government makes it similar to an M-form corporation. Its main strength is the provision of incentives, and its main drawbacks are spillovers and the non-exploitation of some economies of scale. In the case of China, analyzed in detail by Xu (2011), it seems that the incentives worked and the drawbacks did not materialize (see also Caldeira 2012). Markevich and Zhuravskaya (2011) treat Khrushchev's *Sovnarkhoz* reform as an attempt to adopt an M-form of governance and find that it was successful (in terms of economic growth) only for subsets of regions sufficiently diversified, self-contained, and similar.

By itself, that M-form organization of governance does not require that the political regime be autocratic. A blueprint can easily be conceived in which democracy, although perfect, operates exclusively at the level of the central government. The democratic government then appoints prefects and other representatives to administer the different territories. In other words, the nature of the central government, democratic or autocratic, is irrelevant. What counts is, first, that the prefects can be appointed or dismissed discretionarily by the incumbents at the top—at least partly on the basis of comparative performance –and, second, that in administering the territories, they implement the incumbents' policies with due regard to the specificity of local needs and conditions. Because of the assumption of adaptation to local needs and conditions, and also because of the role given to comparative assessments of performance, the blueprint is very different from the way unitary state governance is traditionally modeled in public finance.

There has clearly been a tendency in France toward implementing something like the said blueprint. That tendency arose in the first half of the seventeenth century (with the institutionalization of the *intendants*, ancestors of the prefects) and was stopped or reversed (perhaps only temporally) with the decentralization reforms of the early 1980s (summarized in Salmon, 1987b, 2000a)—municipalities, already made largely autonomous by a law of 1884, being an exception. It is one of the main points made by Tocqueville (1856) that centralization was strengthened by the French Revolution. As he wrote: "The marvelous ease with which centralization was restored in France at the beginning of the nineteenth century should no longer surprise us. The men of 1789 had toppled the edifice, but in the very soul of its destroyers its foundations have remained intact, and upon that foundation it was possible to rebuild it rapidly, and more solidly than before" (ed. 2011, p. 70).[6]

However, no democratic country is completely centralized; nor are autocracies that are not wholly totalitarian. In France, in spite of their ascendancy, the intendants were confronted with many local powers: aristocratic, judiciary or, even (in cities) popular. The prefects, after the said law of 1884, had to interact with elected mayors, many of them simultaneously elected members of parliament. Both intendants and prefects were often by-passed by local or provincial notabilities who negotiated directly with the ministers in the central government. Progressively, and more radically in the early 1980s, the responsibility of elected officials in the territories became as or even more important than that of the representative agents of the central government. That sharing of responsibilities—a form of partial decentralization—could also be called a hybrid, but I will reserve the term for the arrangements in which elected local incumbents themselves are accountable to some authority at another tier as well as to voters. They are the agents of split principals, as discussed below.

Such sharing may take place through political parties rather than within the official governmental machinery.[7] In most democratic countries, competition among national parties is multilevel. Parties are usually concerned with the aggregate electoral success of their candidates in all jurisdictions (national, regional, and local), which gives them an incentive to endorse candidates, including incumbents, who are likely to be assessed positively by voters. Thus, comparisons made by voters across jurisdictions—assumedly, for the moment, at the same jurisdictional tier—remain relevant. However, political parties internalize the effects of policies adopted at one level on outcomes at the same tier as well as at other tiers. This constrains the policy choices of all incumbents. They cannot always adopt the policies most likely to produce outcomes assessed positively by their own voters. As indicated at the outset, their principals are both these own voters and party officials responsible for electoral outcomes overall—see Wrede (2001) for a model along a similar line.

The role of national, centralized, political parties has been noted by many scholars. Enikolopov and Zhuravskaya (2007) attribute to Riker (1964) the view that "only strong national political parties achieve the necessary balance between national and local interests" and that "local politicians internalize interjurisdictional externalities of their policies in the search for promotion and political support by their national governing party because the party cares about national-level performance" (Enikolopov and Zhuravskaya 2007, p. 2262). The assertion is strong because it is based on the assumption that national centralized parties are themselves strong. But this is not always the case, and in a given country party discipline may vary over time as well as in regard of the jurisdictional tier considered. More generally, the "balance between national and local interests" is a question that can be addressed from different perspectives, not necessarily focused on political parties. In Brosio (2007), whatever the decentralization arrangements, voters may consider the central government as keeping a shared responsibility in the provision of local goods. As we saw, the implications can be stability in financing the provision of these goods but also instability in decentralization itself. In the vertical competition framework proposed by Breton (1996), to which we turn now, yardstick vertical competition is hypothesized to ensure that a form of equilibrium obtains that involves all jurisdictional tiers.

## 8.2. VERTICAL COMPETITION AMONG GOVERNMENTS

Vertical competition among governments is associated with the name of Albert Breton who, since 1981, has pleaded for its importance and analyzed many of its aspects.[8] To situate his views on the matter, it is helpful to first characterize different approaches to vertical competition. After the discussion of the main points in Breton's theory, we will discuss the specific problems raised by vertical competition when the assumed setting is that of a unitary state.

### 8.2.1. Competition for what? Three approaches

Among the three main approaches to answering that question, only the third is vertical yardstick competition. The first approach is the most intuitive. The image typically conveyed by the idea of vertical competition is that of a rivalry between governments at different jurisdictional tiers for resources that are, in some sense, scarce (i.e., subject to "rivalry in consumption"). If one tier gets more, that implies that another gets less. An obvious instance of such resources is the tax base. Increased taxes at one tier reduce the tax capacity that can be exploited at another tier. Tax sharing arrangements may hide the underlying competition, which is more visible when there is "fiscal concurrency"—that is, when "distinct levels of government exercise some discretion in levying taxes on substantially the same base" (Keen 1998, p. 459). Actually or potentially, vertical tax competition is a general feature of decentralized fiscal systems.

Other resources used in the production of public services may also be objects of vertical competition. They include office space, qualified staff, promotion in the public media, and so on. Scarcity, understood less literally, may also be found on the other side of the budget or the production functions: the provision of public services and responsibilities or involvements may also be considered scarce resources. Which level of government is to get involved in the organization of the Olympic Games? Will it be the main city? the region? the national state? All of them possibly, but then in what order or to what extent? Again, the existence of agreements is not an objection to a competitive interpretation. Agreements may be the outcomes of a typically opaque competition among government at different tiers to get a greater role or say in the collective undertaking.

The motivation generating the desire to get more taxes or to be more involved may be related to human weaknesses such as vanity or hubris or to the tendency generally ascribed to bureaucracies of seeking ever-larger budgets. It may also reflect a legitimate concern on the part of sub-central jurisdictions with being visible, being recognized by other institutions and by the public.[9]

The second answer to "competition for what?" also refers to rivalry for a scarce resource but this time a particular one, situated at the center of democratic governance: support from the people. The expression Pettys (2003) uses as a title for his interesting article is: "competing for the People's affection." It is directly borrowed from some writings of the framers of the US Constitution, in particular the contributions of Hamilton in the *Federalist Papers*. As Pettys documents, the said framers, as well as many scholars after them, developed the view of a competition between two levels of government (referred to as two "sovereigns") for the affection, trust or loyalty of the People, an "affection" itself based on the perceived comparative performance of governments at the two tiers. For a less romantic or more down-to-earth formulation, let us interpret "affection" as "support" and "the people" as "many citizens."

In the United States, the way support was shared between the two levels of governments changed over time: mainly in favor of the states during most of the nineteenth century (although less so toward the end of that century and at the beginning of the twentieth century), strongly in favor of the federal government during the New Deal and the decades following it, then again in favor of the states since Ronald Reagan. To cite Pettys again:

> Such shifts may reflect broad-based disenchantment with or affection for one sovereign or the other, or they may reflect a narrower judgment that one sovereign is more likely than the other to regulate specific areas of concern in a satisfactory manner. These shifts in sentiment and power do not always occur quickly—they may be more akin to the turns of an ocean freighter than to those of a speedboat—but they do occur. (p. 352)

It is not clear that an analysis focused on federalism in the United States can be applied without substantial change to other federations, not to speak of unitary states. But for a theoretical characterization of the second approach, we need only the skeleton of Pettys's interpretation. It is enough that citizens have preferences (of a quasi-constitutional kind) about the distribution of powers or tasks across jurisdictional tiers, that these preferences may change, notably as a consequence of the relative performance of governments at the different tiers, and that the said citizen preferences count or even prevail. Formulated in this way, the approach may be applied to many settings and phenomena: for instance, in many countries the greater "affection" of citizens for local (municipal) rather than for national or regional government, or, in the European Union the widely-noted "disaffection" of European citizens for "Brussels."

The third approach is vertical yardstick competition, a direct extension of horizontal yardstick competition among governments to the relationship between governments at different tiers. Under that approach, incumbents, more or less absent in our characterization of the first two approaches, are now major decision-makers together with voters. The principal competition in which incumbents are engaged is with their domestic challengers for the support of the voters located in their own jurisdiction. To single out pure vertical yardstick competition, we must say that the electoral success of an incumbent depends on comparisons made by the voters of his or her jurisdiction between what obtains there and what obtains in the other jurisdictions in which *these voters also vote*. Thus, the comparisons made by inhabitants of Toronto who participate in the federal, provincial, and municipal elections are between the federal government of Canada, the provincial government of Ontario, and the municipal government of Toronto. As in the horizontal setting, yardstick competition is generated by each of the three incumbents (the prime minister of Canada, the premier of Ontario and the mayor of Toronto) undertaking to make the government he or she leads well placed in the comparisons made by "his" or "her" voters between its performance and that of the other two.

Obviously, that blueprint calls for some comments. Contrary to what was the case under the second approach, it is now assumed that voters do not have any preferences regarding the assignment of powers. To distinguish the approach from the analysis of Breton discussed later, we must also assume powers to be exogenous (then, as in the horizontal case, the effects of yardstick competition only concern performance, not the assignment of powers). Information asymmetry is assumed to be essential to the yardstick competition mechanism, whether vertical or horizontal. Because voters are physically present in the jurisdictions concerned, they have a more direct knowledge of many policy outcomes in each of the jurisdictions than they can have in the horizontal setting, in which part of the required information is about places in which they do not live.

That superiority is offset, however, by the fact that comparability is structurally problematic. Vertical comparisons of performance cannot concern the simple items typically assumed in the horizontal case (the level or variation of a particular tax for example). Admittedly, some categories of services (e.g., police or museums) may be provided in a comparable way at the two levels (Salmon 1987b, Bodenstein and Ursprung 2005). Another possibility is the comparison of general efficiency indicators such as the "Wicksellian connections" discussed below. Some general features of government activities or behavior may also be compared: for instance, discrimination or gender practices and policies, speed and courtesy of response to demands, displayed frugality of officials, absence of corruption, trustworthiness, quality of web sites, etc. However, most of these features tend to remain somewhat peripheral to the main concerns of citizens. Overall, comparability or commensurability is perhaps the main problem encountered by vertical yardstick competition. The problem is compounded by another difference with horizontal competition, which is that the governments that are compared vertically typically interact in the same policy areas in complex and largely unobservable ways, rendering their respective performance difficult to disentangle.

One should also consider political linkages through multi-tier parties (Santolini 2009). The fact that voters vote for or against incumbents at two or more tiers raises the question of relations between the votes in addition to and complicating that stressed in the yardstick competition mechanism. In particular, if (as is the case in most countries, but not in Canada) centralized political parties have candidates and office-holders at the two levels, then the relatively superior performance of an incumbent at one level may have a positive rather than negative effect on voting for the incumbent at the other level if both incumbents are of the same party.[10] That "coat-tail effect" has been shown to be important in the United States. Another possibility is "split-voting." Voters who want to hedge their bets do not vote for the same party at the two levels. These phenomena and the effects of vertical yardstick competition may be difficult to disentangle in practice (Zudenkova 2011).

Lastly, since the effect of comparisons across jurisdictions is first of all informative (the actual effect on policy-making is more indirect), considering only comparisons made by voters of the several jurisdictions they inhabit is somewhat restrictive. Suppose that the competition is between the federal government of Canada (hereafter Ottawa) and the provincial government of Ontario (hereafter Ontario). Voters in Ontario compare the performance of the two governments and this has an effect on their support for incumbents at the two tiers. What about the observation by voters in Ontario of the performance of the provincial government of Quebec (hereafter Quebec)? Suppose that Ontarians perceive the performance ranking as follows: Quebec first, Ottawa second, Ontario third. This ranking is bad for the Ontario incumbent because of yardstick competition, both vertical and horizontal. What about the Ottawa incumbent? The observation by Ontarian voters of the superior performance of Ottawa over Ontario has a positive impact on their support for the Ottawa incumbent but the observation of the superior performance of Quebec over Ottawa has a negative impact, even though Quebec is not a party to the vertical yardstick competition between Ontario and Ottawa. We may consider the second effect (the negative impact) as a side or external effect of vertical yardstick competition between Ottawa and Quebec. Alternatively, we may contemplate merging vertical and horizontal yardstick competition, which will require a strong assumption about the objects of comparisons. A consistent framework is provided along that line by Breton (1996, 2006), as we will see now .

## 8.2.2. Breton's theory of vertical competition

Breton's views on competition among governments have evolved since they were exposed at length for the first time (Breton 1987). Breton (2006, n. 13, pp. 102–103) indicates that an important turning point was Breton and Fraschini (2003a). As presented in particular there, these views make up a consistent whole, which we might refer to as Breton's theory of intergovernmental competition but which, for reasons explained later, I prefer to refer to as Breton's theory of vertical competition—in any case related to but distinct from his analysis of "intragovernmental" competition (Breton 1996, part 1).

Let me start with a summary of Breton's theory. Governments compete among themselves because office-holders seek the support of citizens, and citizens determine their support on the basis of their comparative assessment of governments' performance. To be precise, office-holders in jurisdiction $J$ want the government of jurisdiction $J$ to be well placed in the comparisons that voters in $J$ make with other jurisdictions. That motivation being also active in other jurisdictions, a yardstick competition among governments ensues. The object of voters' comparisons consists in what Breton calls Wicksellian connections. The expression rings a bell among learned students of public finance but perhaps not very much elsewhere. In Breton's words, "a Wicksellian connection is a link between the quantity of a particular good or service supplied by centers of power and the tax price citizens pay for the good or service."[11] The hypothesis formulated in particular in Breton and Fraschini (2003a) is "that citizens will evaluate the relative performance of governments in terms of the tightness of Wicksellian connections—both horizontally and vertically" (Breton 2006, p. 93). Because tightness can be made a "common standardized variable," citizens can compare tightness in their own jurisdiction with tightness in others situated at the same or at a different tier of the governmental system.

However, vertical competition remains specific because a government has some latitude to occupy the policy domain of governments whose jurisdictions are situated at other tiers (which is impossible horizontally). Given that possibility, whether or not a government will decide to be involved in (i.e., occupy) a particular policy domain will depend on the expected effect of that decision on the tightness of Wicksellian connections. In that way vertical competition is "a mechanism that helps determine equilibrium assignments of powers in federal states and in decentralized unitary states" (Breton 2006, p. 86). As this sentence—which opens the paper—shows, Breton's theory is above all focused on the assignment of powers among different tiers of the governmental system.

This is the first point we will note about Breton's theory. As even more explicitly emphasized in Breton (2015), his long-standing main objective is to provide a positive theory of federalism and decentralization, the positive perspective being, in his opinion, practically absent from the literature. If we understand "assignment of powers" broadly more or less as the distribution of involvements or responsibilities across policy domains Breton's concern is similar to the focus of the first two approaches to vertical competition that we summarized previously. As in these approaches, Breton's analysis purports to explain the distribution of powers or responsibilities among tiers of the governmental system. However, contrary to the first approach, he gives citizens or voters an essential role in the assignment. And, contrary to the second approach, these citizens or voters play that role unwillingly and unconsciously. They have no preferences whatsoever with regard to the question of who does what. In this, they are similar to the voters assumed under the third approach, based on yardstick competition.

Does that similarity of voters' attitude on that particular matter (assignment) imply a similar attitude or role in general? That question brings us to a second point about Breton's theory, one which refers more to his writings in general than to what he says about vertical competition in particular. Breton's views on the relationship between citizens and officeholders are not centrally developed within the principal-agent framework that inspires us throughout the present book.[12] They are more inspired by a public finance tradition of seeing governments as suppliers and citizens as consumers of goods and services, which allows discussing their interaction in terms of supply and demand.[13] Citizens make comparisons across jurisdictions in the same way as consumers make comparisons across supermarkets or restaurants, the difference being, however, that citizens cannot change their supplier (the Tiebout option being excluded by assumption) whereas ordinary consumers can. Their motivation is not to reward or sanction incumbents, after having made sure that their assessment is as fair as possible, but to purchase the goods and services they want at as little cost as possible. The decision to vote for the incumbent or for a challenger is instrumental to that sole objective.

That difference with the agency framework has the following implication. In supply and demand settings, information imperfections in general and asymmetric information in particular tend to be considered secondary complications, of a kind that, at a sufficiently high level of theorization or abstraction, can be glossed over, whereas in the agency framework they remain central whatever the level of abstraction.[14]

Thirdly, an interesting implication of Breton's theory is that (contrary to the first approach to vertical competition) it can account for restraint and withdrawal as well as for expansionism and invasion. To render Wicksellian connections as tight as possible by comparison with other jurisdictions, an incumbent may decide to be less involved in or even withdraw from some policy domain. Thus, the theory can accommodate without difficulty the observed tendency, for instance in domains such as the environment, to "pass the buck" (Harrison 1996, Breton and Salmon 2009). In the context of vertical competition, one example in France is the reluctance of many mayors to create a municipal police, even when it might seem particularly needed and even though it already exists in neighboring communes. These mayors claim that the national police alone should do all that is necessary on their territory to deal with crime whatever its level or nature.

Fourthly, another implication of the theory is a tendency toward asymmetric assignments—Breton (2006, p.101), see also Costa-Font and Rico (2006) on the health system in Spain. The fact that a US state like California gets involved in a policy domain previously occupied exclusively by the federal government does not imply that all other states will follow suit. However, two other mechanisms must be considered that could induce some other states to mimic California: one is horizontal yardstick competition, the other is policy learning. It is not necessary to restate the reasons (given in chapter 4) why in both cases imitation may or may not occur.

The fifth and obviously most needed comment is about Wicksellian connections. In themselves, they are not as distinctive as they seem and giving them a major role not as astonishing. In fact, they are close to the efficiency ratings (i.e., comparative indicators of the technical efficiency of the public sector) on which there is now some significant amount of empirical work both at the level of countries (Alfonso, Schuknecht, and Tanzi 2005) and at that of local jurisdictions (see Kalb, Geys, and Heinemann, 2012, and the references therein).

I have mixed feelings about some aspects of that work. The results are interesting but should be interpreted with even greater care or caution than they typically receive. Intuitively, efficiency ratings compare something like "value for money;" theoretically, they compare something like distance from the production frontier. We do not shop only on the basis of value for money and we are taught at an early stage of economic education that, if consumers' utility counts, a point on the production frontier is not better than an infinity of points inside it. These limitations should be recalled more strongly than there are in most contributions.[15] At the same time, it must be conceded that drawing conclusions from efficiency ratings might be less misleading than drawing conclusions from comparisons of taxation or public spending levels apprehended separately.

These remarks are about that matter in general, but they also have a bearing on Breton's theory. In fact, one may formulate two queries about his hypothesis that the tightness of Wicksellian connections can be estimated and compared across jurisdictions by voters and thus become an object of yardstick competition among governments. One, theoretical or conceptual, is the extension to voters of the reservations just formulated about the lessons one should draw from the empirical findings. Assuming for the moment that voters make correct estimates and comparisons, what implications on support to the incumbent should voters derive from them? Paying more and getting less is unambiguous. But what about paying much more and getting a little more, with the consequence of less comparative technical efficiency (i.e., a looser Wicksellian connection)? Is electoral support to the incumbent likely to be always reduced and never increased as a consequence? It does not seem that Wicksellian connections can do the job assigned to them in that case, which is certainly not untypical (think about spending substantially more to improve only somewhat protection against terrorism).

The other query is about the capacity of voters to estimate and compare efficiency rates across jurisdictions. I have already referred to Breton's solution, which comes down to: "let us assume that voters have that capacity," period. I do sympathize a lot with that, very Chicago School, attitude. If nonetheless we want to delve into the matter, the answer might be different for horizontal and vertical competition. As noted, Geys (2006) finds some spatial interaction among localities in Flanders with regard to efficiency ratings and investigates whether it could be the result of horizontal yardstick competition. He justifies the question by expressing the belief that "people have at least some impression about the efficiency of government provisions in there and neighbouring jurisdictions" (p. 447) and by referring to the proposition that "it is important . . . that voters take into account burdens of taxation as well as public services" (Geys 2006, p. 446, borrowed from Salmon 1987b, p. 33). Although his data provide only "moderate support" for the role played by yardstick competition in the spatial interaction, there is no reason why new attempts along the same line should not prove successful. Indeed, in domains such as education, where the quality or quantity of outputs is relatively measurable and comparisons across jurisdictions by organizations such as the OECD are largely circulated and advertised, some comparisons in terms of value for money have entered the political debate: for instance, voters are informed repeatedly, through a variety of channels, that, per student, their country spends more and gets a less satisfactory result than is the case in some other, designated, countries. This is a clear message based on efficiency comparisons or Wicksellian connections that voters can easily take notice of.

In the case of vertical competition, more or less the same reasoning can be applied when governments at different tiers provide similar services. Voters may observe that, in a particular domain, the government of one of the jurisdictions they inhabit does more or better with limited means than does the government of another of the jurisdictions they also inhabit, even though the latter spends more. That solution, in any case applicable to only a small proportion of governmental activities, is definitely not the one sought with the Wicksellian connections hypothesis. The assumption that citizens will make comparisons across jurisdictions about the value of a single, common standardized variable solves many theoretical difficulties in a way that is much more interesting even if it is also much more demanding.

Demanding does not mean impracticable. We can be reasonably optimistic about the capacity of further empirical research to exploit the assumption in a fruitful way. There are cues that citizens often reason instinctively in terms similar to those assumed in the theory. For instance, the feeling seems widespread among the inhabitants of Northern Italy that their regional and municipal administrations are more efficient, do a better job, than the national administration of Italy as a whole (this often explains their quasi-federalist leanings). A comparable belief can probably be observed in Catalonia, Bavaria, California, or Flanders. Variations in that opinion might be recorded statistically and related in some way to yardstick voting and yardstick competition.

### 8.2.3. The protection of vertical competition in unitary states

The most convenient habitat for the theory of vertical competition is a governmental system that is federal and has two tiers. But that configuration is not that widespread when we consider reality rather than the way it is discussed. To distinguish federal and unitary systems of government, one could refer to constitutional constraints in general, but it is more interesting for our purpose to employ the narrower concept proposed in Breton (2000): ultimate power ownership (in fact also of a constitutional nature). To characterize a governmental system, that criterion should be crossed with the number of tiers. When there are only two tiers, an unambiguous distinction is possible: in a unitary system, all powers are ultimately owned by the central government whereas in a federal system, some powers are ultimately owned by the central government and others by the governments at the second tier.

When there are more than two tiers, one should take into account the unitary or federal nature of the relation between tiers, the criterion remaining ultimate power ownership. The two most common patterns are unitary systems (all ultimate power ownership at the center) and hybrid systems in which the relation between the central government and second-tier governments is federal, but the relation between second-tier and third-tier governments is unitary (no ultimate power ownership at the third tier or below). Consequently, one can say that most observed governmental systems are totally or partially organized around a relation between tiers whose nature is unitary. The United States is generally considered a federal country but the nature of the relation between the government of California and that of Los Angeles is unitary. This increases the practical relevance of the question of vertical competition in unitary states.

A unitary relation between two tiers means that governments at one tier own no ultimate power. The implication for vertical competition is obvious: how can these governments compete with those that can deprive them of some of their powers? In particular, how can winners of a vertical contest get protected against retaliation by the losers when the latter can change the rules? Vertical competition in a unitary state is the topic of Salmon (2000a) with reference to France and of Breton and Fraschni (2003a) with reference to Italy—see also Costa-Font and Rico (2006) on Spain. The following discussion borrows mainly from Salmon (2000a).

Three mechanisms may operate to prevent the central government from eroding the powers that it itself assigns to lower tiers of government. The first is constitutional constraints. In France and Italy, as in many other unitary states, the constitution includes some recognition and protection of subcentral government. The effectiveness of that protection is a moot point. Breton and Fraschini (2003a) are much more sanguine about it with regard to Italy than Salmon (2000a) is with regard to France. Breton and Fraschini stress the role of the judicial system and in particular the Constitutional Court (see also Breton and Fraschini 2003b, and, for Spain, Costa-Font and Rico 2006). They could have relied also on the political difficulty, normally greater in Italy than in France, of modifying the constitution.

The second mechanism is the representation of lower levels of government within the decision-making apparatus of the center. An example is the Bundesrat in Germany (as was originally the Senate in the United States). In Italy the so-called *Conferenze* (state-cities, state-regions, or unified) play a role along that line, as does the Senate in France.

In that country, what counted much more until recently is a phenomenon known in French as *cumul des mandats*, that is, multiple office holding. That practice, whose elimination was completed with the 2017 legislative elections, was an essential characteristic of the way the French institutional system worked. Many decision-makers who counted at the national level (including ministers, until recently) were also important decision-makers at the subnational level and vice versa. About half the members of parliament also had important functions in local, departmental, or regional governments whereas many mayors of large cities and presidents of regional or departmental councils were also members of one of the two houses of parliament (see Foucault (2006), François and Weill (2016) and the references therein). Obviously, the practice had many negative effects but, for our purpose, it had the virtue of giving subcentral governments a means to resist attempts by the central government, including its powerful bureaucracy, to erode their autonomy. Now that the *cumul des mandats* no longer exists, and at a time when the current majority in the lower house of parliament is large (which could facilitate constitutional change), the protection of subcentral government may have to rely even more than before on a third mechanism.

That third mechanism resides in popular opinion. As noted, the assumption that voters have preferences of a quasi-constitutional kind on the assignment of powers is contrary to Breton's views as we interpret them but central to what we called earlier the second approach, presented then in a context of federalism. In the context of decentralization in unitary states, perhaps more than in the case of federal ones, it seems unavoidable. If people are satisfied with or attached to the current state of affairs, it may well prove perilous for the incumbent politicians in the national government to try to change it substantially. That mechanism is likely to be particularly effective to protect municipal government, which is generally more liked by the general public than the other tiers, but some constituencies may also display a strong attachment to these other tiers—sometimes (when historically significant), the regions, sometimes (especially in rural areas), the départements or, in Italy, the provinces.[16]

Public opinion may also have an influence through, ironically, its perception of the fact that the central government owns all the ultimate powers. We saw that effect already when discussing the Brosio index. The central government is evaluated also with regard to what is done at the subcentral level. Since it can change decentralization arrangements, the central government is rightly perceived as ultimately responsible for the performance of the whole governmental system. In federal states such as the United States and Canada, the blame for many things that do not work well can be put on the states or the provinces. This is less easily done in unitary states even when they are quite decentralized.

An important aspect of the existence of more than two tiers should be noted in that context. In many countries there are at least three jurisdictional tiers. In France and Italy there are four: central state, regions, departments or provinces, municipalities. Let us assume three: central, regional, and municipal governments. In federations, as noted, the relationship between regional and municipal government is most often unitary: powers are ultimately owned by regions and cities are at the mercy of regions. In unitary states, powers are ultimately owned by the central state, not by regions. This provides a fourth mechanism for the protection of vertical competition, albeit restricted to the relation between regions and municipalities. The central government monitors and if convenient, protects the vertical competition operating between regional governments and municipalities. In France, as argued in Salmon (2000a), along many dimensions vertical competition was more intense at the bottom—that is, between regional, departmental, and municipal governments (independent from one another)—than at the top—that is, involving the central government.

At the time of writing that paper, except possibly with regard to the French départements and Italian provinces, whose extinction I predicted if not recommended, I tended to judge that competition rather favorably.[17] This was in the late 1990s. I think that the perspective has changed. In the public debate, in France in particular, the costs of decentralization have become more prominent than its benefits, with competition among subcentral tiers being considered a major reason for those costs to have increased. Of course, more decentralization might be a way to control costs if it took the form of less reliance on grants and greater subcentral tax autonomy and responsibility. That could still happen. Still, currently, there seems to be less interest in decentralization and its virtues in general. In France as in Italy, underperformance of the country as a whole has become the major concern. As noted in chapter 7, when this happens, all existing arrangements might be reconsidered as a consequence. As we will see next, systemic implications of European integration also have some influence on the way decentralization in general is considered (Salmon 2002).

## 8.3. THE EU CONTEXT

European integration matters for our discussion in several ways. Many of the rules under which Europeans live are decided in Brussels. The EU institutions (hereafter Brussels) make up in many respects (especially regulation) an additional jurisdictional tier of the governmental systems of the member states. As such, one is tempted to determine in normative terms which powers should be assigned to Brussels and which should be left to the member states. The large literature inspired by that agenda is not without merits but on the whole, it has not really proved very realistic.

European integration is a peculiar process, mainly political, whose distinctive nature has misled eminent economists into formulating distressingly naïve or simplistic predictions. The Eurozone has not collapsed, Greece has remained a member, Italy has not defaulted, no other country has emulated Brexit, and populism has been at least as successful in countries outside rather than inside the Eurozone. As I argued in Salmon (1995), the European integration project is very much about generating, through a convoluted process, attachments or ties that will prove sufficiently strong to resist disintegrating shocks, whatever their origin. It definitely is a conspiracy, but fundamentally by the peoples themselves against themselves rather than against them by their governments or so-called elites.[18] Recent events confirm that the undertaking was worthwhile. There have been very serious shocks but so far, the ties have held. What are the implications of these features for the relationship between European integration and yardstick competition? Let us distinguish again between the horizontal and the vertical relationship and start this time with the latter, even though its relation with yardstick competition is more indirect.

### 8.3.1. Vertical relationships: the centralization process

At a popular level of discussion, it is claimed from different quarters that there is a competition between Brussels (or the bureaucrats there) and the governments, or perhaps directly the peoples, of the member countries. That claim suggests the existence, at least from a systemic perspective, of a vertical competition between the two tiers. But the scope for vertical competition involving the European Union is quite limited. At any rate, we should not start the reflection from its possible existence. With regard to vertical relationships, the main phenomenon, and the one most discussed in the public debate, is the centralization of regulatory power at the level of Brussels (only some narrow-minded economists are more concerned with the EU budget or the size and remuneration of the staff in Brussels). In Salmon (1995), it is assumed that the ties mentioned are generated in parallel with a slow transfer of powers or responsibilities from the member states to Brussels.

But seeking stronger ties is not the only cause of centralization. In Salmon (2003a), three underlying forces are distinguished. The first is the closest to the objective of generating ties. The form it takes is close to the so-called Jean Monnet method (ascribed to that *éminence grise* of the European project in its early stages). Its ingredients are opportunism, disequilibrium, and monotonicity. Opportunism means that every realistic occasion to move forward in the direction of greater integration should be seized and that any force working in that direction should be, a priori, welcome. Most integrative changes generate as many problems as they solve. Disequilibrium is typically their immediate outcome and it is also an essential part of the Monnet method because it provides an incentive to seek remedies. Then we have monotonicity, our third ingredient, which means that the remedies that are sought must never represent a step toward less integration. Several rules or legal tools are mobilized to implement monotonicity. A fascinating instance is the way extensions of the *acquis communautaire* (something like accumulated legislation and regulations) became legally binding on the occasion of each of the treaties required for the enlargement to new members (Salmon 2004).

The creation of the Euro or of the Schengen space have clearly generated many serious problems most of which were anticipated (especially in the case of the Euro). For the proponents of these important moves toward more integration, remedies would certainly be found that would enhance further integration. Although this may still happen, or perhaps is beginning to happen, the delays are certainly longer and the disequilibrium costs higher than anticipated. Yet, moving backward seems even more costly than mitigating ill-effects through new integrative undertakings.

The second force possibly underlying centralization is a desire by Brussels (as embodied in the European Commission, the European Court of Justice, and their personnel) to increase its role in as many domains as possible. That attitude is similar to that ascribed to governments in general under the first approach to vertical competition presented in section 8.2. If that force was the main factor of centralization, this would give some plausibility to the view that the relationship between Brussels and the governments of the member states is above all competitive. An obvious difficulty is the need to take also national bureaucracies and courts into account. Indeed, supporters of European integration have often claimed that integration was stalling because of the hostility and resistance of the powerful bureaucracies of the member states. One way, also noted in Salmon (2003a), to reconcile the interests of the bureaucrats in the member countries and the bureaucrats in Brussels may have been the institution of "comitology," in a broad sense—that is, of specialized networks associating departments of the EU institutions in Brussels and departments at the level of the member states. Bureaucrats of each country concerned with a given domain gain additional strength vis-à-vis politicians, voters, or ministries of finance in their own country from their membership of transnational networks specialized in that domain and coordinated by a department of Brussels. This also can be understood as a form of centralization.

Contrary to the first two, the third force on which I will now insist is generally overlooked in the analyses of centralization at the level of the European Union. Ironically, the new impulse that it received from the Single Act of 1987 (including the 1992 project) was approved by the United Kingdom in the person of Margaret Thatcher. One of its two

main ingredients was a renewed emphasis on the achievement of a perfect internal market, implying the eradication of all barriers to trade and
competition distortions.[19] The other was, thanks to greater allowance of
majority-voting in the Council of Ministers, a much-enhanced capacity to
make laws or regulate at the level of the European Union. This necessary
institutional change was considered a necessary condition for pursuing the
main objective.

Why has that important pro-market move led to considerable centralization and little deregulation?[20] To understand that effect, it is necessary to take into account the nature of impediments to trade within
"internal" or "domestic" markets (Breton and Salmon 2001). To satisfy
the demands of their constituents, decentralized governments innovate,
whether by making new services available or by finding more efficient
ways to deliver the existing ones. However, a government that departs
from what other governments are doing almost always fragments the
common economic space. As a side-effect of its innovativeness and responsiveness toward its constituents, it creates unwillingly non-tariff
and non-border barriers to trade—implying additional transaction
costs for private-sector activities that straddle jurisdictions and rents
for those that do not—and/or distortions of competition. Regulations
in particular have side-effects that fragment some markets and can
thus be considered as barriers to trade, whereas subsidies, "state aids"
to domestic activities, and in particular to firms, distort competition
and jeopardize the prospect of maintaining a level playing field among
competing firms.

A policy, such as that decided with the Single Act, which pursues the
objectives of eliminating all kinds of fragmentation of the single market
and of distortion of competition among firms implies, under modern
conditions, a massive transfer of responsibilities in the area of regulation and policy-making from the level of the member states to that of the
union. In contemporary democracies, any drastic reduction in the levels of
regulation, public services, and welfare provisions to which the population
is accustomed is politically unrealistic (Rodden and Rose-Ackerman 1997).
If governments at one level are prevented from providing the goods that
are demanded, a government at another level will have to do the job.

In the end, as explained in particular in Salmon (2003a), the driving
force behind centralization is the first one—that is, the combination of
the "strengthening ties" (or "ever closer union") objective and the Monnet
method, in particular in what we called its opportunistic dimension. This
does not mean that the other two forces do not also play a role. But this role
is contrived or manufactured in the service of the first.

More than elsewhere, the bureaucracy in Brussels has a proclivity to seek ways to expand. But that proclivity is part of the original design. As noted by Ross (1995): "The European Commission was meant constitutionally to be an institution whose explicit task it was to work for change—generating greater Europeanization" (p. 6); or: "the founding fathers wanted to establish [the Commission] as an activist motor at the center of the Community whose most important job would be to expand the EC's mandate over time" (p. 23). Other EU institutions are also genetically biased in favor of centralizing solutions.[21]

At the same time, nothing important can happen in the European Union that runs against the will of a sufficiently large number of member states. This applies to centralization as to other issues. Thus, contrary to what may be the case of genuine federations—in which, in spite of constitutional protection, de facto centralization can be forced on junior governments[22]—centralization in the setting of the European Union is to be ascribed first of all to a desire for, or at least some acquiescence to, centralization present among most of the governments of the subcentral units—that is, in the present case, of the member countries. Supporters of the European integration project will tend to welcome all occasions to transfer new responsibilities to the Brussels level. For that purpose, they will be prone to conclude alliances with various other constituencies pursuing completely different objectives. To return to the question mentioned at the outset, and simplifying a bit, the main reason why the governments of the member states cannot engage in vertical competition, yardstick or otherwise, with the Brussels level is a simple one: they have pledged to build up that level.

### 8.3.2. Horizontal yardstick competition in the EU context

Most of the points that follow have been at least alluded to:

(1) Horizontal yardstick competition among member countries is probably more intense than elsewhere. Citations of Mark Leonard and of Roger Congleton in chapter 6 reflected that. A particular high intensity of voters' cross-border comparisons among the founding member countries of the European Union was also assumed in the empirical discussion of the first model presented in chapter 7. There the variable considered was economic growth. It is clear that currently comparisons of growth rates are at the center of political debates in France and Italy. With regard to the circulation of comparative data, it is not clear that

the European Union does better than the OECD. Whether in general more should be done is discussed in the next chapter.

(2) An implication of that first model, which is not formulated in its discussion but was developed in the earlier version of that model presented in Salmon (1991), concerns the possible effect of an increasing degree of yardstick competition, in terms of economic growth, between the European Union as whole and non-member countries such as the United States, Japan, and China. The perspective of such yardstick competition was more plausible at the time (1991) than it would be today. One of the factors leading governments to agree to the Single Act of 1987 and the 1992 project was the mood of "Europessimism" and the impression of "Eurosclerosis" widespread at the time. Public opinion in EU countries was relatively attentive to a tendency of Europe to fall behind in comparisons with rapid growth elsewhere. It is not the case that Europessimism has evaporated, but for some reasons its basis on relative economic growth seems to be much less politically relevant today. Currently, the focus of cross-jurisdiction comparisons of economic growth seems steadfastly located within the European Union, among member countries, rather than between the European Union and the rest of the world.

(3) There is another analysis developed in Salmon (1991) which has lost some of its relevance. The tendency of the European economy to underperform could be explained then by an asymmetry of cross-country comparisons (e.g., the German economy being the yardstick) associated with the underperformance of the German economy in the wake of German unification. I will return in the next chapter to the possibility in general for yardstick competition to have an effect of that kind. Anyhow, the superior performance of the German economy makes the configuration irrelevant in the European Union setting for the time being.

(4) If in some countries (those most concerned with falling behind), yardstick competition on economic growth crowds out other worthy policy objectives, this may provide a case for entrusting these policies to subnational jurisdictional tiers. In retrospect, I am not sure that the doubts about that argument expressed in Salmon (2003b) are really justified. Contrary to what I suggested there, the argument does not necessarily belong to the optimal assignment approach to decentralization and federalism whose relevance is limited in the EU context because of the nature of the integration process. Decentralization at the subnational level is not on the agenda of Brussels seriously, if at all. Each country can decide autonomously the way powers are distributed

among the different tiers. Its decisions have no direct bearing on the integration process itself. Thus, it is possible that the awareness of a bias toward sacrificing everything to keeping in line in terms of growth leads the government of a country or its voters to favor some reassignment of tasks in the direction of more decentralization.

(5) However, the opposite effect is also plausible. As noted with a reference to France and Italy, when a high priority is given to reaching growth rates comparable to what is obtained in other member countries, the desire to save costs may lead to recentralization. More generally, the process of federalization at the EU level, in spite of being so slow, may generate a desire to reduce the number of tiers at the national level.

(6) Finally, as noted, the completion of the common market, with the stress it puts on establishing a level playing field and eliminating all distortions of competition stifles the working of a yardstick competition enhanced by policy innovations. This might inspire a change in the policy followed by Brussels and, underlying that, by the member states.[23] What would be the effect of such a change—toward a less strict interpretation of internal market completion and relatedly toward less regulatory centralization—on the monotonicity characteristic of the integration process is a difficult question. Anyway, if that inflexion in the interpretation of the internal market is considered a recommendation, it is subject to the interrogations we raise in the next chapter about recommendations in general.

## 8.4. CONCLUSION

For scholars living in federal countries or in countries in which federalist arrangements are on the agenda, for instance Canada, Italy, or Spain, a competitive perspective on the vertical relationship between governments placed at different tiers may be far more exciting than competition among governments placed at the same level. But most scholars will consider vertical interactions as being above all intricate and their characterization as competitive as interestingly challenging rather than fully compelling. As is the case with the extension of the yardstick competitive perspective to international settings discussed in chapter 6, an obstacle to its extension to vertical interactions is a lack of research manpower. In particular, if this chapter has been completely silent about empirical work on the topic, it is essentially because there is none, or almost none. Contrary to what I did in chapter 6, I will not try to explain the fact but formulate instead the hope that ways to investigate empirically vertical yardstick competition, in particular along the line suggested by Breton, will be found.

## NOTES

1. One problem, though, is when competition is submitted to constraints on spending or taxation decided at a higher tier. Some recent empirical work on that matter is surveyed in Revelli (2015, pp. 112–13).
2. For the United States, see Sigman (2003).
3. I am referring to the "framers" of the US constitution as interpreted in particular by Pettys (2003).
4. As noted, a similar argument for equalization is suggested in particular by Allers (2012). A counter-argument could refer to Kotsogiannis and Schwager (2008), who present some evidence that equalization has a negative effect on accountability.
5. Another pattern is proposed by Bodenstein and Ursprung (2005). In their contribution, both horizontal and vertical yardstick comparisons play a role: voters' yardstick comparisons of governors' performance influence the election of one of them as president, while re-election of the president is mostly based on vertical yardstick competition.
6. The story of the French Revolution is still sufficiently alive in the minds of many Frenchmen today for the division of French politicians into those whose instincts are *jacobins* (pro-centralization) and those whose instincts are *girondins* (pro-decentralization) to be still generally understood.
7. Admittedly, in France, mayors, in addition to representing the inhabitants of their communes, are supposed by law to represent the nation or the state as a whole. But this does not amount to much.
8. For the 1981 dating, see Breton (1987) p. 263.
9. Manifestations of that concern are numerous. See Chandler (2007, pp. 75–76) for the motivation underlying the construction of the "grandiose" and "magnificent" Victorian edifices that were to serve as town halls in English cities such as Liverpool, Leeds, and Manchester. In France, a similar effect is observable in the architectural display of regional capitals. Dijon, a city of about 260,000 inhabitants (including the suburbs) is a case in point. In it, five large buildings are occupied by the headquarters and administrations of five interlocking jurisdictions (I neglect some effects of the merging of French regions decided in 2015). The two palaces completed or built in the eighteenth century are occupied respectively by the municipality of Dijon and by the prefect (i.e., the representative of the national government). The département of Côte d'Or (one of the 83 départements created in 1790) recently left a building specially constructed for it in 1898–1901 for a new one, while the regional council of Burgundy (one of 22 regions progressively endowed with some reality in the 1970s and a full democratic status in the early 1980s) occupies an impressive building constructed for it in 1975–1981. *Dijon Métropole* (as the metropolitan area is now called) occupies former military barracks whose beautiful restoration and enlargement was completed in 2005. It is difficult not to consider the impressive size of these buildings as reflecting as noted a concern with visibility and recognition.

10. In horizontal yardstick competition, comparisons may also take into account the fact that politicians in office in different same-tier jurisdictions belong to the same political party (Geys and Vermeir 2008), but the complication implied seems greater in the case of vertical competition.

11. The concept is situated historically, elaborated on, and justified at length by Breton in the context of his analysis of "intragovernmental" competition (1996, part 1).

12. Breton's disinclination to reason in a principal-agent framework in which citizens are the principals and governments or incumbents their agents (our approach in this book) is relatively mild and tacit compared to his strong refusal to use—as recommended in particular by Bird (1993)—that framework with the central government as the principal and junior governments as its agents. See Bird (2000).

13. Of course, in the case of some types of goods, particularly services, the difference between the two settings is blurred or even vanishes. Here, when referring to supply and demand, I neglect that possibility.

14. In the analysis of intragovernmental competition (Breton 1996, part 1), competitive equilibrium was derived under the assumptions of perfect information and perfectly tight Wicksellian connections. In the analysis of vertical competition among governments, Breton and Fraschini (2003a) and Breton (2006) ascribe to information imperfection the fact that tightness is itself imperfect.

15. Even though perfectly understandable as a diminishing return effect, the positive relation between small provision and high efficiency generally found in the studies based on rankings is particularly in need of more comments than it receives. I am less surprised, for instance, by the finding that Cyprus ranks first in terms of efficiency, than by the fact that there is no comment about its significance. A problem here, perhaps, is that the term "efficiency" is so *persuasive*, as was analyzed already by Little (1950).

16. In that context, the grandiose edifices mentioned earlier (with reference to Victorian England and to Dijon) may signal the resilience that the subcentral governments concerned would display if it were attempted to deprive them of their powers (I owe that remark to Giorgio Brosio).

17. As an instance of that inclination, a view I "ventured" in Salmon (2000a) was that "the growth of expenditures at some of the levels," although a problem whose "seriousness could not be denied," would "prove to be transitory" (p. 253, note 23). It has not. With regard to predicting the extinction of the départements (p. 256, note 26), we may observe that, two decades later, the French départements and the Italian provinces are still around and their extinction still discussed.

18. In Britain, most politicians and voters have never really shared that concern. On February 19, 2016 (that is, before the Brexit referendum), Britain's singularity on that matter found an official, belated, recognition with the agreement by European leaders (obtained by David Cameron within his so-called renegotiation deal) that the Treaties will "make it clear that the references to ever closer union do not apply to the United Kingdom." Whether ties involving Britain have or have not been generated is another matter.

19. The mutual recognition principle, as spelled out notably by the European Court of Justice in a famous *Cassis de Dijon* ruling (1979), is also part of the new approach adopted in the Single Act. It says that although the production of a good remains regulated by the government of the jurisdiction where this production takes place, the good can be freely exported to another jurisdiction whatever the regulation applicable to its production in that other jurisdiction. In the domains in which

it applies, the mutual recognition principle eliminates one barrier to the free trade of goods. The economic space remains, however, fragmented in the sense that imposed modes of production goods can be different across jurisdictions. If the objective is a completely unique market, mutual recognition will have to be superseded by full harmonization.

20. Member-state governments have been deprived of a substantial part of their autonomy in some areas, but the lost regulatory capacity has been firmly relocated at the center of the governmental system (Brussels)—not quite the division of responsibilities prescribed in Weingast (1995) as a condition for "market-preserving federalism."

21. This has often been noted. The European Parliament has a "general bias for more integration of any kind," according to Scharpf (1999, p. 69) and the European Court of Justice is more likely to represent "in euro-speak," "an engine of integration" than "a 'bulwark' against centralization" according to Vaubel (1994, p. 153).

22. For the case of Canada see Winer (2000) and Bird and Vaillancourt (2006).

23. The fact that Canada and Switzerland do not have a perfect internal common market might inspire some restraint in the efforts of some to create one at all costs within the European Union. Bird and Vaillancourt (2006) observe: "It should be understood that Canada is not, and never has been, a full internal common market. There has been a long tradition of accepting that provinces not only have their own economic policies but can and do sometimes implement them in ways that reduce national economic efficiency" (p. 236).

# CHAPTER 9

# Final comments: perverse effects, advice, and arguments

T here is a reason why topics as heterogeneous in appearance as perverse effects, advice, and arguments can be treated in a same final chapter. That reason is the status or situation one would like to give to yardstick competition among governments. There are different possibilities, more or less realistic. Thanks mainly to the work done since Besley and Case (1995) in the context of fiscal federalism (as surveyed in chapter 5), it is certainly not illegitimate to consider yardstick competition as a theoretical hypothesis supported by some empirical evidence. Future work will certainly confirm that status.

However, given the broader and more informal nature of the analyses presented in the other chapters of this book, the said status when considered alone may seem at the same time too ambitious and too limited. We should draw the implications of treating political yardstick competition as a mechanism and situate its most natural habitat in the world of debates and arguments at least as decidedly as in the category of well-supported empirical hypotheses. To justify that choice, it is helpful (in addition to being independently necessary) to acknowledge the possibility that yardstick competition has perverse effects. It is also necessary to explain why, in part for that reason and in part because of the said habitat, it may be wise to abstain from any serious effort at deriving advice or recommendations. The excursion in methodology that follows the discussion of perverse effects and advice is centered on three concepts with which methodology and the philosophy of science are still ill at ease: models, mechanisms, and arguments. The conclusion of the chapter purports to

show how, when apprehended together, the three provide some methodological justification for the way yardstick competition is presented and
discussed in this book.

## 9.1. PERVERSE EFFECTS

We want to eschew a purely normative approach, and thus we will not refer
to optimality. We also want to stay away from moral and political philosophy, so we will not embark on deep questions such as the limits of individualism. Indeed, we will only consider here, in a pragmatic mode, effects
that turn out to be contrary to stated objectives, generally related to various characterizations of the interest of citizens. The causes of these perverse effects can be sought in two directions: the competence of voters and
the incentives of incumbents.[1]

### 9.1.1. Incompetent voters

The belief that voters or ordinary citizens do not engage in comparisons
with other jurisdictions is widespread and was referred to several times in
the preceding chapters. Here, we are interested in the view that if voters
engage in cross-jurisdiction comparisons they do so in an incompetent
way. As a consequence, cross-border observations generate a pressure on
office-holders that makes them adopt policies detrimental to voters' welfare. It is interesting that in a review of policy diffusion stressing "seven
lessons for scholars and practitioners," Shipan and Volden (2012) allude to
voters (more exactly to "the voting public") only once and only to stress the
wrong kind of policy diffusion or imitation they are likely to bring about.
"Imitation may be thought of as the policy diffusion equivalent of "keeping
up with the Joneses," with all the associated negative aspects of such an
approach. The voting public may demand the adoption of policies that they
have seen or experienced elsewhere, regardless of whether those policies
are ultimately suitable in their home community" (p. 791).

Although their analysis is incomplete (and excessive), Shipan and
Volden do point to a real phenomenon. The general issue involved here is
governments pandering to voters' demands that, in some sense, should
not be satisfied. That the demands are themselves inspired by what obtains
elsewhere is only an aspect of the more general question.

There are two ways to analyze pandering. One involves questioning
voters' true preferences, the other only those wishes that are based on

insufficient information or attention.[2] The first is more problematic than the second, at least for economists. The tradition in economics is to respect consumer sovereignty—that is, individual preferences—except in the presence of externalities or perhaps addiction. Even then, reluctance to condemn remains the norm. This applies to many kinds of motives, including status seeking—keeping up with the Joneses. In that case, although there is nothing to say about the motive itself, the rank-competition it triggers does generate negative externalities and can be seen as a collective-action failure (a kind of prisoners' dilemma). It may be argued that all participants would benefit from its absence. Nonetheless, the traditional recommendation from economics is still to do nothing (implement no sumptuary taxation for instance), not even reprove. One reason is the uncertainty of the diagnosis. People who have never driven a Ferrari may judge that buying a Ferrari can only be motivated by the desire to impress others, but people who have driven a Ferrari might well think otherwise. The macroeconomic consequences (on economic growth, etc.) of conspicuous consumption are even more uncertain.

Many recent developments in economics, in particular in domains such as the philosophy of economics and the empirical study of happiness, suggest qualifications to that traditional position; consumer sovereignty is now challenged along many dimensions. However, we do not really need to discuss here the implications of the said developments because a second way to address pandering, focused this time on information and political institutions, is both more secure and generally sufficient. In a nutshell, voters may be insufficiently aware of or concerned with the costs or negative effects entailed by the decisions they ask their government to make, and that failure may not be corrected at the policy-making level. Voters may disregard the costs because they do not have to bear them or because they are unaware of bearing them. And the attitude of voters interacts with the behavior of policy-makers in a way that depends on institutional arrangements.

As compared to Switzerland, many localities in France give the impression of spending much more on flowers and concrete (the latter generously spent on sidewalks, roundabouts, and speed-bumps). Assuming that the difference exists and that it has something to do with yardstick competition,[3] what could account for it? The most plausible answer is that their institutions make the Swiss inhabitants of the concerned localities particularly conscious of costs. Imitation tendencies that potentially induce more spending do exist in both countries,[4] but they are better contained by attention to costs in Switzerland than in France. One reason is more fiscal responsibility of local governments because of less reliance on grants and subsidies. Another is less separation at the level of each jurisdiction between deciding about expenditures and about taxation. This is true of all Swiss localities but particularly of those that rely more on direct consultation of voters (Feld and Kirschgässner 2000, Feld, Kirschgässner, and Schaltegger 2010). Overall, in Switzerland many proposed expenditures are directly or indirectly vetoed by the population.

In both countries, spending is restrained by the reluctance of support-conscious mayors to raise tax rates, but that mechanism tends to be the only one in France whereas it is only one element in a set of forces limiting, often at birth, both expenditures and taxation in the case of Switzerland. The highly mobile inhabitants of Swiss localities are exceptionally well informed about neighboring jurisdictions; they cannot but rapidly take notice of innovations that might be imitated. At the same time, they are also particularly well informed about costs and much more able than in any other country to have their views respected. Thus, in Switzerland both voters' inducements to imitate and voters' control of the effects of imitation are strong. For that reason, pandering to voters' wishes is probably less of a problem in that country than in others. This suggests that the problem emphasized by Shipan and Volden, also raised by excessive local expenditures in France, should be ascribed mainly to an insufficient democratic control of costs rather than to the presumed incompetence or superficiality of voters.

In fact, it may be argued that if voters have some responsibility for the ill-effects of yardstick competition, this is first of all because of the negativity bias in their votes discussed in chapter 3. Simplifying somewhat, if voters sanction incumbents when their jurisdictions fall behind others but do not reward them when they do better, incumbents are given incentives that reduce yardstick competition to mimicking. And in turn mimicking can have effects detrimental to voters.

The negativity bias suggests that yardstick comparisons will focus on policy outcomes that seem better in other jurisdictions than in one's own. This may be combined with, or take the form of, a second bias, consisting in overestimating the situation in other jurisdictions. Not much empirical evidence exists on the matter. An exception is the interesting contribution of Huang (2015) on relative perceptions in China. It is based on a college survey (involving about 1,200 students of a provincial university) and three online survey experiments. The findings of both types of studies are similar. The respondents have a tendency to overestimate the socioeconomic performance of OECD countries, in particular the United States.[5] The main result is that the higher the overestimation, the lower the evaluation of China and the Chinese government. The online experiments also show that correcting the misperceptions of the respondents who overestimate foreign socioeconomic conditions improves their evaluation of China. In Huang and Yeh (2017), a survey experiment on Chinese Internet users shows that having pro-Western inclinations tends to induce more reading of Western media but that more reading of Western media tends to produce a higher, rather than a lower, evaluation of China. The explanation provided or suggested, given the bias mentioned, is that "reputable Western media" are generally more realistic than the "rosy" information about foreign socioeconomic conditions that "popularly" circulates in China. These two complementary analyses are important for our general purpose because they provide some evidence of citizens making cross-border comparisons. They are also relevant for the discussion of whether ordinary citizens are or are not competent. However, what is their implication with regard to perverse effects? Huang and Yeh suggest that foreign media may enhance regime stability by making regime critics less critical. A link between that audacious proposition and the possibility of perverse effects of yardstick comparisons might not be so difficult to formulate but might also seem far-fetched or at least require more distinctions among the types of cross-jurisdiction comparisons citizens make than has seemed sufficient so far.

### 9.1.2. Incumbents' incentives

As explained already in chapter 2, an implication of the trade-off between incentives and selection is that more information, in particular when enhanced by cross-jurisdiction comparisons, can have a perverse effect on the welfare of voters (Besley 2006, Besley and Smart 2007). But the mechanism involved is only one among several that can generate perverse effects of yardstick competition. Three others—herding, multitasking, and manipulating—are particularly noteworthy. Let us consider the four in turn.

First, the trade-off between incentives and selection, discussed in chapter 2, yields the intellectually attractive possibility of a perverse effect of yardstick comparisons. The idea is grafted on the more general proposition that getting more information may be bad for voters. Better-informed voters induce "bad-type" incumbents to give up "pooling"—that is, to cease mimicking in the present the behavior of "good-type" incumbents. This increases their rent in the present (the so-called incentive effect) but also the probability that they will not be in office, thus getting no rent, in the future (the selection effect). The balance between the two effects determines the sign of the aggregate effect (regarding total rents and the voters' welfare) of improved information. It is negative (i.e., welfare decreasing) if the so-called incentive effect is larger than the selection effect.

One could simply treat cross-jurisdiction comparisons as one of the forms that improved information can take and directly apply the reasoning above. The analysis developed in Besley and Smart (2007) is more ambitious. They write: "Yardstick competition is welfare decreasing when politicians' reputations are poor because rents are increased with little advantage from the improved information generated as most politicians who are kicked out are replaced by an incumbent of the same type" (p. 768). That the selection effect is small in the setting indicated is obvious. But why do yardstick comparisons induce bad-type incumbents to give up yardstick competition and grab rents in the present? The reason provided is that, when it is likely (also in the eyes of citizens) that incumbents in other jurisdictions are bad-type the signal provided by engaging in yardstick competition (i.e., mimicking) would be too weak to be worthwhile. Better take as much rent as possible and run away.

That argument is dependent on the specific way the situation is modeled. Ambiguity produced by yardstick comparisons in the context of a trade-off between incentives and selection could be derived from different assumptions and take a different form. In particular, we could assume that being in a world in which bad-type incumbents dominate could make each bad-type incumbent more rather than less inclined to engage in yardstick competition—if only because the involved sacrifice required in the present would be less than in a world in which good types dominate. As a consequence, average rents would be reduced in the present and (because of diminished selection) increased in the future. The net result would still be ambiguous but for reasons opposite to those assumed in Besley and Smart (2007).

How relevant is the mechanism? The setup imagined by Besley and Smart is close in substance to that analyzed in Svolik (2013)—even though in the latter there are no cross-jurisdiction comparisons and bad-type incumbents maximize short run rents by definition of their type rather than by calculation. The image conveyed in both cases is that of a succession at each election of new, bad-type incumbents. For reasons explained by Svolik, young democracies are particularly likely to display the syndrome. It is certainly possible that yardstick comparisons among them make the matter worse—although not necessarily via that channel.

There are not so many young democracies—that is, if we reserve the word democracy for regimes in which incumbents can be removed easily by way of fair elections. Rapid rotation is definitely not a prominent feature of the numerous existing regimes referred to as autocracies, illiberal democracies, or hybrids (see, e.g., Levitsky and Way 2010). Even among "tinpot" dictators (Wintrobe 1998), particularly eager to grab rents, long-lived incumbency seems the rule. That characteristic makes the incentive-selection framework irrelevant in the context of the present discussion. If there is a perverse effect of yardstick competition also in the case of authoritarian regimes, it must be sought elsewhere.

But the same seems true of well-established democracies. In chapter 2 we suggested that in those, bad-type incumbents are relatively few. Admittedly, if we consider that enjoying the quiet life is a form of rent and that being lazy is a constitutive way for an incumbent to be bad, more office-holders would qualify. Even then, there are theoretical frameworks better than Besley and Smart's to yield perverse effects.

I am referring here to frameworks that generate or allow herding, our second mechanism. In the first, as just discussed, a perverse outcome is associated with opting out of cross-jurisdiction mimicking (based on yardstick competition).[6] With the second mechanism, the source is exactly the opposite: perfect mimicking.

An early contribution making such result possible is Feld, Josselin, and Rocaboy (2002, 2003). Their model takes the form of a non-cooperative game between the incumbents of two jurisdictions. Each is re-elected only if the tax rate he or she sets is equal or inferior to the tax rate set by the other. Tax rates are strategic complements. Nash equilibrium requires that the two incumbents decide the same rate. There are an infinite number of mimicking or Nash equilibria, all except one implying the existence of rents. Since the adoption of a non-cooperative setting precludes collusion, the Nash equilibrium that would maximize rents is not necessarily reached. The model makes rents likely and predicts a convergence of tax-rate variations, leaving its direction unexplained or indeterminate.[7]

What to think in general of the hypothesis that mimicking induces rents? In most of the literature on yardstick competition—my own work included—the possibility is glossed over.[8] There is an implicit presumption that yardstick competition tends to reduce rents. In my case, why that implicit presumption? One reason is that I started from competition for rank (see Salmon 1987b), along the lines of Lazear and Rosen (1981) and their immediate successors. Competition for rank suggests a more dynamic form of yardstick competition than does mimicking, which focuses on not falling behind. Another reason is that I also started from a counterfactual vision of quasi-abysmal rents in the absence of cross-jurisdiction openness to comparisons (Salmon 1987a). This reduces the likelihood that openness can increase rents further.

When mentioned in the literature, the significance of the effect of yardstick competition being to enhance rents is sometimes overstated. For Dafflon and Madiès (2009), yardstick competition means that "elected officials will have a tendency to imitate each other to avoid being stigmatized" and "this mimicry will result in tax rates that are higher than necessary to finance the level of public goods desired by voters, leaving elected officials with a rent" (p. 25). That formulation suggests that the perverse effect of mimicking is the rule, whereas it is only a possibility.

It may be useful at this stage to elaborate on our discussion of mimicking in chapter 3. The case of tax rates is special in the sense that it supposes no distance between decisions by government and their direct effect on citizens. There is no need for a production function relating inputs and outputs, or instruments and outcomes. But in the case of other types of variables—those related to economic growth, health, or education in particular—there is no instantaneity and automaticity between decision and outcome. And the distance between the two is often important. As argued in chapter 3, this renders legitimate a distinction between three meanings of mimicking: mimicking as a decision, mimicking as an objective, and mimicking as a statistical result. Even if we assume that the objective is mimicking, risk-averse incumbents may want to play safe, and this will make them try to do better than others rather than merely as well. Another reason for such behavior is uncertainty about the accuracy of voters' evaluations and the possibility that voters average between different dimensions their assessments of comparative performance. Doing comparatively less well in some respects may be compensated in the eyes of voters by doing comparatively better in other respects. The effect of the negativity bias ascribed to voters is mitigated as a consequence. Since, in the absence of collusion, the herding equilibrium discussed here is fragile, concerns with playing safe, even if shared by few, may well trigger tournaments generating a downward pressure on rents—as implicitly assumed in general in the literature on yardstick competition.

All this being said, it seems true that low performance associated with high rents (whether in a literal sense or only of the quiet life variety) may characterize for extended periods of time groups of neighboring jurisdictions. Although the responsibility of yardstick competition in that situation is difficult to document, it is certainly plausible. In these settings, voters who do look across borders, albeit not far afield, find no reason to be dissatisfied with their own incumbents. Incumbents feel safe as long as their jurisdiction does not fall behind its also failing neighbors. Illustrations that come to mind are West Africa, South America, Eastern Europe or, for that matter, Western Europe over some periods of time. With some optimism, one may argue that such periods are not unlimited. Eventually, public opinion enlarges its perspective to more distant continents. Then, feelings like Europessimism and concerns of the Eurosclerosis type (mentioned in chapter 8) do make their way among the citizenry and into the public debate.

The following remark applies to the first two mechanisms: Whether yardstick comparisons have perverse effects depends very much on where we start from—how we perceive the situation in their absence. Our imagined benchmark can be catastrophic or simply bad. In the contributions just mentioned, the benchmark situation is simply bad. Voters are disadvantaged but not totally in the dark. For instance, they know some characteristics of the population of candidates or of incumbents in other jurisdictions. Rents are assumed but are not totally out of control (more rents now implies fewer rents later). Under these assumptions, the impact of yardstick competition can be marginal and easily conceivable as negative. In the way I have generally described it, the imagined situation without cross-jurisdiction comparisons is, in the policy domains concerned, more extreme. For instance, in the absence of cross-jurisdiction yardsticks, citizens are assumed to be at a complete loss when it comes to judging economic growth or improvement in health care. On such matters at least, it is unlikely that their situation could be worsened by becoming informed about what obtains elsewhere.

The third and fourth mechanisms (to which I turn now) are straightforward compared to the first two. The third mechanism concerns multitasking. As analyzed in particular in chapter 7 in the setting of the first model, yardstick competition induces a change in the allocation of government's effort between policy domains or tasks. Even if yardstick competition does reduce rents (that is, resources incumbents can employ discretionarily), some domains or tasks are allocated less effort than would be the case in the absence of yardstick competition. To various degrees, these domains or tasks are sacrificed. That negative effect may dominate and thus justify the view that yardstick competition has perverse effects overall.

Implications of multitasking are well understood in economics in general since Holmstrom and Milgrom (1991). The two main solutions, adopted in particular by business firms, are separation of tasks when that is possible or convenient and lower-powered incentives when that is not. In the present context, the first solution was mentioned in our discussion of multitier government and decentralization. It could introduce a new dimension to the discussion of assignment in the context of European integration (Salmon 2003b). Lower-powered incentives is another matter. In labor or industrial economics, it means less reliance on pay-for-performance schemes. Here the pay-for-performance incentive of incumbents is exclusively in terms of information and votes. A major way to have lower-powered incentives, then, is to have less yardstick competition, a policy question discussed in the next section.

The fourth mechanism concerns manipulation. Comparisons may be biased by manipulating indicators or their results—that is, "gaming" indicators (Besley 2015). Let us concentrate on league tables. If cross-jurisdiction comparisons show that a jurisdiction is badly placed in a ranking, it is tempting for its government to seek a higher rank directly in terms of the signal or indicator itself without trying to deal with the real phenomenon it is meant to reflect. The way many governments react to bad positions in rankings suggests that such behavior or motivation might be frequent.

Focusing directly on an indicator is widespread. Examples in the case of the *Doing Business* rankings include President Putin and Prime Minister Modi targeting for Russia and India the twentieth and fiftieth ranks respectively (Besley 2015). Indeed, such focus is faithful to the spirit of the *Doing Business* undertaking. Thus, one can read in the *Doing Business Report* of 2007: "In 2006 Georgia targeted the top 25 list and used Doing Business indicators as a benchmark of its progress. It now ranks 18 on the ease of doing business, and the government has set an even more ambitious goal. Saudi Arabia and Mauritius have targeted the top 10. Both have made tremendous progress: Saudi Arabia now ranks 23, and Mauritius 27" (p. 7).[9] The mediocre position of French universities and *grandes écoles* (Ecole Polytechnique, Ecole Normale Supérieure, etc.) in the Shanghai Jiao Tong Academic Ranking of World Universities—and, less publicized, in the Times Higher Education Supplement ranking—had a strong impact on public opinion. The most visible response of the government has been arm twisting universities and *grandes écoles* into consolidation, at least on paper (Ecole Polytechnique finally rebelled in 2017). I do not think that it is unfair to say that the driving rationale was arithmetic: since the numbers of Nobel laureates and Fields medalists count in the rankings, a virtue of consolidated units is that they have a higher probability than their single components to include some in their staff.

It is certain that league tables and rankings have good and bad effects. This is clear from discussions among statisticians (see Goldstein and Spiegelhalter 1996) and from the large quantity of comments each important rating has received from specialists of the domain concerned—some of the comments, when concerned with bad effects, quite emotional. But I think that there is a difference between well-established democracies and other regimes. In the former, rankings will find a place in public debates—in particular, new rankings may arouse considerable public attention—without triggering reckless responses on the part of governments. Typically, there will be an extensive public and professional discussion about the validity and interpretation of the rankings, and governments will encounter many obstacles if they try to "game" or adopt hasty remedies for the purpose of improving the jurisdiction's position. Thus, at least in democracies, the balance of positive and negative effects is likely to be positive.

To complement Besley's discussion of the *Doing Business* reports (Besley 2015), let me elaborate on a point I made in Salmon (2005). The great contribution of these reports is calling attention to the combined side-effects on business transactions of completely independent concerns and policies—e.g., protection of the supposedly weak side of contracts (consumers, buyers, tenants, employees, borrowers, etc.), health care, the environment, contractual security, industrial risks, crime and laundering prevention, national defense, protection of monuments, urbanism, decentralization, taxation, and so on. All or most of these concerns and policies, although operationalized in different sections and at different tiers of the governmental system, can have an impact on a single category of transactions (e.g., property transfers) and that category may be important for doing business. A country having a bad rank regarding that particular category may reflect a specific organizational defect, relatively easy to remedy, or the impact, impossible to modify in the short run, of many separate policies pursuing different objectives and supported by different constituencies. It cannot be expected, in well-entrenched democracies, that a sufficient number of such policies can be truncated at a stroke just to gain a better position, along a single dimension, in the *Doing Business* rankings.

The matter is quite different in the case of most authoritarian regimes. Open political debates are generally non-existent or limited. Instead of being first an object of public discussion, a bad position in a ranking may directly trigger a prompt response at the higher level of government. Political obstacles are more swiftly overcome. Thus, there is a serious possibility that—just to please public opinion, international investors, or the *Doing Business* team at the World Bank—insufficiently thought-out responses will be decided on.[10]

I have focused on the *Doing Business Reports* of the World Bank. One might consider that they concern mainly investors or governments and seek less clearly to inform citizens or public opinion than some other indicators (*Transparency International, Human Watch*, PISA, etc.) do. Yet, the *Doing Business* reports are clearly related to yardstick competition in Besley (2015), as they were also in Salmon (2005). Even if in the course of time the attention of the general public has weakened, when the reports first came out (2003, 2004), their large echo in several countries cannot be doubted, and the way many governments responded is clearly a manifestation of yardstick competition. It is also at this early stage that the likelihood of perverse effects was highest.

## 9.2. ADVICE (OR THE ABSENCE THEREOF)

Although I am sure that some have popped up here and there, I have endeavored to avoid recommendations. Three areas in which the temptation is particularly strong are assignments of tasks across tiers of the governmental system, constitutional provisions, and the provision of comparative information. Advice about assignments emerges readily from the implications of the first model of chapter 7 and more generally from the analysis of yardstick competition in a context of multitasking. Yardstick competition over economic performance, in particular growth rates, may induce national governments to reduce their efforts in other domains. The fear that this goes too far may provide one reason to reassign and, in particular, decentralize powers in these domains. Constitutional or quasi-constitutional provisions were discussed in particular in chapters 7 and 8. They may be important to discipline competition among governments especially in multi-tier systems. Finally, it seems almost evident that providing more information on comparative performance can do no harm and may do some good. The presumption that their contribution in that matter will be beneficial applies to various actual or potential public producers of comparative information, at the subnational, national, and supranational levels, and to non-governmental institutions such as universities, research centers, and associations. It seems natural to recommend supporting them.

However, we have seen why more information, in particular of a comparative kind, can be harmful by itself, as can be, more indirectly, the additional workability or intensity of yardstick competition that it may foster. One major problem with both constitutional solutions and decentralization is the dependence of their effects on the particulars of each country. Even within Western Europe, countries are so profoundly different that it is difficult to imagine recommendations about constitutional solutions or decentralization that would have some validity or relevance for all. More generally, there are two main reasons to avoid recommendations. One is uncertainty about effects, especially over time. The other is the difficulty of weighing positive and negative effects, gains and losses, generally experienced by or affecting different subsets of the population.

The attitude defended here does not imply giving up policy relevance. Advising, recommending, prescribing, or even suggesting are not necessary for contributing to reflections and debates about policies, constitutional rules, or decentralization. One of the aims of the methodological views we turn to now is to justify that proposition.

## 9.3. A METHODOLOGICAL EPILOGUE

Methodological norms have become very demanding in economics. The time has passed when functions could be said to be "well behaved" or correlation coefficients sufficient indicators of empirical significance. The change is most welcome in many respects. Still, in the case of this book, I fear that the said norms may prevent some readers from taking as seriously as they deserve (irony sign needed here) the analyses I developed or the points I made. The following remarks concern models, mechanisms, and arguments whose common characteristics are, first, that they have been for a long time relatively neglected in the philosophy of science and, second, that their relevance is enhanced when they are apprehended together.

### 9.3.1. Models

To characterize models, we may start from a philosophical position called "the semantic interpretation of theories," more particularly the variant proposed in Giere (1987). For our purpose, the main idea is simple: a model is an artificial, non-linguistic entity. In the case of economics, political science, and political economy, one may say that it is an imaginary economy, polity, or society. That entity can be apprehended in our minds even if we do not find the words to describe it. But usually it is characterized in words, possibly with the help of equations and diagrams. There is a risk of confusion if we stop at that, for we cannot overlook the usual interpretation of models as sets of formal statements or equations. The solution I proposed in Salmon (2000b) is a distinction between the described non-linguistic model and, *if there is one*, the describer model, which is a form of language.[11] That dichotomy is part of a larger, fourfold, distinction, in which the two elements added are the real world, in all its complexity, and the aspect of the real world we want to focus on, which we will call (following Giere) the "real system." The intellectual process which allows the focus of our attention to move from the real world to the real system is one of isolation or abstraction (we want to discuss tax competition without being bothered by all the other relations that may exist between governments or jurisdictions). However, the intellectual process typically (but not necessarily) involved in the construction of the "described model" is one of simplification or idealization. Inasmuch as the furniture (e.g., elections, incumbents, voters) is broadly the same in the real system and in the described model, it is simplified or idealized in the latter. The use of ceteris paribus (or more to the point "ceteris absentibus") clauses is natural for isolation (we want to discuss yardstick competition independently of other interactions), but it is inappropriate for idealization. Thus, in an idealized analysis of political agency, it would make little sense to say that ceteris paribus incumbents are either good or bad.

Ways to describe a non-linguistic model can be clumsy or elegant, unnecessarily pretentious or insufficiently precise, good or bad. But this should not matter as much (except perhaps for doctoral dissertations and journal referees) as whether the described, non-linguistic, model is a good or a bad one given the objective pursued. It seems clear that Keynes (1938) had our described models in mind when he wrote: "Progress in economics consists almost entirely in a progressive improvement in the choice of models. Economics is a science of thinking in terms of models joined to the art of choosing models which are relevant to the contemporary world." (pp. 296–97).[12]

The relation between models and reality is of course important but let us forget about it for a moment and concentrate on described models.[13] As non-linguistic entities, they cannot be true or false (they can be incoherent). As noted, many of the items (actors, actions, institutions, constraints, etc.) that we find in described models are idealized or simplified versions of items that also exist in real systems or directly in the real world. Thus, in a neo-classical model of growth, the described model is a closed economy in which consumers are identical, competition is perfect, one homogeneous good (wheat) is consumed and invested, the production function of that good is linear and continuous and has two arguments, capital and labor, both homogeneous, technical progress and population growth are exogenous, etc. The specific-factors model of Jones (1971), which inspired the first model of chapter 7, is a simplified international economy whose distinctive characteristic is that some but not all of the factors of production are immobile across sectors. In the theory of voting, the seminal model of Black (1948) is a short-lived committee using a simple majority rule to decide on a single and unidimensional issue, each member having unimodal preferences, being ignorant of the preferences of other members and voting sincerely.

As illustrated by these instances, described models are usually less messy and more uniform than the real world; the objects included in models usually have more stable properties and interact in a more regular way. Hence one may relate law-like properties of models deductively, deduce theorems, etc. If one prefers causal forms of explanation, one may concentrate on processes and mechanisms.

In spite of being less messy than the real world, described models are usually deep or rich. They can be explored and one may make in them discoveries of unforeseen properties. Questions that can be raised in the context of a model are numerous (sometimes infinite). They can be raised simply by varying the values of exogenous variables.[14] Consequently, discussing aspects of a described model and discussing the real world is formally very similar, which cannot but generate many confusions.

With regard to the description of models, let me stress again that there are many alternative or complementary ways to describe a (non-linguistic) model: with words, geometrically, mathematically, or even physically (as did Irving Fisher). The main form of description in economics has become mathematical models. It is well adapted to the uniformity introduced, as we saw, in the described (non-linguistic) models. But the description or characterization, whether formal or informal, is always incomplete, as is unavoidable when attempting to describe reality itself. Much remains tacit (background assumptions and results, common knowledge, etc.). In particular, causal mechanisms and processes are typically tacit—that is, unmentioned by mathematical models, which are often formulated in terms of equilibrium relations. Hence the mistaken view that there are no or few mechanisms in economic models (Mäki 1998). In fact, the inclusion of mechanisms constitutes a main strength of models.

Let us consider now the relation between models and reality and start with views that are better not held. Thus, the idealization process just mentioned for the construction of the non-linguistic model should not count when the question is whether the model is a good or a bad one. Very good models can be the product of pure imagination, pure invention, rather than idealization. Relatedly, the question is not whether the model is a good or bad representation of reality. Seeing it in those terms would lead one to prefer more exact, detailed mappings, which is not at all what model designers seek or should seek in general. The solution I defended in Salmon (2000b, 2007) is very simple: the relation between the model and the real system is a link between a "thing" in the model and a "thing" in the real system. What are those "things"? There are many possibilities: they can be equilibrium results, regularities, trade-offs, properties, inequalities, differences, impossibilities, explanations, processes, mechanisms, etc. Currently, the dominant view in economics implies that they are regularities.[15]

What is claimed about the link? What is its status? The dominant view suggests that the link should be asserted. Under our interpretation of models, the assertion cannot be justified by deduction ("deductivism" and "apriorism" are philosophical positions that do not refer to models). The assertion can be given the status of a hypothesis—a conjecture, in the language of Popper—to be tested. Then, in principle, there is no need of justification before testing. Less demandingly, the assertion may be based on a mixture of induction and plausibility, as argued by Sugden (2000) in his analysis of the social segregation model of Schelling (1978). Changing somewhat Sugden's formulation, the idea is as follows: the mechanism in the model (i.e., in the non-linguistic model) is plausible; it has consequences that are observable also in reality; hence there are good reasons to think that a similar mechanism is at work in reality. With regard to empirical evaluations, three points must be noted: experimentation is particularly well suited to the methodology of models (Guala 2005); just accounting for stylized facts is generally criticized but may be justified from a perspective emphasizing the dynamics of scientific inquiry; and the status given by researchers to their contributions is often implicit, uncertain, and flexible as illustrated by the widespread use of the grammatical forms "may," "might," or "could."

In fact, very often the link between something in the model and something in the real system is not truly asserted. That feature is important to understand the argumentative nature of economics and social science. To elaborate on that point, we must also consider mechanisms.

### 9.3.2. Mechanisms

The title of Salmon (1998) was "free riding as mechanism." The written comments on the essay and the extended oral discussion that followed my presentation, published in the same volume, are a very good illustration of the uncertainty that prevailed at the time (in 1996) and perhaps still prevails today among economists and philosophers about the nature and role of mechanisms in economics or more generally.[16] Explanation by mechanisms rather than by empirical laws, or together with them, has been defended or contemplated for a long time by some isolated philosophers (see Bunge 1997), but it has become a more widely supported philosophical position only since the writings of philosophers of science such as Nancy

Cartwright (1983) on the laws of nature and especially Wesley Salmon (1984) on causal explanation.

The matter is philosophically or methodologically complicated. However, economists do speak of mechanisms without waiting for their nature to be elucidated. And I do refer constantly to yardstick competition as a mechanism. Thus, some attention to the concept seems justified. I will not try to reproduce here the relatively detailed analyses that I presented in Salmon (1998). For our purpose the following points are relevant.

First, to serve as a definition we may simply say that a mechanism is the set of causal processes and interactions connecting causes and effects. Thus, the chief mechanism of transmission of the plague "is a flea that bites infected rats and then bites other organisms" (W. Salmon 1984, p. 271). Or, "cognitive dissonance reduction" is a psychological mechanism which makes people cease desiring what they cannot get (Elster 1989, p. 4). One fact need not be the causal antecedent of another: an "internal or underlying causal mechanism" may account for the nature of a fact, for instance "that humid air is less dense than dry air" (W. Salmon 1984, p. 269).

Second, as is clear from these citations, mechanisms are part of the real world. How, otherwise, could it be said that the mechanism of something is unknown or poorly understood? However, mechanisms can also be included in non-linguistic models (which is not surprising since those models can accommodate everything). Indeed, mechanisms can be important components of non-linguistic models, even when, as noted, they are absent from their description, formal or not.

The fact that the location of a given mechanism is simultaneously in a non-linguistic model and in reality, makes discussions about it often very confused. In particular, the habitat of perfect, optimizing, rationality is the world of models, not the real world. A major research strategy of economists has always been to ask what would happen if humans were perfectly rational and self-interested, and that strategy has proved fruitful. It has led to the discovery of interesting mechanisms first (we would now say) within non-linguistic models, and from there, with some adaptation, into the real world at large. Although anticipated by Hume, Wicksell, and possibly Hegel, free riding is a mechanism discovered in that way. It is a product of the rational choice approach within models. But now that it is here, now that we have become familiar with it, we must not treat it as an implication of that approach or relevant only in models. Free riding, in a more flexible and less precise sense than in the models, has become part of our practical knowledge. We all know, through introspection or casual observation, that we and others around us sometimes but not always free ride when it is narrowly rational to do so. A similar analysis could apply to other mechanisms, adverse selection for instance.

Third, mechanisms do not have to be active all the time. Frequently, we understand fairly well how a mechanism works without understanding as well what causes or prevents its activation—in the examples provided earlier, why some flees bite and others do not bite infected rats, or if they do bite why the infection is not always transmitted to other organisms; or, in Elster's example, why some individuals are more prone than others to engage in a reduction of cognitive dissonance or when there is some inclination to do so. Even when we have an idea of the factors that are favorable or unfavorable to the activation of the mechanism, that idea is often less precise than our understanding of the mechanism itself.

Fourth, mechanisms may work, influence things, just through the knowledge of their existence. Many things would be organized differently if potential free riding was not there, in the background, to make these alternatives difficult or impossible. In that role, free riding contributes to the explanation of present arrangements.[17] Similarly, as stressed at the outset (chapter 1), yardstick competition among governments can be an important element in the explanation of actual policies even when governments do not engage in it.

### 9.3.3. Arguments

Economics is a critical or argumentative science in a way that physics is no more or only marginally. In both disciplines, researchers do exchange among themselves arguments about aspects of the world. Thus, both can be viewed as critical, argumentative sciences. But in economics that exchange takes place in the context of a voluminous exchange of views with society whereas, in contemporary physical sciences, this the case only on some issues like global warming.

Let us first consider the exchange of views with society. The starting point of our reflection should be the fact that, even without the contribution of economics and other social sciences, society would know a lot, so to say, about itself. Politicians, businessmen, journalists, civil servants, and people in general have a detailed practical knowledge of the domains they are mostly concerned with, and today they are also well informed about more general matters. A major limit of their knowledge, however, is with regard to underlying interactions or mechanisms. Social sciences, and especially, economics, have thrived from the exploitation of that limit. One of their main contributions to society has consisted from the beginning in uncovering, bringing to light, mechanisms—or the possibility thereof.

That the main task of social sciences is the study of the unwanted and unforeseen consequences of individual actions is a theme one tends to associate with Hayek or Popper. That formula, however, may give to the insistence on underlying mechanisms an association with individualism and an ideological connotation we can eschew by referring instead to Marshall (1890):

> And it happens that in economics, neither those effects of known causes, nor those causes of known effects which are most patent, are generally the most important. "That which is not seen" is often better worth studying than that "which is seen". For experience shows, as might have been anticipated, that common sense, and instinct, are inadequate for this work; that even a business training does not always lead a man to search for those causes of causes, which lie beyond his immediate experience; and that it does not always direct that search well, even when he makes the attempt. For help in doing that, everyone must perforce rely on the powerful machinery of thought and knowledge that has gradually been built up by past generations." (ed. 1962, annex C, "The scope and method of economics," p. 642)

The tradition in economics of elaborate arguments critical of widespread perceptions inspired by common sense is still alive. There is a methodological continuity between Smith's invisible hand, Say's law of markets, Ricardo's theory of comparative advantage, Malthus's and Marx's dynamics, Keynes's (and Mandeville's) saving paradox, Olson's logic of collective action, Tullock's theory of rent-seeking, Stigler on regulation capture, Akerlof's market for "lemons," Ricardian equivalence, new classical economics, etc. In each case an underlying mechanism is put forward that is interesting in itself but also challenges received views, shared in general both in society and in academia. The contributions cited are well-known but many others, pertaining to a variety of topics or issues, have as one of their dimensions the same pattern: an underlying mechanism put forward at least in part as an argument critical of received opinion.

Among the questions raised by that pattern (Mingat, Salmon, and Wolfelsperger 1985, Salmon 1994), I will only consider the following three. First, to what extent is some empirical support needed for the arguments to make sense? What is put forward as a critical argument in the examples listed is (or is mainly) a mechanism, or an interaction, rather than an empirical law or regularity. Of course, there are also many empirical regularities, with no reference to mechanisms, that are exposed by economists as critiques of received opinion or more generally as contributions to public debates. It is also true that in some of these examples, the display of the mechanism is complemented and its assertion supported by conventional (econometric or statistical) empirical results. Still, often, the reference to the real world consists only in showing in an informal way that the mechanism may account for some facts. As we saw, this is Sugden's interpretation of the methodology underlying Shelling's contribution. But our presentation may be too static. From a perspective on science that focuses on its dynamics, accounting for some facts may be only a first step in a process in which other facts will be brought forward, critiques will trigger new investigations, and so on.

The argumentative interpretation suggests other patterns. In particular, showing that "something" is possible is uninteresting if it is not an objection to the view that this "something" is impossible or inconceivable. Smith's invisible hand is the basis of a critique of the view that only voluntary coordination can produce the variety of individual actions and collective outcomes that characterize a complex economy. Similarly, Olson's theory of collective action shows that it is not necessarily because of divergence of interests that a collective action does not take place.

Second, although the word model is not used in the oldest contributions, and not always in the more recent ones, the way each of the mechanisms mentioned earlier may be thought of in retrospect is typically as a central element in a non-linguistic model, in the sense given before to that term. The early contributions also confirm that the way, formal or informal, concise or convoluted, in which that model was described in the first place does not really matter (Adam Smith was no Walras or Debreu). But, as noted, whether or not the mechanism is supposed to be also present in the real world depends on the relation stated between the model and the real system or the real world. The thing in the model which is said to have a counterpart in reality, or *possibly* to have a counterpart in reality, may be the mechanism itself or only a relation (or something else) derived in the model from the mechanism.

The dynamics of argumentation within the profession is partly influenced by what it is vis-à-vis society—partly autonomous, partly similar, partly specific. Arguments typically take the form of vast scientific research programs in which often nowadays hundreds if not thousands of scholars participate (Mingat, Salmon, and Wolfelsperger, 1985, chapter 1). The division of labor and other sociological necessities related to large numbers require individual contributions to be highly specialized, which may well cause the general purpose of the program to become invisible. Only tiny sub-segments of the program are signaled as such. Yet, much changed but still identifiable, the invisible hand, comparative advantage or the logic of collective action are still with us, in the world of models and arguments but also, if only sometimes in an indirect way, of reality

## 9.4. CONCLUSION

An aim of this chapter is to justify the approach adopted in the book. One feature of that approach is the absence both of normative discussions and of advice, recommendations, prescriptions, or even suggestions. Another is the relatively limited place given to empirical findings and to formal modeling. Perhaps the best way to characterize the whole contribution is to say that it is a discussion. This is perhaps particularly suitable in the case of this book (given its topic) but we can also interpret science in general, social science and economics in particular, as a critical discussion, a process in which the objects exchanged are arguments. A difference between natural and social sciences is the importance, greater in the latter, of discussion with society at large. To contribute to the reflections and debates that take place in society, not only empirical findings but also reference to possible relations, causes, processes, or mechanisms may be valuable, especially when their uncovering has required (beyond common sense) reasoning within artificial settings—that is, within non-linguistic models, described or not with formal tools.

The main intellectual objective pursued in this book is to contribute to the recognition of yardstick competition among governments as something that must be kept in mind, something—like free riding or comparative advantage, but more modestly—that is part of our intellectual furniture, baggage, or landscape. It does not matter too much that it is often found unimportant or irrelevant. As a mechanism it may also lie in the background, at rest for the moment but available, and possibly influential merely because of awareness within government that some event could get it started. If that event is a policy, awareness that the policy could trigger actual yardstick competition may condition in one direction or the other the decision to adopt it. Both the objective of the book and the mechanism itself seem simple, but the real world (contrary to models) is definitely not. Since our interest is above all in the real world, this explains the painstaking discussions developed in the different chapters.

## NOTES

1. Ashworth and Bueno de Mesquita (2014) focus on the interaction between the two (incompetence of voters and motivation of politicians).
2. An argument for representative government is that politicians are more able than voters to judge the effects of policies. The reason traditionally provided for the difference is that politicians are more qualified, or more specialized in policy decision-making, than are voters (Manin 1997, Maskin and Tirole 2004). The reason underlying our analysis in this book is based on information asymmetry faced by voters, which affects policies or instruments rather than outcomes. The question discussed now, in the text, is about governments pandering to voters' demands about outcomes, not policies.
3. Mimicking and yardstick competition do play a role according to Choumert (2009).
4. There is a *village fleuri* label and, related to it, a competition for prizes in the two countries.
5. Their estimates are compared to standard, supposedly objective, figures on per-capita income, unemployment, life expectancy, income inequality, years of schooling, home ownership, air and water pollution, and homicide.
6. In Bordignon, Cerniglia, and Revelli (2004), yardstick comparisons between two governments may lead to a negative rather than a positive correlation between their responses to shocks. In other words, yardstick competition may lead to the inverse of mimicking.
7. The empirical part of their contribution is about the tax rates decided by the French regions between 1984 and 1999. It consists both of descriptive statistics, showing a high degree of convergence upward of some of the taxes, and an econometric analysis on panel data, showing some spatial interdependence among neighboring regions. The authors consider that mimicking is confirmed and, because of its upward direction, the convergence process unlikely to be caused by tax competition. To what extent may mimicking account for the observed overall convergence? French regions became full-scale decentralized jurisdictions only in 1981–82 and, as the authors themselves note, were given fiscal autonomy only in 1986, which means that they were still building up their role or influence during much of the period studied. The spatial econometric evidence is more significant but with no bearing on overall convergence—and also, as noted by Elhorst and Fréret (2009, p. 941), with no attempted identification of yardstick competition as the mechanism underlying mimicking.
8. Or, in a more general setting, denied (Auriol 2000)
9. Cited in Høyland, Moene, and Willumsen (2012).
10. However, the prevalence in the countries concerned of informal ways to do business suggests that changes in formal procedures may be less important than they look (Hallward-Driemeier and Pritchett 2015). Possible perverse effects may be less serious as a consequence.
11. I used to refer to "describing" models; but "describer," the word used in Crespo (2013), seems preferable.
12. More generally, for Harré (1972, p. 174), a philosopher of science, "the proper use of models is the very basis of scientific thinking."
13. Although I developed my views on models without knowledge of Mary Morgan's important work (see Morgan 2012), there is clearly a relation between the two

analyses. One source of differences is, I think, my reliance on Giere's interpretation of models (i.e. described models) as non-linguistic entities and the implications of that interpretation. See a criticism of Morgan and Morrisson (1999) along that line in Giere (1999, p. 53). Note also that for Morgan and Morrison, "economic modelling emerged in the 1930s and only became a standard method in the post-1950 period" (p. 6), whereas I argue that reasoning in terms of models has been a central feature of economics since its beginnings.

14. Lucas (1982) refers to "fully articulated, artificial economic systems that can serve as laboratories" (p. 271), For Guala (2005), "you do things with models, you don't just contemplate them or put them is correspondence with reality" (p. 212).

15. In that case, the underlying methodology is not very different in practice from that proposed in Friedman (1953) when interpreted correctly—that is, by giving its proper hierarchical position to what Friedman says therein about the domain or scope of the hypothesis (Mingat, Salmon, and Wolfelsperger 1985, chapter 6).

16. Salmon (2000b) includes a response to some of these comments, in particular those made by Mäki (1998). Uncertainty about the nature of mechanisms is still present if we believe Illari and Williamson (2012), who write: "After a decade of intense debate about mechanisms, there is still no consensus on characterization" (p. 119). The ten-year debate they refer to started with Machamer, Darden, and Craver (2000).

17. A similar logic underlies the seminal article of Tullock (1967) on what was to become the theory of rent-seeking.

# REFERENCES

Acemoglu, Daron, and James A. Robertson (2005). *Economic Origins of Dictatorship and Democracy*. Cambridge and New York: Cambridge University Press.

Acemoglu, Daron, and James A. Robertson (2012). *Why Nations Fail*. New York: Crown Business.

Adsera, Alicia, Carles Boix, and Mark Payne (2003). "Are you being served? Political accountability and the quality of government," *Journal of Law, Economics, and Organization* 19(2): 445–90.

Ahmad, Ehtisham, and Bob Searle (2006). "On the implementation of transfers to subnational governments," in: G. Brosio and E. Ahmad (eds.), *Handbook of Fiscal Federalism*. Cheltenham: Edward Elgar, pp. 381–404.

Aidt, Toke S., and Jayasri Dutta (2017). "Fiscal federalism and electoral accountability," *Journal of Public Economic Theory* 19(1): 38–58.

Alfonso, Antonio, Ludger Schuknecht, and Vito Tanzi (2005). "Public sector efficiency: an international comparison," *Public Choice* 123(3–4): 321–47.

Allers, Maarten A. (2012). "Yardstick competition, fiscal disparities, and equalization," *Economics Letters* 117: 4–6.

Allers, Maarten A. (2014). "Are we getting value for our tax money? Improving the transparency of subnational government performance," MS. Center for Research on Local Government Economics (COELO), University of Groningen.

Allers, Maarten A., and J. Paul Elhorst (2005). "Tax mimicking and yardstick competition among local governments in the Netherlands," *International Tax and Public Finance* 12: 493–513.

Allers, Maarten A., and J. Paul Elhorst (2011). "A simultaneous equations model of fiscal policy interactions," *Journal of Regional Science* 51: 271–91.

Ambrosiano, Flavia, and Massimo Bordignon (2015). "Normative versus positive theories of revenue assignments in federations," in: G. Brosio and E. Ahmad (eds.), *Handbook of Multilevel Finance*. Cheltenham: Edward Elgar, pp. 231–63.

Ansolabehere, Stephen (2006). "Voters, candidates, and parties," in: B.R. Weingast and D.A. Wittman (eds.), *The Oxford Handbook of Political Economy*. Oxford and New York: Oxford University Press, pp. 29–49.

Ashworth, John, and Bruno Heyndels (1997). "Politicians' preferences on local tax rates: an empirical analysis," *European Journal of Political Economy* 13: 479–502.

Ashworth, Scott (2012). "Electoral accountability: recent theoretical and empirical work," *Annual Review of Political Science* 15: 183–201.

Ashworth, Scott, and Ethan Bueno de Mesquita (2014). "Is voter competence good for voters? Information, rationality, and democratic performance," *American Political Science Review* 108(3): 565–87.

Auriol, Emmanuelle (2000). "Concurrence par comparaison: un point de vue normatif," *Revue Economique* 51(3): 621–34.

Aussaresses, General Paul (2001). *Services spéciaux Algérie 1955–1957*. Paris: Perrin. English version: *The Battle of the Casbah: Counter-Terrorism and Torture*. New York: Enigma Books, 2005.

Aussaresses, General Paul (2008). *Je n'ai pas tout dit: ultimes révélations au service de la France*. Paris: Editions du Rocher.

Baiman, Stanley, and Joel S. Demski (1980). "Economically optimal performance evaluation and control systems," *Journal of Accounting Research* 1 (Supplement): 184–220.

Banks, Jeffrey S., and Rangarajan K. Sundaram (1993). "Adverse selection and moral hazard in a repeated elections model," in: W.A. Barnett, M.J. Hinich and N.J. Schofield (eds.), *Political Economy: Institutions, Competition, and Representation*. Cambridge and New York: Cambridge University Press, pp. 295–311.

Banks, Jeffrey S., and Rangarajan K. Sundaram (1998). "Optimal retention in agency problems," *Journal of Economic Theory* 82: 293–323.

Bardhan, Pranab (2002). "Decentralization of governance and development," *Journal of Economic Perspectives* 16(4): 185–205.

Bartolini, David, and Raffaella Santolini (2012). "Political yardstick competition among Italian municipalities on spending decisions," *Annals of Regional Science* 49(1): 213–35.

Baskaran, Thushyanthan (2014). "Identifying local tax mimicking with administrative borders and a policy reform," *Journal of Public Economics* 118: 41–51.

Bell, David A. (2001). "Culture and religion," in: W. Dyle (ed.), *Old Regime France 1648–1788*. Oxford and New York: Oxford University Press, pp. 78–104.

Bellaigue, Christopher de (2017). *The Islamic Enlightenment: The Struggle between Faith and Reason, 1798 to Modern Times*. London and New York: Norton.

Belleflamme, Paul, and Jean Hindriks (2005). "Yardstick competition and political agency problems," *Social Choice and Welfare* 24: 155–69.

Benz, Arthur (2012). "Yardstick competition and policy-learning in multi-level systems," *Regional and Federal Studies* 22(3): 251–67.

Berman, Harold J. (1983). *Law and Revolution: The Formation of the Western Legal Tradition*. Cambridge (Mass.) and London: Harvard University Press.

Bernholz, Peter, Manfred E. Streit, and Roland Vaubel (eds) (1998). *Political Competition, Innovation and Growth*. Berlin and Heidelberg: Springer.

Besley, Timothy (2006). *Principled Agents? The Political Economy of Good Government*. Oxford and New York: Oxford University Press.

Besley, Timothy (2015). "Law, regulation, and the business climate: the nature and influence of the World Bank Doing Business project," *Journal of Economic Perspectives* 29(3): 99–120.

Besley, Timothy, and Anne Case (1995). "Incumbent behavior: vote-seeking, tax-setting, and yardstick competition," *American Economic Review* 85(1), 25–45.

Besley, Timothy, and Michael Smart (2007). "Fiscal restraints and voter welfare," *Journal of Public Economics* 91: 755–73.

Bhagwati, J.N., and T.N. Srinivasan (1969). "Optimal intervention to achieve non-economic objectives," *Review of Economic Studies* 36(1): 27–38.

Bianchini, Laura, and Federico Revelli (2013). "Green polities: urban environmental performance and government popularity," *Economics and Politics* 25(1): 72–90.

Bird, Richard M. (1993). "Threading the fiscal labyrinth: some issues in fiscal decentralization," *National Tax Journal* 46: 207–27.

Bird, Richard M. (2000). "Fiscal decentralization and competitive governments," in: G. Galeotti, P. Salmon, and R. Wintrobe (eds.), *Competition and Structure. The Political Economy of Collective Decisions: Essays in Honor of Albert Breton.* Cambridge and New York: Cambridge University Press, pp. 129–49.

Bird, Richard M., and François Vaillancourt (2006). "Changing with the times: success, failure and inertia in Canadian fiscal arrangements, 1945–2002," in: J.S. Wallack and T.N. Srinivasan (eds.), *Federalism and Economic Reforms: International Perspectives.* Cambridge and New York: Cambridge University Press, pp. 189–248.

Black, Duncan (1948). "On the rationale of group decision-making," *Journal of Political Economy* 56(1): 23–34.

Blendon, Robert J., Minah Kim, and John M. Benson (2001). "The public versus the World Health Organization on health system performance," *Health Affairs* 20(3): 10–20.

Boadway, Robin (2015). "Intergovernmental transfers: rationale and policy," in: G. Brosio and E. Ahmad (eds.), *Handbook of Multilevel Finance.* Cheltenham: Edward Elgar, pp. 410–36.

Boarnet, Marlon G., and Amihai Glazer (2002). "Federal grants and yardstick competition," *Journal of Urban Economics* 52: 53–64.

Bodenstein, Martin, and Heinrich Ursprung (2005). "Political yardstick competition, economic integration, and constitutional choice in a federation: a numerical analysis of a contest success function model," *Public Choice* 124: 329–52.

Borck, Rainald, Frank M. Fossen, and Thorsten Martin (2015). "Race to the debt trap? Spatial econometric evidence in German municipalities," *Regional Science and Urban Economics* 53: 20–37.

Bordignon, Massimo (2015). "Exit and voice: yardstick versus fiscal competition across governments," *Italian Economic Journal* 1(1): 117–37.

Bordignon, Massimo, Floriana Cerniglia, and Federico Revelli (2003). "In search of yardstick competition: a spatial analysis of Italian municipal property tax setting," *Journal of Urban Economics* 54: 199–217.

Bordignon, Massimo, Floriana Cerniglia and Federico Revelli (2004). "Yardstick competition in intergovernmental relationships: theory and empirical predictions," *Economics Letters* 83(3): 325–33.

Bordignon, Massimo, Matteo Gamalerio, and Gilberto Turati (2013). "Decentralization, vertical fiscal imbalance, and political selection," CESifo Working Paper 4459.

Borooah, Vani K. (2014). *Europe in an Age of Austerity.* Heidelberg: Springer.

Bosch, Núria, and Albert Solé-Ollé (2007). "Yardstick competition and the political costs of raising taxes: an empirical analysis of Spanish municipalities," *International Tax and Public Finance* 14: 71–92.

Brennan, Geoffrey, and James M. Buchanan (1980). *The Power to Tax: Analytical Foundations of a Fiscal Constitution.* Cambridge and New York: Cambridge University Press.

Breton, Albert (1987). "Towards a theory of competitive federalism," *European Journal of Political Economy* 3(1–2): 263–329.

Breton, Albert (1996). *Competitive Governments: An Economic Theory of Politics and Public Finance.* Cambridge and New York: Cambridge University Press.

Breton, Albert (2000). "Federalism and decentralization: ownership rights and the superiority of federalism," *Publius* 30(2): 1–16.

Breton, Albert (2006). "Modelling vertical competition," in: Ehtisham Ahmad and Giorgio Brosio (eds.), *Handbook of Fiscal Federalism.* Cheltenham: Edward Elgar, pp. 86–105.

Breton, Albert (2015). "Toward a positive theory of federalism and political decentralization," in: G. Brosio and E. Ahmad (eds.), *Handbook of Multilevel Finance*. Cheltenham: Edward Elgar, pp. 66–84.

Breton, Albert, Alberto Cassone, and Angela Fraschini (1998). "Decentralization and subsidiarity: toward a theoretical reconciliation," *University of Pennsylvania Journal of International Economic Law* 19(1): 21–51.

Breton, Albert, and Angela Fraschini (2003a). "Vertical competition in unitary states: the case of Italy," *Public Choice* 114(1–2): 57–77.

Breton, Albert, and Angela Fraschini (2003b). "The independence of the Italian Constitutional Court," *Constitutional Political Economy* 14(4): 319–33.

Breton, Albert, and Pierre Salmon (2001). "External effects of domestic regulations: comparing internal and international barriers to trade," *International Review of Law and Economics* 21(2): 135–55.

Breton, Albert and Pierre Salmon (2009). "Compliance in decentralized environmental governance," in: A. Breton, G. Brosio, S. Dalmazzone. and G. Garrone (eds.), *Governing the Environment: Salient Institutional Issues*. Cheltenham and Northampton: Edward Elgar, pp. 174–207.

Breton, Albert, and Heinrich Ursprung (2002). "Globalization, competitive governments, and constitutional choice in Europe," in: H: Kierzkowski (ed.), *Europe and Globalization*. Basingstoke: Palgrave Macmillan, pp. 274–301.

Brosio, Giorgio (1994). *Equilibri instabili: politica ed economia nell'evoluzione dei sistemi federali*. Turin: Bollati Boringhieri.

Brosio, Giorgio (1996) (ed.). *Governo decentralizzato e federalismo: problemi ed esperienze internazionali*. Naples: FORMEZ.

Brosio, Giorgio (2007). "Cases for and against transparency/obfuscation in intergovernmental relations," in: A. Breton, G. Galeotti, P. Salmon, and R. Wintrobe (eds.), *The Economics of Transparency in Politics*. Aldershot and Burlington: Ashgate, pp. 173–87.

Brosio, Giorgio, and Juan Pablo Jimenez (2015). "Maintaining taxes at the center despite decentralization: interactions with national reforms," in: J-P. Faguet and C. Pöschl (eds.), *Is Decentralization Good for Development? Perspectives from Academics and Policy Makers*. Oxford and New York: Oxford University Press, pp. 179–95.

Brueckner, Jan K. (2003). "Strategic interaction among governments: an overview of empirical studies," *International Regional Science Review* 26: 175–88.

Buchanan, James M. (1995/96). "Federalism and individual sovereignty," *Cato Journal* 15(1–2): 259–68.

Bunge, Mario (1997). "Mechanism and explanation," *Philosophy of the Social Sciences* 27(4): 410–65.

Buruma, Ian, and Avishai Margalit (2004). *Occidentalism: the West and its Enemies*. New York: Penguin Press.

Caldeira, Emilie (2012). "Yardstick competition in a federation: theory and evidence from China," *China Economic Review* 23: 878–97.

Caldeira, Emilie, Martial Foucault, and Grégoire Rota-Graziosi (2015). "Decentralization in Africa and the nature of local governments' competition: evidence from Benin," *International Tax and Public Finance* 22(6): 1048–76.

Carruthers, Bruce G., and Naomi R. Lamoreaux (2016). "Regulatory races: the effects of jurisdictional competition on regulatory standards," *Journal of Economic Literature* 54(1): 52–97.

Cartwright, Nancy (1983). *How the Laws of Physics Lie*. Oxford and New York: Oxford University Press.

Case, Anne (1993). "Interstate tax competition after TRA86," *Journal of Policy Analysis and Management* 12(1): 136–48.

Case, Anne C., James R. Hines, and Harvey S. Rosen (1988). "Copycatting: fiscal policies of States and their neighbors," NBER working paper n. 3032.

Case, Anne C., Harvey S. Rosen, and James R. Hines (1993). "Budget spillovers and fiscal policy interdependence," *Journal of Public Economics* 52: 285–307.

Cassette, Aurélie, Jérôme Creel, Etienne Favarque and Sonia Paty (2013). "Governments under influence: country interactions in discretionary fiscal policy," *Economic Modelling* 30: 79–89.

Cassette, Aurélie, and Sonia Paty (2008). "Tax competition among Eastern and Western European countries: with whom do countries compete?" *Economic Systems* 32(4): 307–25.

Caves, Richard E., and Ronald W. Jones (1985). *World Trade and Payments: An Introductio*ⁿ 4th edition. Boston: Little, Brown and Company.

Chandler, J.A. (2007). *Explaining Local Government: Local Government in Britain since 1800*. Manchester and New York: Manchester University Press.

Charbonneau, Etienne, and Gregg G. Van Ryzin (2015). "Benchmarks and citizen judgments of local performance: findings from a survey experiment," *Public Management Review* 17(2): 288–304.

Chiu, Y. Stephen (2002). "On the feasibility of unpopular policies under re-election concerns," *Southern Economic Journal* 68(4): 841–58.

Choumert, Johanna (2009). "Analyse économique d'un bien public local: les espaces verts." Université d'Angers, doctoral dissertation.

Christoffersen, Henrik, Michelle Beyeler, Reiner Eichenberger, Peter Nannestad, and Martin Paldam (2014). *The Good Society: A Comparative Study of Denmark and Switzerland*. Heidelberg: Springer.

Clark, Andrew E., and Andrew J. Oswald (1998). "Comparison-concave utility and following behaviour in social and economic settings," *Journal of Public Economics* 70: 133–55.

Congleton, Roger D. (2006). "The story of Katrina: New Orleans and the political economy of catastrophe," *Public Choice* 127(1–2): 5–30.

Congleton, Roger D. (2007a). "Informational limits to democratic public policy: the jury theorem, yardstick competition, and ignorance," *Public Choice* 132(3–4): 333–52.

Congleton, Roger D. (2007b). "The globalization of politics: rational choice and the internationalization of public policy," MS. Center for Study of Public Choice, George Mason University.

Congleton, Roger D. (2011). *Perfecting Parliament: Constitutional Reform, Liberalism, and the Rise of Western Democracy*. Cambridge and New York: Cambridge University Press.

Congleton, Roger D., and Yongjing Zhang (2013). "Is it all about competence? The human capital of US presidents and economic performance," *Constitutional Political Economy* 24(2): 108–24.

Costa-Font, Joan, and Ana Rico (2006). "Vertical competition in the Spanish National Health System (NHS)," *Public Choice* 128(3–4): 477–98.

Crespo, Ricardo F. (2013). *Philosophy of the Economy: An Aristotelian Approach*. Heidelberg: Springer.

Dafflon, Bernard, and Thierry Madiès (2009). *Decentralization: A Few Principles from the Theory of Fiscal Federalism*. Paris: Agence Française de Développement.

Dassonneville, Ruth, and Marc Hooghe (2015). "Are voters benchmarking the economy? An experimental test on the impact of pre-benchmarked economic information," MS. Universities of Montreal and Leuven.

Davies, Ronald B., and Krisna Chaitanya Vadlamannati (2013). "A race to the bottom in labor standards? An empirical investigation," *Journal of Development Economics* 103: 1–14.

Davis, Kevin E, Angelina Fisher, Benedict Kingsbury, and Sally Engle Merry (2012). *Governance by Indicators: Global Power Through Quantification and Rankings.* Oxford and New York: Oxford University Press.

Delgado, Francisco J., Santiago Lago-Peñas, and Matias Mayor (2015). "On the determinants of local tax rates: new evidence from Spain," *Contemporary Economic Policy* 33(2): 351–68.

Devereux, Michael P., Ben Lockwood, and Michela Redoano (2008). "Do countries compete over corporate tax rates?" *Journal of Public Economics* 92: 1210–35.

Dijk, Oege (2012). *Keeping up with the Medici: three essays on social comparison, consumption and risk*, European University Institute, Florence, Italy, doctorate thesis.

Dincer, Oguzhan C, Christopher J. Ellis, and Glen R.Waddell (2010). "Corruption, decentralization and yardstick competition," *Economic Governance* 11: 269–94.

Dobbins, Michael, and Kerstin Martens (2012). "Towards an education approach à la finlandaise? French education policy after PISA," *Journal of Education Policy* 27(1): 23–43.

Dubois, Eric, and Sonia Paty (2010). "Yardstick competition: which neighbours matter?" *Annals of Regional Science* 44: 433–52.

Duch, Raymond M., and Randoph T. Stevenson (2008). *The Economic Vote: How Political and Economic Institutions Condition Election Results.* Cambridge and New York: Cambridge University Press.

Duru-Bellat, Marie (2011). "From the appealing power of PISA data to the delusions of benchmarking: does that challenge any evaluation of educational systems?" in: M.A. Pereyra, H-G. Kotthoff, and R. Cowen (eds.), *PISA under Examination: Changing Knowledge, Changing Tests, and Changing Schools.* Rotterdam: Sense Publishers, pp. 157–67.

Edmark, Karin, and Hanna Agren (2008). "Identifying strategic interactions in Swedish local income tax policies," *Journal of Urban Economics* 63: 849–57.

Elhorst, J. Paul, and Sandy Fréret (2009). "Evidence of political yardstick competition in France using a two-regime spatial Durbin model with fixed effects," *Journal of Regional Science* 49(5): 931–51.

Elster, Jon (1989). *Nuts and Bolts for the Social Sciences.* Cambridge and New York: Cambridge University Press.

Elster, Jon (1999). "Accountability in politics," in: Adam Przeworski, Susan C. Stokes, and Bernard Manin (eds.), *Democracy, Accountability and Representation.* Cambridge and New York: Cambridge University Press, pp. 253–78.

Elster, Jon (2007). *Explaining Social Behavior: More Nuts and Bolts for the Social Sciences.* Cambridge and New York: Cambridge University Press.

Enikolopov, Ruben, and Ekaterina Zhuravskaya (2007). "Decentralization and political institutions," *Journal of Public Economics* 91: 2261–90.

Epple, Dennis, and Allan Zelenitz (1981). "The implications of competition among jurisdictions: does Tiebout need politics?" *Journal of Political Economy* 89(6): 1197–217.

Esteller-Moré, Alejandro, and Leonzio Rizzo (2014). "US excise tax horizontal inter-dependence: yardstick versus tax competition," *The Annals of Regional Science*, 52(3): 711–37.

Fearon, James D. (1999). "Electoral accountability and the control of politicians: selecting good types versus sanctioning poor performance," in: Adam Przeworski, Susan C. Stokes, and Bernard Manin (eds.), *Democracy, Accountability and Representation*. Cambridge and New York: Cambridge University Press, pp. 55–97.

Fearon, James D. (2011). "Self-enforcing democracy," *Quarterly Journal of Economics* 126(4): 1661–708.

Feld, Lars P. (2007). "Regulatory competition and federalism in Switzerland: diffusion by horizontal and vertical interaction," in: Peter Bernholz and Roland Vaubel (eds.), *Political Competition and Economic Regulation*. London: Routledge, pp. 200–40.

Feld, Lars P., Jean-Michel Josselin, and Yvon Rocaboy (2002). "Le mimétisme fiscal: une application aux régions françaises," *Économie et Prévision* 156(2002–5): 43–49.

Feld, Lars P., Jean-Michel Josselin, and Yvon Rocaboy (2003). "Tax mimicking among regional jurisdictions," in: A. Marciano and J.-M. Josselin (eds.), *From Economic to Legal Competition: New Perspectives on Law and Institutions in Europe*. Cheltenham: Edward Elgar, pp. 105–19.

Feld, Lars P., and Gebhard Kirchgässner (2000). "Direct democracy, political culture, and the outcome of economic policy: a report on the Swiss experience," *European Journal of Political Economy* 16: 287–306.

Feld, Lars P., Gebhard Kirchgässner, and Christoph A. Schaltegger (2010). "Decentralized taxation and the size of government: evidence from Swiss state and local governments," *Southern Economic Journal* 77(1): 27–48.

Feld, Lars P., and Emmanuelle Reulier (2009). "Strategic tax competition in Switzerland: evidence from a panel of the Swiss cantons," *German Economic Review* 10(1): 91–114.

Ferejohn, John (1986). "Incumbent performance and electoral control," *Public Choice* 50(1–3): 5–26.

Fertig, Michael (2003). "Who's to blame? The determinants of German students' achievement in the PISA 2000 study," IZA discussion paper No. 739.

Fiorina, Morris P. (1981). *Retrospective Voting in American National Elections*. New Haven: Yale University Press.

Fiva, Jon H., and Jørn Rattsø (2007). "Local choice of property taxation: evidence from Norway," *Public Choice* 132: 457–70.

Foucault, Martial (2006). "How useful is the '*cumul des mandats*' for being re-elected? Empirical evidence from the 1997 French legislative elections," *French Politics* 4(3): 292–311.

Foucault, Martial, Thierry Madies, and Sonia Paty (2008). "Public spending interactions and local politics: empirical evidence from French municipalities," *Public Choice* 137: 57–80.

François, Abel, and Laurent Weill (2016). "Does holding a local mandate alter the activities of deputies? Evidence from the French Assemblée Nationale," *French Politics* 14(1): 30–54.

Fredriksson, Per G., John A. List, and Daniel L. Millimet (2004). "Chasing the smoke-stack: strategic policymaking with multiple instruments," *Regional Sciences and Urban Economics* 34: 387–410.

Friedman, Milton (1953). "The methodology of positive economics," in: *Essays in Positive Economics*. Chicago: University of Chicago Press, pp. 3–43.

Fu, Qiang, and Jingfeng Lu (2012). "Micro foundations of multi-prize lottery contests: a perspective of noisy performance ranking," *Social Choice and Welfare* 38: 497–517.

Fukuyama, Francis (2011). *The Origins of Political Order: From Prehuman Times to the French Revolution*. London: Profile Books Ltd.

Fukuyama, Francis (2014). *Political Order and Political Decay: From the Industrial Revolution to the Globalization of Democracy*. London: Profile Books Ltd.

Fukuyama, Francis (2015). "Why is democracy performing so poorly?" *Journal of Democracy* 26(1): 11–20.

Gentzkow, Matthew, and Jesse M. Shapiro (2008). "Competition and truth in the market for news," *Journal of Economic Perspectives* 22(2): 133–54.

Gérard, Marcel, and Laurent Van Malderen (2012). "Tax interaction among Walloon municipalities: Is there room for yardstick competition, intellectual trend and partisan monopoly effect?" CESifo WP 4025.

Geys, Benny (2006). "Looking across borders: a test of spatial policy interdependence using local government efficiency ratings," *Journal of Urban Economics* 60: 443–62.

Geys, Benny, and Jan Vermeir (2008). "On party cues and yardstick voting," *European Journal of Political Economy* 24(2): 470–77.

Ghosh, Arpita, and Patrick Hummel (2015). "Cardinal contests," MS. Cornell University and Google Inc., International World Wide Web Conference Committee (IW3C2).

Giere, Ronald N. (1987). *Explaining Science: A Cognitive Approach*. Chicago and London: The University of Chicago Press.

Giere, Ronald N. (1999). "Using models to represent reality," in: L. Magnani, N.J. Nersessian, and P. Thagard (eds.), *Model-based Reasoning in Scientific Discovery*. New York: Kluwer/Plenum, pp. 41–57.

Glaeser, Edward L., and Andrei Shleifer (2005). "The Curley effect: the economics of shaping the electorate," *Journal of Law, Economics, and Organization* 21(1): 1–19.

Glazer, Amihai (2009). "Learning and imitation in theocracies," in: M. Ferrero and R. Wintrobe (eds.), *The Political Economy of Theocracy*. New York: Palgrave Macmillan, pp. 203–11.

Goldstein, Harvey, and David J. Spiegelhalter (1996). "League tables and their limitations: statistical issues in comparisons of institutional performance," *Journal of the Royal Statistical Society. Series A (Statistics in Society)* 159(3): 385–443.

Green, Jerry R., and Nancy L. Stokey (1983). "A comparison of tournaments and contracts," *Journal of Political Economy* 91(3): 349–64.

Grillo, Michele, and Michele Polo (1993). "Political exchange and allocation of surplus: a model of two-party competition," in: A. Breton, G. Galeotti, P. Salmon, and R. Wintrobe (eds.), *Preferences and Democracy*. Dordrecht: Kluwer, pp. 215–44.

Guala, Francesco (2005). *The Methodology of Experimental Economics*. Cambridge and New York: Cambridge University Press.

Hall, Joshua C., Justin M. Ross (2010). "Tiebout competition, yardstick competition, and tax instrument choice: evidence from Ohio school districts," *Public Finance Review* 38(6): 710–37.

Hallward-Driemeier, Mary, and Lant Pritchett (2015). "How business is done in the developing world: deals versus rules," *Journal of Economic Perspectives* 29(3): 121–40.

Hansen, Kasper M., Asmus L. Olsen, and Mickael Bech (2015). "Cross-national yardstick comparisons: a choice experiment on a forgotten voter heuristic," *Political Behavior* 37(4): 767–89.

Hanson, Gordon H. (2010). "Why isn't Mexico rich?" *Journal of Economic Literature* 48(4): 987–1004.

Hanushek, Eric A., and Ludger Woessmann (2010). "Schooling, educational achievement, and the Latin American growth puzzle," *Journal of Development Economics* 99: 497–512.

Harré, Rom (1972). *The Philosophy of Science: An Introductory Essay*. Oxford and New York: Oxford University Press.

Harrison, Kathryn (1996). *Passing the Buck: Federalism and the Canadian Environment*. Vancouver: University of British Columbia Press.

Hayashi, Masayoshi, and WataruYamamoto (2017). "Information sharing, neighborhood demarcation, and yardstick competition: an empirical analysis of intergovernmental expenditure interaction in Japan," *International Tax and Public Finance* 24(1): 134–63.

Hettich, Walter, and Stanley L. Winer (1988). "Economic and political foundations of tax structure," *American Economic Review* 78(4): 701–12.

Heyndels, Bruno, and Jeff Vuchelen (1998). "Tax mimicking among Belgian municipalities," *National Tax Journal* 51(1): 89–101.

Hillman, Arye L. (2003). *Public Finance and Public Policy*. Cambridge and New York: Cambridge University Press.

Hindriks, Jean, and Ben Lockwood (2009). "Decentralization and electoral accountability: incentives, separation and voter welfare," *European Journal of Political Economy* 25: 385–97.

Hirschman, Albert O. (1970). *Exit, Voice, and Loyalty: Responses to Decline in Firms, Organizations, and States*. Cambridge (Mass.): Harvard University Press.

Hochman, Harold M., and James D. Rogers (1969). "Pareto optimal redistribution," *American Economic Review* 59(4): 542–57.

Holmstrom, Bengt (1979). "Moral hazard and observability," *Bell Journal of Economics* 10(1): 74–91.

Holmstrom, Bengt (1982). "Moral hazard in teams," *Bell Journal of Economics* 13(2): 324–40.

Holmstrom, Bengt, and P. Milgrom (1991). "Multitask principal-agent analyses: incentives contracts, asset ownership, and job design," *Journal of Law, Economics, and Organization* Special Issue, 7: 24–52.

Hory, Marie-Pierre (2018). "Delayed mimicking: the timing of fiscal interactions in Europe," *European Journal of Political Economy* 55: 97-118.

Houston, R.A. (2002). *Literacy in Early Modern Europe: Culture and Education 1500–1800*. 2nd Edition. London: Longma (Pearson Education).

Howitt, Peter, and Ronald Wintrobe (1995), "The political economy of inaction," *Journal of Public Economics* 56(3): 329–53.

Høyland, Bjørn, Karl Moene, and Fredrik Willumsen (2012). "The tyranny of international index rankings, *Journal of Development Economics* 97(1): 1–14.

Huang, Haifeng (2015). "International knowledge and domestic evaluations in a changing society: the case of China," *American Political Science Review* 109(3): 613–34.

Huang, Haifeng, and Yao-Yuan Yeh (2017). "Information from abroad: foreign media, selective exposure and political support in China," *British Journal of Political Science* 1–26. doi: 10.1017/S0007123416000739.

Hugh-Jones, David (2009). "Constitutions and policy comparisons: direct and representative democracy when states learn from their neighbours," *Journal of Theoretical Politics* 21(1): 25–61.

Huntington, Samuel P. (1991). *The Third Wave: Democratization in the Late-Twentieth Century*. Norman: University of Oklahoma Press.

Illari, Phyllis McKay, and Jon Williamson (2012). "What is a mechanism? Thinking about mechanisms across the sciences," *European Journal for the Philosophy of Science* 2(1): 119–35.

James, Oliver, and Alice Moseley (2014). "Does performance information about public services affect citizens' perceptions, satisfaction and voice behaviour? Field experiments with absolute and relative performance information," *Public Administration* 92(2): 493–511.

Joanis, Marcelin (2014). "Shared accountability and partial decentralization in local good provision," *Journal of Development Economics* 107: 28–37.

Johnson, Harry G. (1973). *The Theory of Income Distribution*. London: Gray-Mills Publishing Ltd.

Jones, Ronald W. (1971). "A three-factor model in theory, trade, and history," in: J. Bhagwati, R.W. Jones, R.A. Mundell, and J. Vanek (eds.), *Trade, Balance of Payments and Growth*. Amsterdam: North Holland, pp. 3–21.

Kalb, Alexander, Benny Geys, and Friedrich Heinemann (2012). "Value for money? German local government efficiency in a comparative perspective," *Applied Economics* 44(2): 201–18.

Kammas, Pantelis (2011). "Strategic fiscal interaction among OECD countries," *Public Choice* 147(3–4): 459–80.

Kayser, Mark Andreas, and Arndt Leininger (2013) . "A benchmarking forecast of the 2013 Bundestag election," MS, Hertie School of Governance, Berlin.

Kayser, Mark Andreas, and Arndt Leininger (2016). "A predictive test of voters' economic benchmarking: the 2013 German Bundestag election," *German Politics* 25(1): 106–30.

Kayser, Mark Andreas, and Michael Peress (2012). "Benchmarking across borders: electoral accountability and the necessity of comparison," *American Political Science Review* 106(3): 661–84.

Keen, Michael (1998). "Vertical tax externalities in the theory of fiscal federalism," *IMF Staff Papers* 45(3): 454–85.

Keohane, Robert O. (1984). *After Hegemony: Cooperation and Discord in the World Political Economy*. Princeton: Princeton University Press.

Keohe, Timothy J., and Kim J. Ruhl (2010). "Why have economic reforms in Mexico not generated growth? *Journal of Economic Literature* 48(4): 1005–27.

Keynes, John Maynard (1938). Letter of 4 July 1938 to R.F. Harrod, in: *Collected Writings*, vol. 14. London: Macmillan, pp. 295–97.

Kindleberger, Charles P. (1976). "Systems of international economic organization," in: D. Calleo (ed.), *Money and the Coming World Order*. New York: New York University Press, pp. 15–39.

Kirchgässner, Gebhard, and Werner W. Pommerehne (1996). "Tax harmonization and tax competition in the European Union: lessons from Switzerland," *Journal of Public Economics* 60(3): 351–71.

Knoeber, Charles R. (1989). "A real game of chicken: contracts, tournaments, and the production of broilers," *Journal of Law, Economics, and Organization* 5(2): 271–92.

Konrad, Kai A. (2009). *Strategy and Dynamics in Contests*. Oxford and New York: Oxford University Press.

Kotsogiannis, Christos, and Robert Schwager (2008). "Accountability and fiscal equalization," *Journal of Public Economics* 92: 2336–49.

Ladd, Helen F. (1992). "Mimicking of local tax burdens among neighboring counties," *Public Finance Quarterly* 20(4): 450–67.

Lafay, Jean-Dominique (1993). "The silent revolution of probabilistic voting," in: A. Breton, G. Galeotti, P. Salmon. and R. Wintrobe (eds.), *Preferences and Democracy*. Dordrecht: Kluwer, pp. 159–91.

Laffont, Jean-Jacques (1994). "The new economics of regulation ten years after," *Econometrica* 62(3): 507–37.

Lau, Richard R. (1985). "Two explanations for negativity effects in political behaviour," *American Journal of Political Science* 29(1): 119–38.

Lazear, Edward P., and Sherwin Rosen (1981). "Rank order tournaments as optimal labor contracts," *Journal of Political Economy* 89(5): 841–64.

Leigh, Andrew (2009). "Does the world economy swing national elections?" *Oxford Bulletin of Economics and Statistics* 71(2): 163–81.

Leonard, Mark (2005). *Why Europe will Run the 21st Century*. London and New York: Fourth Estate (Harper and Collins).

LeSage, James P. (2008). "An introduction to spatial econometrics," *Revue d'Economie Industrielle* 123(3): 19–44.

Levitsky, Steven, and Lucan A. Way (2010). *Competitive Authoritarianism: Hybrid Regimes after the Cold War*. Cambridge and New York: Cambridge University Press.

Lewis-Beck, Michael S., Bruno Jérôme, and Véronique Jérôme-Speziari (2001). "Evaluation économique et vote en France et en Allemagne," in: D. Rénié and B. Cautrès (eds.), *L'opinion européenne 2001*. Paris: Presses de Sciences Po, pp. 101–22.

Lewis-Beck, Michael S., and Mary Stegmaier (2013). "The VP-function revisited: a survey of the literature after over 40 years," *Public Choice* 157(3–4): 367–85.

Lingens, Hans (2005). "PISA in Germany: a search for causes and evolving answers," in: J. Zadja (ed.), *International Handbook on Globalization, Education and Policy Research*. Dordrecht: Springer, pp. 327–36.

Linos, Katerina (2013). *The Democratic Foundations of Policy Diffusion: How Health, Family and Employment Laws Spread Across Countries*. Oxford and New York: Oxford University Press.

Little, I.M.D. (1950). *A Critique of Welfare Economics*. Oxford: Clarendon. Revised ed. 1957.

Lucas, Robert E. (1982). *Studies in Business Cycle Theory*. Cambridge (Mass.): MIT Press.

Lundberg, Johan (2014). "On the definition of W in empirical models of yardstick competition," *The Annals of Regional Science* 52(2): 597–610.

Lyytikäinen, Teemu (2012). "Tax competition among local governments: evidence from a property tax reform in Finland," *Journal of Public Economics* 96: 584–95.

Machamer, Peter, Indley Darden, and Carl F. Craver (2000). "Thinking about mechanisms," *Philosophy of Science* 67(1): 1–25.

Mainwaring, Scott (2003). "Introduction," in: S. Mainwaring and C. Elna (eds.), *Democratic Accountability in Latin America*. Oxford and New York: Oxford University Press, pp. 3–33.

Mäki, Uskali (1998). "Comment: mechanisms, models and free riders," in: R. Backhouse, D. Hausman, U. Mäki, and A. Salanti (eds.), *Economics and Methodology: Crossing Boundaries*. London: Macmillan, pp. 97–112.

Mandel, Philipp, and Bernd Süssmuth (2015). "Public education, accountability, and yardstick competition in a federal system," *BE Journal of Economic Analysis and Policy* 15(4): 1679–703.

Manin, Bernard (1997). *Principles of Representative Government*. Cambridge and New York: Cambridge University Press.

Manin, Bernard, Adam Przeworski, and Susan S. Stokes (1999). "Elections and representation," in: Adam Przeworski, Susan C. Stokes, and Bernard Manin (eds.), *Democracy, Accountability and Representation*. Cambridge and New York: Cambridge University Press, pp. 29–54.

Manski, Charles F. (1993). "Identification of endogenous social effects: the reflection problem," *The Review of Economic Studies* 60(3): 531–42.

Markevich, Andrei, and Ekaterina Zhuravskaya (2011). "M-form hierarchy with poorly-diversified divisions: a case of Khrushchev's reform in Soviet Russia," *Journal of Public Economics* 95(11–12): 1550–60.

Marshall, Alfred (1890). *Principles of Economics*. 8th Edition 1962. London: Macmillan and Co Ltd.

Martens, Kerstin, and Dennis Niemann (2010) . "Governance by comparison: how ratings and rankings impact national policy-making in education," MS. Universities of Bremen and Oldenburg, Transtate Working Papers No 139.

Martens, Kerstin, and Dennis Niemann (2013). "When do numbers count? The differential impact of the PISA rating and ranking on education policy in Germany and the US," *German Politics* 22(3): 314–32.

Maskin, Eric, and Jean Tirole (2004). "The politician and the judge: accountability in government," *American Economic Review* 94(4): 1034–54.

Maskin, Eric, Yingyi Qian, and Chenggang Xu (2000). "Incentives, information, and organizational form," *Review of Economic Studies* 67(2): 359–78.

Mattozzi, Andrea, and Antonio Merlo (2015). "Mediocracy," *Journal of Public Economics* 130: 32–44.

Meade, James Edward (1952). *A Geometry of International Trade*. London: George Allen & Unwin Ltd.

Mingat, Alain, and Pierre Salmon (1986). "Choisir sa population pour gagner les élections? Une étude empirique sur les élections municipales de 1953 à 1983," *Revue Française de Science Politique* 36(2): 182–204.

Mingat, Alain, and Pierre Salmon (1988). "Alterable electorates in the context of residential mobility," *Public Choice* 59(1): 67–82.

Mingat, Alain, Pierre Salmon, and Alain Wolfelsperger (1985). *Méthodologie économique*. Paris: Presses Universitaires de France.

Morgan, Mary S. (2012). *The World of the Model: How Economists Work and Think*. Cambridge and New York: Cambridge University Press.

Morgan, Mary S., and Margaret Morrison (1999). Chapters 1 and 2, in: M.S. Morgan and M. Morrison (eds.), *Models as Mediators: Perspectives on Natural and Social Science*. Cambridge and New York: Cambridge University Press, pp. 1–37.

Morrisson, Christian (2015). "Le déclin économique de la France depuis 1981," *Commentaire* 151: 537–43.

Nalebuff, Barry J., and Joseph E. Stiglitz (1983). "Information, competition and markets," *American Economic Review* 73(2): 278–83.

Nannestad, Peter, and Martin Paldam (1994). "The VP-function: A survey of the literature on vote and popularity functions after 25 years," *Public Choice* 79(3–4): 213–45.

Nannestad, Peter, and Martin Paldam (1997). "The grievance asymmetry revisited: a micro study of economic voting in Denmark, 1986–92," *European Journal of Political Economy* 13: 81–99.

North, Douglas C, John Joseph Wallis, and Barry R. Weingast (2009). *Violence and Social Orders: A Conceptual Framework for Interpreting Recorded Human History*. Cambridge and New York: Cambridge University Press.

Oates, Wallace E. (1972). *Fiscal Federalism*. New York: Harcourt Brace Jovanovich.

Oates Wallace E., and Robert M. Schwab (1988). "Economic competition among jurisdictions: efficiency enhancing or distortion inducing?" *Journal of Public Economics* 35: 333–54.

O'Donnell, Guillermo A. (1998). "Horizontal accountability in new democracies," *Journal of Democracy* 9(3): 112–26.

O'Keefe, Mary, W. Kip Viscusi, and Richard J. Zeckhauser (1984). "Economic contests: comparative reward schemes," *Journal of Labor Economics* 2(1): 27–56.

Olsen, Asmus Leth (2017). " Compared to what? How social and historical reference points affect citizens' performance evaluation," *Journal of Public Administration Research and Theory* 27(4): 562–80.

Olson, Mancur (1965). *The Logic of Collective Action: Public Goods and the Theory of Groups*. Cambridge (Mass.): Harvard University Press.

Olson, Mansur (1982). *The Rise and Decline of Nations: Economic Growth, Stagflation, and Economic Rigidities*. London and New Haven: Yale University Press.

Ozouf, Mona (1988). "Public opinion at the end of the Old Regime," *Journal of Modern History* 60 (Supplement): S1–S21.

Pacheco, Julianna (2012). "The social contagion model: exploring the role of public opinion on the diffusion of antismoking legislation across the American States," *The Journal of Politics* 74(01): 187–202.

Padovano, Fabio, and Ilaria Petrarca (2014). "Are the responsibility and yardstick competition hypotheses mutually consistent?" *European Journal of Political Economy* 34: 459–77.

Paldam, Martin (2009). "An essay on the Muslim gap: religiosity and the political system," in: M. Ferrero and R. Wintrobe (eds.), *The Political Economy of Theocracy*. New York: Palgrave Macmillan, pp. 213–342.

Parks, Roger B., and Elinor Ostrom (1981). "Complex models of urban services systems," in: T.N. Clark (ed.), *Urban Policy Analysis: Directions for Future Research, Urban Affairs Annual Reviews*. Beverly Hills: Sage, vol. 21. pp. 171–99. Reprinted in M.D. McGinnis (ed.), *Polycenticity and Local Public Economics: Readings from the Workshop in Political Theory and Policy Analysis*. Ann Arbor: University of Michigan Press, 1999, pp. 355–80.

Persson, Torsten, Gérard Roland, and Guido Tabellini (1997). "Separation of powers and political accountability," *Quarterly Journal of Economics* 112(4): 1163–202.

Persson, Torsten, and Guido Tabellini (2000). *Political Economics: Explaining Economic Policy*. Cambridge (Mass.): The MIT Press.

Pettys, Todd E. (2003). "Competing for the People's affection: federalism's forgotten marketplace," *Vanderbilt Law Review* 56(2): 329–91.

Pitlik, Hans (2007). "A race to liberalization? Diffusion of economic policy reform among OECD economies," *Public Choice* 132: 159–78.

Popper, Karl R. (1945). *The Open Society and its Enemies*. London: Routledge and Kegan Paul. 5th edition 1966 Routledge Paperbacks.

Popper, Karl R. (1963). *Conjectures and Refutations: The Growth of Scientific Knowledge*. London: Routledge and Kegan Paul.

Pritchett, Lant, and Michael Woolcock (2004). "Solutions when *the* solution is the problem: arraying the disarray in development," *World Development* 32(2): 191–212.

Przeworski, Adam, Susan C. Stokes, and Bernard Manin (1999) (eds.). *Democracy, Accountability and Representation*. Cambridge and New York: Cambridge University Press.

Redoano, Michela (2007) . "Fiscal interactions among European countries: does the EU matter?" CESifo WP 1952.

Redoano, Michela (2014). "Tax competition among European countries: does the EU matter?" *European Journal of Political Economy* 34: 353–71.

Reulier, Emmanuelle, and Yvon Rocaboy (2006). "Finite-lived politicians and yardstick competition,"*Journal of Public Finance and Public Choice* 24(1): 23–40.

Revelli, Federico (2002). "Local taxes, national politics and spatial interactions in English district election results," *European Journal of Political Economy* 18: 281–99.

Revelli, Federico (2005). "On spatial public finance empirics," *International Tax and Public Finance* 12(4): 475–92.

Revelli, Federico (2006). "Performance rating and yardstick competition in social service provision," *Journal of Public Economics* 90(3): 459–75.

Revelli, Federico (2008). "Performance competition in local media markets," *Journal of Public Economics* 92(7): 1585–94.

Revelli, Federico (2009). "Spend more, get more? An inquiry into English local government performance," *Oxford Economic Papers* 62(1): 185–207.

Revelli, Federico (2015). "Geografiscal federalism," in: E. Ahmad and G. Brosio (eds.), *Handbook of Multilevel Federalism.* Cheltenham: Edward Elgar, pp. 107–23.

Revelli, Federico, and Per Tovmo (2007). "Revealed yardstick competition: local government efficiency patterns in Norway," *Journal of Urban Economics* 62: 121–34.

Riker, William (1964). *Federalism: Origins, Operation, Significance.* Boston: Little, Brown.

Rincke, Johannes (2009). "Yardstick competition and public sector innovation," *International Tax and Public Finance* 16: 337–61.

Rodden, Jonathan, and Susan Rose-Ackerman (1997). "Does federalism preserve markets? *Virginia Law Review* 83(7): 1521–72.

Rose-Ackerman, Susan (1980). "Risk-taking and reelection: does federalism promote innovation?" *Journal of Legal Studies* 9(3): 593–616.

Ross, George (1995). *Jacques Delors and European Integration.* Cambridge: Polity Press.

Ross, Lee, and Richard N. Nisbett (1991). *The Person and the Situation.* New York: McGraw-Hill. Revised ed. 2011, London: Pinter & Martin.

Salmon, Pierre (1987a). "The logic of pressure groups and the structure of the public sector," *European Journal of Political Economy*: 3(1–2): 55–86.

Salmon, Pierre (1987b). "Decentralisation as an incentive scheme," *Oxford Review of Economic Policy* 3(2): 24–43.

Salmon, Pierre (1991). "Checks and balances and international openness," in: A. Breton, G. Galeotti, P. Salmon, and R. Wintrobe (eds.), *The Competitive State.* Dordrecht: Kluwer, pp. 169–84.

Salmon, Pierre (1992). "Leadership and integration," in: G. Bertin and A. Raynauld (eds.), *L'intégration économique en Europe et en Amérique du Nord / Economic Integration in Europe and North America.* Paris: Clément Juglar, pp. 367–84.

Salmon, Pierre (1993). "Unpopular policies and the theory of representative democracy," in: A. Breton, G. Galeotti, P. Salmon, and R. Wintrobe (eds.), *Preferences and Democracy*, Dordrecht: Kluwer, pp. 13–39.

Salmon, Pierre (1994). "Outrageous arguments in economics and Public Choice," *European Journal of Political Economy* 10(3): 409–26.

Salmon, Pierre (1995). "Nations conspiring against themselves: an interpretation of European integration," in: A. Breton, G. Galeotti, P. Salmon, and R. Wintrobe (eds.), *Nationalism and Rationality*, Cambridge and New York: Cambridge University Press, pp. 290–311.

Salmon, Pierre (1997). "Democratic governments, economic growth and income distribution," in: A. Breton, G. Galeotti, P. Salmon, and R, Wintrobe (eds.), *Understanding Democracy: Economic and Political Perspectives.* Cambridge and New York: Cambridge University Press, pp. 144–60.

Salmon, Pierre (1998). "Free riding as mechanism," in: R. Backhouse, D. Hausman, U. Mäki, and A. Salanti (eds), *Economics and Methodology: Crossing Boundaries.* London: Macmillan, pp. 62–87 (62–119 incl. discussion).

Salmon, Pierre (2000a) "Vertical competition in a unitary state," in: Gianluigi Galeotti, Pierre Salmon, and Ronald Wintrobe (eds.), *Competition and Structure. The Political Economy of Collective Decisions: Essays in Honor of Albert Breton.* Cambridge and New York: Cambridge University Press, pp. 239–56.

Salmon, Pierre (2000b). "Modèles et mécanismes en économie: essai de clarification de leurs relations," *Revue de Philosophie Economique* 1: 105–26.

Salmon, Pierre (2002). "Decentralization and supranationality: the case of the European Union," in: E. Ahmad and V. Tanzi (eds.), *Managing Fiscal Decentralization.* London and New York: Routledge, pp. 99–121.

Salmon, Pierre (2003a). "Accounting for centralisation in the European Union: Niskanen, Monnet or Thatcher?" in: J.M. Josselin and A. Marciano (eds.), *From Economic to Legal Competition: New Perspectives on Law and Institutions in Europe.* Cheltenham: Edward Elgar, pp.165–91.

Salmon, Pierre (2003b). "Assigning powers in the European Union in the light of yardstick competition among governments," *Jahrbuch für Neue Politische Ökonomie* 22: 197–216.

Salmon, Pierre (2004). "The assignment of powers in an open-ended European Union," in: C.B. Blankart and D.C. Mueller (eds.), *A Constitution for the European Union,* Cambridge (Mass.): The MIT Press, pp. 37–60.

Salmon, Pierre (2005). "L'apport informatif des rapports *Doing Business* est précieux mais attention aux effets pervers," in: G. Canivet, M.-A. Frison-Roche, and M. Klein (eds), *Mesurer l'efficacité économique du droit.* Paris: L.G.D.J, pp. 109–22.

Salmon, Pierre (2006). "Political yardstick competition and corporate governance in the European Union," in: G. Ferrarini and E. Wymeersch (eds.), *Investor Protection in Europe.* Oxford and New York: Oxford University Press, pp. 31–58.

Salmon, Pierre (2007). "Réflexions sur la nature et le rôle des modèles en économie," in: A. Leroux and P. Livet (eds.), *Leçons de philosophie économique, Tome III: Science économique et philosophie des sciences.* Paris: Economica, pp. 355–84.

Salmon, Pierre (2010). "Decentralization as an incentive scheme when regional differences are large," in: *La finanze locale in Italia: Rapporto 2009.* Milan: FrancoAngeli, pp. 263–82.

Salmon, Pierre (2014). "How significant is yardstick competition among governments? Three reasons to dig deeper," in: F. Forte, R. Mudambi, and P.M. Navarra (eds.), *A Handbook of Alternative Theories of Public Economics.* Cheltenham: Edward Elgar, pp. 323–41.

Salmon, Pierre (2015). "Horizontal competition in multilevel governmental settings," in: G. Brosio and E. Ahmad (eds.), *Handbook of Multilevel Finance.* Cheltenham: Edward Elgar, pp. 85–106.

Salmon, Wesley C. (1984). *Scientific Explanation and the Causal Structure of the World.* Princeton: Princeton University Press.

Sand-Zantman, Wilfried (2004). "Economic integration and political accountability," *European Economic Review* 48(5): 1001–23.

Santolini, Raffaella (2007). "La letteratura empirica sull'interdependenza e sul comportamento imitativo nelle scelte di politica fiscale," *Studi e Note di Economia* 12(3): 417–33.

Santolini, Raffaella (2009). "The political trend in local government tax setting," *Public Choice* 139: 125–34.

Schaltegger, Christoph A., and Dominique Küttel (2002). "Exit, voice, and mimicking behavior: evidence from Swiss cantons," *Public Choice* 113(1–2): 1–23.

Scharfstein, David S., and Jeremy C. Stein (1990). "Herd behavior and investment," *American Economic Review* 80(3): 465–79.

Scharpf, Fritz W. (1999): *Governing in Europe: Effective and Democratic?* Oxford and New York: Oxford University Press.

Schelling, Thomas C. (1978). *Micromotives and Macrobehavior*. New York: Norton.

Schnellenbach, Jan (2008). "Rational ignorance is not bliss: when do lazy voters learn from decentralised policy experiments?" *Jahrbücher für Nationalökonomie und Statistik* 228: 372–93.

Schulze, Günther G., and Heinrich W. Ursprung (1999). "Globalization of the economy and the nation state," *World Economy* 22(3): 295–352.

Scitovsky, Tibor (1976). *The Joyless Economy: An Inquiry into Human Satisfaction and Consumer Dissatisfaction*. Oxford and New York: Oxford University Press.

Seabright, Paul (1996). "Accountability and decentralization in government: an incomplete contract model," *European Economic Review* 40: 61–91.

Shipan, Charles R., and Craig Volden (2012). "Policy diffusion: seven lessons for scholars and practitioners," *Public Administration Review* 72(6): 788–96.

Shleifer, Andrei (1985). "A theory of yardstick competition," *Rand Journal of Economics* 16: 319–27.

Sigman, Hilary (2003). " Letting states do the dirty work: State responsibility for federal environmental regulation," *National Tax Journal* 56(1, Part 1): 107–22.

Sisak, Dana (2009). "Multi-prize contests: the optimal allocation of prizes," *Journal of Economic Surveys* 23(1): 82–114.

Snidal, Duncan (1985a). "The limits of hegemonic stability," *International Organization* 39(4): 579–614.

Snidal, Duncan (1985b). "Coordination versus prisoners' dilemma: implications for international cooperation and regimes," *American Political Science Review* 79(4): 923–42.

Sobbrio, Francesco (2014). "The political economy of news media: theory, evidence and open issues," in: F. Forte, R. Mudambi, and P.M. Navarra (eds.), *A Handbook of Alternative Theories of Public Economics*. Cheltenham: Edward Elgar, pp. 278–320.

Solé Ollé, Albert (2003). "Electoral accountability and tax mimicking: the effects of electoral margins, coalition government, and ideology," *European Journal of Political Economy* 19: 685–713.

Soroka, Stuart N. (2006). "Good news and bad news: asymmetric responses to economic information," *Journal of Politics* 68(2): 372–85.

Stigler, George J. (1965). *Essays in the History of Economics*. Chicago: The University of Chicago Press.

Stigler, George J. (1974). "Free riders and collective action: an appendix to theories of economic regulation," *Bell Journal of Economics and Management Science* 5(2): 359–65.

Stokes Susan C. (2009). "Political clientelism," in: R.E. Goodin (ed.), *The Oxford Handbook of Political Science*. Oxford and New York: Oxford University Press, pp. 648–72.

Sugden, R. (2000). "Credible worlds: the status of theoretical models in economics," *Journal of Economic Methodology* 7(1): 1–31.

Svolik, Milan W. (2013). "Learning to love democracy: electoral accountability and the success of democracy," *American Journal of Political Science* 57(3): 685–702.

Terra, Rafael, and Enlinson Mattos (2017). "Accountability and yardstick competition in the public provision of education," *Journal of Urban Economics* 99: 15–30.

Tiebout, Charles M. (1956). "A pure theory of local expenditures," *Journal of Political Economy* 64: 416–24.

Tocqueville, Alexis de (1856). *L'ancien régime et la Révolution*. New translation and edition, Jon Elster (ed.), Arthur Goldhammer (trans.), *Tocqueville: The Ancien Régime and the French Revolution*. Cambridge and New York: Cambridge University Press, 2011.

Tommasi, Mariano, and Federico Weinschelbaum (2007). "Centralization vs decentralization: a principal-agent analysis," *Journal of Public Economic Theory* 9(2): 369–89.

Tsebelis, George (2002). *Veto Players: How Political Institutions Work*. New York: Russell Sage Foundation.

Tsoulouhas, Theofanis (2015). "A primer on cardinal versus ordinal tournaments," *Economic Inquiry* 53(2): 1224–35.

Tullock, Gordon (1967). "The welfare costs of tariffs, monopolies, and theft," *Economic Inquiry* 5(3): 224–32.

Van Malderen, Laurent and Marcel Gérard (2013). "Testing yardstick competition through a vote-function: evidence from the Walloon municipalities," *Economics and Business Letters* 2(4): 206–14.

Vanberg, Viktor, and Wolfgang Kerber (1994). "Institutional competition among jurisdictions: an evolutionary approach," *Constitutional Political Economy* 5(2): 193–219.

Vaubel, Roland (1994). "The political economy of centralization and the European Community," *Public Choice* 81(1–2): 151–90.

Vaubel, Roland (2008). "A history of thought on institutional competition," in: A. Bergh and R. Höijer (eds.), *Institutional Competition*. Cheltenham: Edward Elgar, pp. 29–66.

Vermeir, Jan, and Bruno Heyndels (2006). "Tax policy and yardstick voting in Flemish municipal elections," *Applied Economics* 38(19/20): 2285–98.

Vihanto, Martti (1992). "Competition between local governments as a discovery procedure," *Journal of Institutional and Theoretical Economics* 148: 411–36.

Walker, Jack L. (1969). "The diffusion of innovations among the American States," *American Political Science Review* 63(3): 880–99.

Weingast, Barry R. (1995). "The economic role of political institutions: market-preserving federalism and economic development," *Journal of Law, Economics, and Organization* 11(1): 1–31.

Werck, Kistien, Bruno Heyndels, and Benny Geys (2008). "The impact of 'central places' on spatial spending patterns: evidence from Flemish local government cultural expenditures," *Journal of Cultural Economics* 32: 35–58.

Winer, Stanley L. (2000). "On the reassignment of fiscal powers in a federal state," in: G. Galeotti, P. Salmon, and R. Wintrobe (eds.), *Competition and Structure. The Political Economy of Collective Decisions: Essays in Honor of Albert Breton*. Cambridge and New York: Cambridge University Press, pp. 150–73.

Wintrobe, Ronald (1998). *The Political Economy of Dictatorship*. Cambridge and New York: Cambridge University Press.

Wrede, Matthias (2001). "Yardstick competition to tame the Leviathan," *European Journal of Political Economy* 17: 705–21.

Wrede, Matthias (2006). "Uniformity requirement and political accountability," *Journal of Economics* 89(2): 93–113.

Wyplosz, Charles (2010). *The failure of the Lisbon strategy*, MS. http://www.voxeu.org/index.php?q=node/4478.

Xu, Chenggang (2011). "The fundamental institutions of China's reforms and development," *Journal of Economic Literature* 49(4): 1076–151.

Zheng, Xiaoyong, and Tomislav Vukina (2007). "Efficiency gains from organizational innovation: comparing ordinal and cardinal tournament games in broiler contracts," *International Journal of Industrial Organization* 25: 843–59.

Zudenkova, Galina (2011). "A political agency model of coattail voting," *Journal of Public Economics* 95: 1652–60.